... book gives a balanced historical perspectiv
eSwatini, in the liberation of South Africa. We have always ...
Kingdom's positive contribution to the liberation of the Republic of South Africa, would one day be
brought to the limelight – for all to appreciate; and you have done just that... The Swazi Nation
thanks you... **His Majesty, King Mswati III, June 2007**

... It is the time to tell the story of our struggle... about ourselves, the guerrillas of the ANC, what
type of people they were, their bravery, their ... understanding of Swaziland... When I read this
book, I was touched. Firstly, because it talks about comrades I worked with, who died in Swaziland
- others, in South Africa.

One of the moving stories was that of a girl who was caught in the cross-fire... It was also the
story of the Pretoria bombers. It is not what happened to them, but what happened to their families
thereafter... I want to meet up with those families... It is a great story. ... You and I still need to
meet to talk about September. ... who was September? **Deputy President of the ANC, Jacob
G Zuma, June 2007**

... House Number 43 as a place for reconciliation, peace and harmony. UMagogo never cared
whether you were a member of the PAC or ANC... Nalabancane bata kwati kutsi bekwentekani
ngesikhatsi semzabalazo... (Even the young ones will know what used to happen during the days
of liberation...) **Absalom Themba Dlamini, Prime Minister of Swaziland, 23 June 2007**

... the book is not only a history. It is also a description of the characteristics that defined the
politics in exile, shaping the movement that later swept to power. ... the book reads partly as a
thriller and partly as a study in heroism that even those on the opposing side of the political divide
cannot deny. What it achieves overall is an insight into the ANC on the ground and, importantly,
a warts-and-all look at the place Swaziland holds in the anti-apartheid legacy. **Allan Greenblo,
South Africa, July 2007**

This book deals with only activities that were associated with House Number 43. Nevertheless,
what happened to those people who were in that house has the ability to keep a constant flow of
tears from my eyes. When any relative has died, I never shed a tear. Yet, the continuous suffering
sustained by the South African freedom fighters as described in the book managed to keep my
eyes flowing with tears. **Dr Ben Dlamini, Commentator and Educationist, Swaziland, June
2007**

For full readers' commentary visit :http://www.number43trelawneypark.com

TRELAWNY PARK ESTATE

Swaziland Agents,
Bambi Stewart (Pty.) Ltd.
P.O. Box 130,
Manzini,
SWAZILAND

P.O. Box 32
KRUGERSDORP
Transvaal
Telephone 660-2738

S. Masilela,
P.O. Box 18,
~~MANKAIANA~~   *137*
Manzini

17th August, 1967

DEBITED TO TRELAWNY PARK TOWNSHIP

Balance due on Purchase Price of Stand 43 Trelawny Park Township at 30th June, 1967	R 729-00 *Less*
~~Less~~ Payment July, 1967	29-00
	R 700-00 *R 10*
Assessment Rates to 31st March, 1968	37-00 *R 10*
Total Due	R 737-00
	20

Less Paid 1.8.67 R20.   *717 00*

Monthly Instalment of R27 on balance of purchase price.   *27*   *pd: 9/9/*
R 690

All amounts now payable at the office of:

Bambi Stewart (Pty) Ltd., Manzini

or

P.O. Box 130, Manzini

Trelawney Park was managed by a Krugerdorp-based estate agency. Over time, developer SB Williams slightly altered the spelling of the name of the suburb. Shown above is a rates bill sent to uButhongo in August 1967.

NUMBER 43
TRELAWNEY PARK
KwaMagogo

*Untold stories of ordinary people caught up in
the struggle against apartheid*

Elias Masilela

Foreword by John Kgoana Nkadimeng

dp davidphilip

First published in 2007 in southern Africa
by David Philip Publishers,
an imprint of New Africa Books (Pty) Ltd,
99 Garfield Road, Claremont 7700,
South Africa

www.newafricabooks.co.za
second impression 2011

ISBN 978-0-86486-706-3

Editor: John Kench
Typesetter: Nazli Jacobs
Cover designer: Nathalie Scott
Proofreader: Sandra Cattich

Printed and bound in South Africa by Impressum

This book is dedicated to
my mother and father as well as
all those who fell – siblings, comrades and friends.
May their souls rest in peace.

Table of Contents

Biggest defection:

Links to the Pretoria Church Street bomb blast:

Other significant activities:

Acknowledgements

This book is a product of an arduous collective effort that involved many people. As such, I can never hope to thank every person, individually. But there are certain people who require singling out.

First and foremost, I would like to thank my parents, uMagogo and uButhongo as they are referred to herein, for making me who I am today. Above all, for allowing me the freedom to write about the family at liberty; for availing themselves to be subjected to many torturous hours of interviews and debates, as well as occasionally facing up to difficult and challenging questioning. I found myself having to jettison some of the values that characterised the relationship I had with my parents, from childhood. I had never before questioned my parents about their private lives. With this project, I was forced to do so. It was not an easy exercise, but one I had to go through.

Secondly, I would like to thank my wife for having endured the torture and the deprivation of her rightful family time. At no point did she complain or indicate that the encroachment was not welcome. She saw beyond the short-term pain.

Thirdly, warmest gratitude goes to all the comrades and friends who availed themselves for the taxing interviews sharing their experiences, follow-up interviews (where these were necessary), reading the scripts over, editing and giving their approval. This book would not have been written without you. A lot was unknown to the family and yet a lot was revealed by this journey. We now know more about the relationships that developed during those dark days. Even more so, we now know more about ourselves as a family and how the world perceived us then and how it is likely to perceive us in the future. On behalf of the family, I would like to thank you for having shaped us into what we are today.

Amongst these, I would like to single out uNtate Nkadimeng –

whom uMagogo referred to as 'Ng'bolekeni' back then – who was like a godfather to the project and gracefully agreed to do the fore-word. I am deeply indebted to him.

Fourthly, acknowledgment goes to my boys, uRakgomo and uTinga, who encouraged and goaded me on the journey to write. Their youth-ful and inquisitive quest for information about what their grand-mother, uMagogo, was admired for and their final discovery that we had kept a valuable piece of history from them was an essential im-petus that drove me into action. They contributed significantly to the long list of reasons to write this book.

Fifthly, I would like to thank my siblings, nieces and nephews, as well as brothers and sisters-in-law, who at the final stages of writing got themselves closely involved with the production. That helped me sharpen many of the memories reflected herein. However, I still do not know what jolted them into this action. I hope it was not for fear that the project would fail.

There are many more people who did work in the background, en-suring that the book stayed on track. I would like to single out a for-mer colleague, friend and critic, uKevin Fletcher, who volunteered and spent cold London nights doing some of the initial language edit-ing. When I requested him to take on the task and explained what I was doing, he responded in an interesting manner, saying, "Remem-ber that those we engage with, those that we draw close to and those that we let into our inner circles are often reflections of different parts of our characters...". He went on to reveal that he agreed to help with a purpose in mind. However, he has not yet revealed whether he has realised his purpose.

Volumes of appreciation go to another wonderful person behind the production of this book, uAlettah Masilela. She used her family time to type out every single one of the fifty or so interviews that form the fundamental building blocks of this book. Without her, the book would not have been produced in the period it was. She was magnificent.

I would also like to thank the team at New Africa Books, and every-one involved in this production. The editor, John Kench, has done an excellent job, balancing the demands of the publisher with the need to preserve the content and messages conveyed during the interview process. Most importantly, I take my hat off to Alfred Le Maitre for his creativity, vision and patience. He ended my gruelling search for a publisher and was prepared to put every resource into this production to ensure that it succeeds. He seems to have infected me with the desire-virus to write more – not just for the sake of writing but to break traditional boundaries.

Finally, I salute Swaziland and its people. Swaziland was not only a place of refuge for us, but also a home away from home. That is where I gained my basics in life and sharpened my teeth as an economist, even though this training is not relevant to the production of this book. Like many other countries from which the ANC and PAC operated, the struggle against apartheid would not have succeeded in the way it did, had it not been for the Swazi people. The community of Manzini, and particularly that of Trelawney Park, embraced the Masilela family from the day they arrived, up to this present day. Over the years, many have come and gone, but their memories remain vividly inscribed both in our minds and hearts.

In spite of the attendant difficulties, I am sure that this book will, appropriately, bridge an information gap left by the perceptions that have developed over time, about the role of Swaziland in the liberation struggle. I trust that the experiences shared herein will provide fair insights into that country's contribution.

ELIAS MASILELA
March 2007

The Property Specialists
in Swaziland

VJR
AGENCIES

Mbabane
Tel: 43553
42726

Manzini
Tel: 53898
53973

The Times
OF SWAZILAND

Price 17 cents   Monday, April 16, 1984   Vol.82 No.74

'ANC MUST GET OUT'

'No shooting to kill'

By TIMES
Reporter

THERE was massive military activity in Manzini yesterday following the fatal showdown between security forces and ANC insurgents at the weekend.

A police spokesman was quoted as saying the raids would be carried out until all members of the ANC had been flushed out of the country.

Commenting on the developments on the ANC/police clash a top police officer said in Manzini over the weekend that this was a strange type of confrontation with the was being carried out throughout the Hub, an Assistant Superintendent was shot in the eye during the clash on Saturday and an Inspector was killed on the spot at Zakhele.

Late yesterday Commissioner of Police Mr. Titus Msibi denied reports that the police shot and killed an ANC man. "They shot at our men in cold blood. Even the ANC itself knows very well that Swazi police don't townships ran into hundreds.

Eye witnesses at Zakhele said the shootings were the most frightening thing they had ever seen.

"The shooting was all over the place," said Mrs Joyce Khumalo of Zakhele. "I have never seen so many armed soldiers before. We huddled together with my children and hid under the bed. The whole thing was so loud one would think it was happening outside the house," Mrs Khumalo said.

"They came back this morning but there was no

COMMISSIONER OF POLICE Mr. Titus Msibi, asked about the Saturday morning Manzini shootout, told the Times:

"When the police conducted the raid, some of the ANC men came out and surrendered themselves to the them for unlawful possession of arms, ammunition and other explosives," said the Commissioner of police.

An official spokesman from R.F.M. Hospital in Manzini confirmed that the four police officers and a member of the ANC were admitted on Saturday morning with shot wounds.

It was also reported that police in Mbabane arrested the house loading and arming himself with the AK 47 rifle.

Police, however, suspected something and asked the four ANC who had surrendered themselves if there are any of them in the house. They told the police that one is inside and they told him to come out. At first he resisted the warning by his colleague, but he later responded to the warning.

When police were satisfied that they had all surrendered themselves to them they then raided the house.

They found four AK 47, six hand-grenades and other explosives.

After many years of uneasy coexistence, the period after 1982 was characterised by heightened discomfort on the part of the Swazi authorities with the activities of the ANC in Swaziland.

Foreword

For those of us who experienced life in Swaziland, this book is captivating. It is so relevant, not only to my own life history, but to many ANC operatives who lived in Swaziland. It is a fair and honest account of our experiences. I have found the whole concept and the title most appropriate. Number 43 Trelawney Park was, simply, our home in exile.

What fascinates me even more is that the author, whom I have always called 'young Masilela', grew up right under my eyes. After all these years, I still consider him as such. The author's mother and father, who are well covered in the book, were literally like family to me, as they continue to be.

To me, this is a blessing in disguise, particularly that I was given the opportunity to contribute to its writing. But it is a blessing for many reasons. Most importantly, it gives me an opportunity to engage with my family and friends about our past, on the basis of documented evidence.

I have given many an interview since I returned from exile. None of these have resonated with me in the way that this book does. This time around, I was humbled by the manner in which 'young Masilela' was able to relate our experiences – with accuracy, passion and succinctness. There is no doubt that this is the fairest reflection, so far, of what we went through while in Swaziland.

May I, however, hazard that the stories being told in this book are by no means a complete picture of the life of the ANC in Swaziland. It is only a part, but I may say, a very important part.

The other house cited in the book, that we came to know as 'Come Again', was the base for the President (Thabo Mbeki) and former Deputy President (Jacob Zuma) while they were residing in Swaziland. I am glad that this house is being given the prominence it deserves in the book, along with Number 43 and the 'White House'.

In my first engagement with the author, I found him a bit too humble with his intent. He introduced the subject of writing the book merely as an initiative that would document the experiences of people who had had a relationship with Number 43. I thought, "How noble!" At no point did he refer to himself as being part of the story – that is, until I read the script. Clearly, this book and history could not have been told without him in the picture. It would simply be incomplete. This is despite the fact that the bulk of the period in question coincides with his tender youth. I have known him to be the quiet type, who was always in the background. Little did I know that his demeanour allowed him to absorb, like a sponge, a lot of the developments that took place around him. All this plays out in the book. This is displayed by the manner in which he introduces himself, in almost every event. Young and quiet as he was, he was instrumental in the struggle, as waged from Swaziland. His footprint and that of the Masilela family is indelible.

I am pleased by the attention that has been given to each character in the book. Each one of us, whether cited or not, can see ourselves in this mosaic.

I implore all those who have a history to tell to document it as Number 43 has been documented in this book. Each of us who passes on takes a wealth of information and history, which can never be represented by others. This valuable information is lost to generations – forever. I can only commend 'young Masilela' for having taken this initiative. He has filled a void in my conscience. I will confess that ever since I returned from exile, I have contemplated doing something similar. I simply could not make the time for it, owing to busy schedules and creeping old age. I am sure that I am not alone suffering under this cloak of culpability. From now on, I can comfort myself for the failure to do it myself; 'young Masilela' has done it, not only for me, but also for many other comrades who will be able to see themselves in this book.

The twelfth chapter deals with a very delicate subject that threatened my life. I hope, as the last chapter of the book does, that it will provide closure to my history and that of many more of my friends and comrades who worked from the beautiful Kingdom of Swaziland. This is particularly so for families who lost their loved ones on Swazi soil.

JOHN KGOANA NKADIMENG
Kew, Johannesburg, 2007

All members of the family were exposed to arrest, and often torture, by the Swazi police. However, the author is the only one whose arrests received media attention, as shown above.

Preface

Writing this book was motivated by numerous defining moments in the life and history of the Masilela family, as I observed them through the eyes of a young boy growing in an environment full of tumult. The urge to write has gone through peaks and troughs – with the final peak coming in December 2004.

I had harboured this thought for a long time. To the best of my recollection, the first time the idea crossed my mind was during my student days, at the University of Swaziland (UNISWA), following the signing of the Nkomati Accord in March 1984. The signing followed the assassination in Mamelodi of my brother-in-law by the South African security forces. His story is discussed in detail in chapters 21 and 23. In the period immediately before his death he had been classified as one of the most wanted terrorists in Swaziland.

The idea of writing would come back when uNelson Mandela (Madiba) visited Swaziland in November 1990 as a guest of the King. What triggered the thought was a rude awakening to the acute disparity of views within the ANC on various policy issues.

During his stay in Swaziland, uMadiba made a call to South Africans to assemble at Manzana Guest House, where he was being hosted, to meet with him. Only a handful of families heeded the call and found their way to Manzana. Judging from the turnout, one would be tempted to believe that only those South Africans who were active in the struggle for South Africa's liberation attended. It could also have been a result of self-selection, since at that stage many non-active South Africans wanted little or nothing to do with the ANC or its members.

On entering the room where the gathering took place, I identified familiar faces in Madiba's entourage. They included uColin Coleman, a former fellow-pupil at Salesian High School. I later learned that he was one of Madiba's bodyguards. Other leading members of the ANC delegation included people such as uTito Mboweni, uSaki Macozo-ma, uJomo Mavuso, uTokyo Sexwale, and uZwai Piliso.

Following his address to the gathering on a wide range of issues, including how the high command of the ANC envisioned the future of South Africa, uMadiba invited questions from the floor.

After a number of what I considered uninspired questions, I raised my hand to ask a question on nationalisation and how feasible that policy stance was, given what I saw as an extremely fragile economy at the time. Little did I know that what I deemed not only intellectu-ally stimulating but also an innocent query would not go down well with uMadiba. He was visibly irritated by the question, to the extent that he clearly felt it did not warrant a response. Not only that, he sud-denly lost the appetite for the meeting and immediately stood up and walked out of the room.

This sudden turn of events abruptly brought the evening to a sour end, to the disappointment of all present. I felt extremely guilty, feel-ing that I had ruined what was seen as an important historical event. I thought to myself, "People have been waiting a lifetime to meet this world-renowned figure, their Comrade-leader, and in a split second I have destroyed what could have otherwise been a wonderful and edu-cative evening."

Driving back to Manzini, my brother uTodd chastised me the whole way for a wrong I had already recognised. I could not defend myself and could only concede that he was right. Up until the day I started writing this book, this turn of events remained a source of guilt and wonder.

When I began writing, I promised my wife and children that if ever I had an opportunity to meet uMadiba, no matter how awkward it might be, I would ask him about the experience at Manzana. As if the gods were listening, this dream came true in February 2005, thanks to the Minister of Finance, Trevor Manuel.

During an official trip to London, where I was to attend a meeting of the Commission for Africa (CfA), uMadiba happened to be in the City to fundraise and to lend support to the CfA initiative. On 5 Febru-ary, uTrevor arranged that we pay a courtesy call to uMadiba, who was staying at the Dorchester Hotel. To my surprise, as soon as we stepped into the hotel room, in his typical fatherly voice, he said "Young man, I have been following you in the press, and watching you grow in the policy environment. You are doing very well!" I was confounded by the observation, but more confused as to whether he was referring to me then, or was linking me to the Manzana event. I did not believe it could be the latter. It was fifteen years since the Manzana event. "There is no way he could remember what happened so far back" I thought to myself.

However, in the ten minutes or so that we had, I was determined to establish the truth and deliver on the promise I had made to my wife and children. Using his privileged position, uTrevor suggested that we take pictures with uMadiba, to which he agreed. Just as we were about to leave the room, I found the gap to ask my question.

I tried to phrase the question in what I thought was the most polite, inoffensive manner: "Tata, do you remember, many moons ago, when you visited Swaziland as guest of the King and you called South Africans to meet with you? There was this young man who stood up to ask a question on nationalisation . . ." In his usual stately manner he stopped me in my tracks and said, "It was you, I know!" I am not sure whether I was embarrassed or relieved. But I do know that I was content that my life-long wish had been fulfilled. I could not wait to get back home and relate the experience to my family and friends.

However, I did not get to ask the other part of my question, why he became so angry on that eventful night. This, notwithstanding, cemented my resolve to write this book.

People may wonder why uMadiba is such an important part of the decision. To a large extent it is due to the underlying theme of the book. This relates to a parallel that has been drawn by a number of comrades between Liliesleaf Farm in Rivonia and my parents' house in Swaziland, from which the book takes its title. These comrades argued that both these properties contributed to the liberation of South Africa. However, it can also be maintained that Number 43, certainly from a military perspective, contributed more to the struggle. This conclusion is based on the period the house was used as a key strategic point for the ANC and its armed wing, Umkhonto weSizwe

(MK), and the fact that, unlike Liliesleaf, it lived to see liberation. While it is true that the Swazi security police arrested many people at Number 43 and that others were tailed by the South African death squad from the house and disappeared or were killed, none of these events incapacitated the ANC in Swaziland.

However, given the complexity of the comparative exercise, I do not attempt to motivate for the argument. Instead this is left to the life stories and experiences of people who had relationships of a wide-ranging nature with Number 43. This decision also determined the design of the book. Rather than having a flowing thematic story line, it is written as a series of what one might characterise as people's testimonials. Each of these contributes towards testing the conclusion made above.

The book shows that almost every ANC and PAC activist who went through Swaziland used Number 43 in one way or another in carrying out their various activities. It can be shown that it was the principal base for launching the armed struggle against South Africa, particularly in the period after 1982, when King Sobhuza II died.

Other considerations

The final decision point came during the Christmas weekend of 2004. As part of family tradition, we assemble at Number 43 every Christmas as a family, accompanied by numerous friends and comrades. Christmas Day 2004 was one of those days when we gathered to reminisce about 'the good old days'. It is rather ironic, of course, to talk about the good old days, as these were characterised by fear, trepidation and sometimes hate. However, we were schooled to manage the latter and to stay objective.

In one of our discussions, we talked about how important Number 43 was during the days of liberation and how it continues to be central to people's history. After a lengthy debate, I remember one comrade, uPeter Dambuza, said, "If Liliesleaf Farm can qualify to be declared a national monument, I do not see why Number 43 should not. . ." That statement rang long and hard in my mind, firming my decision to start writing. That was the day I settled on the title of the book.

In a later discussion with uCassius Motsoaledi, I was fascinated by the way in which he paralleled the two houses. He noted that all the command units from the various provinces used Liliesleaf as a central point for information consolidation, distribution and strategic decision-making. He argued that the same could be said of Number 43. As he put it, "It was almost the nerve centre for the receiving and dissemination of strategic information amongst all the machineries that operated from Swaziland."

Four machineries operated from Number 43. These were the Transvaal urban, Transvaal rural, Natal and special operations machineries. As a result, Number 43 became a key point of contact for most senior members of the ANC who operated from Swaziland, as well as other operatives. It also attracted a lot of attention from both the Swazi and South African security police. For both sides, it was strategic and needed to be preserved. This led to the house being spared all the bombings and kidnappings that other safe houses suffered in Swaziland.

Most of the major military operations that the ANC launched in the period covered by this book were finalised, launched, received and celebrated from Number 43. They included the gunning down of the notorious police officer, Hlubi, in Soweto (1978), the Venda police station attack (1981), the Voortrekker army base attack (1981), the Tonga army base operation (1982), the Hectorspruit fuel depot operation (1982), the Pretoria Church street bomb blast (1983) – and many more. Some of these and some of the people who were directly or indirectly behind these operations are discussed elsewhere in the book.

In subsequent discussions and interviews I had further encouragement. I remember one comrade, uWally 'Gordon' Mabuza, quoting uSiphiwe Gebhuza Nyanda as saying, "For every death that we observe, a big part of our history is lost forever, never to be recovered." "How true!" was my response. Coincidentally, a few months later Ntate John Nkadimeng repeated these exact words.

For its significance, at the time of writing this book Number 43 was presented to the Manzini City Council as part of an exercise to identify historical sites in the Manzini urban area.

Closing a gap

Not much has been written about the South African struggle from the perspective of operations launched from Swaziland. This is a major omission, given the contribution of the country, its people and the ANC cadres who operated from it to the liberation of South Africa. According to one of the submissions to the Truth and Reconciliation Commission (TRC) report, during the period from August 1979 to March 1984, machineries in Swaziland and Mozambique launched most of the armed operations. In turn, machineries operating from Mozambique used Swaziland as their passage into South Africa. Even more notable is that Number 43 was the nerve centre for most, if not all of these, making it an indispensable piece of South Africa's liberation jigsaw.

Rationale

This, therefore, is the story of a modest family that quietly yet effectively contributed to the struggle for the liberation of South Africa, over a period of more than forty years. It is an attempt to give a well-deserved recognition to this important yet little-known place, one which is hardly talked about but which provided essential shelter, refuge and pilgrimage for many people, as it continues to do to this day.

This is the story of Number 43 Trelawney Park, affectionately called 'kwaMagogo', meaning 'place of the grandmother' in isiZulu, by those who have had a relationship with it, told through the eyes and ears of the Masilela family, comrades and friends.

The book covers a broad time frame, but the core of this period runs from 1965 to 2004. Whilst a significant number of the events described fall outside this core period, they are dealt with in such a way that they provide the larger context.

The starting point of the observation period was when uButhongo and uMagogo, the key architects behind Number 43, made their historic journey to Swaziland in search of a better education for their children. At the outset, the decision was not politically motivated, nor were uButhongo and uMagogo political, but the long-term result was of phenomenal political consequence from both a Swazi and a South African perspective.

Throughout this period, the Masilela family lived a life of risk, fear and uncertainty owing to the many activities in which they found themselves involved and the many people they harboured at their residence. Two of these marked the most conspicuous peaks of danger in the history of the family. The first was uNkosinathi Maseko, a brother-in-law who was pursued in 1983 after being labelled the most wanted person in Swaziland for his involvement in the Pretoria Church Street bomb blast as well as an armed robbery in Manzini. This resulted in the biggest manhunt in the history of Swaziland. The other was uGlory 'September' Sedibe, who was kidnapped in 1986 and ultimately defected.

His defection would go down in my analysis as the biggest defection from the ANC, after that of Bartholomew Hlapane in the 1980s. This event inflicted untold suffering on the Masilela family and ANC operatives in Swaziland. He wreaked havoc across Swaziland, with people disappearing, being maimed or killed. Whilst the suffering the family sustained was not physical, it had far-reaching emotional consequences. We had many questions, but no one could give us the answers.

The characters in the book, the people interviewed and the events described, have been carefully selected for their relevence to the liberation struggle, especially in their proximity to Number 43. To a large extent, the names are real, but where it was found inappropriate to cite a person's name, this was omitted. In many cases, the names used are operative names, which may not necessarily relate to birth names, which are often forgotten. Indeed, long after liberation most of the people continue to be identified by their operative names.

Special care was taken to protect the identities of people, where this was found necessary, and careful attention was given to detail, ensuring that we achieved an accurate representation of people and events. However, providing detail while at the same time preserving confidentiality proved to be a difficult balance with respect to certain events and individuals. In order to ensure the highest level of accuracy, a thorough verification and approval process was undertaken. Where errors are found, these are clearly unintended and purely a function of failing memory, as the main part of the book relies on individual recollections of events, mostly many years in the past.

Clearly many more people and events could have been featured. I am sure that there will be many people who would have wished to be part of this story. However, owing to resource constraints this could not be done.

The rest of the book is divided into four parts. Each part has a prelude that gives a general perspective of the theme, from the viewpoint of the writer. Each prelude sets the scene for the individual experiences that follow.

Part I looks at the origins of Number 43 Trelawney Park and the two architects of its creation, uButhongo and uMagogo.

Part II describes the contributions of each member of the Masilela family and how they jointly and individually supported the struggle as it was waged from this house.

Part III is the main body of the book. It describes the many relationships that developed between Number 43 and the various members of the ANC, both its leadership and general operatives. It also looks at the key operations that were launched from Number 43 as well as at some of the people behind each operation.

The chapters in this section are clustered into three broad subcategories. Chapters 12 to 15 deal with the leadership of the ANC at that time in Swaziland, both from a political and military standpoint. Chapters 16 to 20 cover the biggest defection in the history of the ANC and the responses to this occurrence. Chapters 21 to 23 look at events linking particular operatives to the Pretoria Church Street bomb blast. Finally, chapters 24 to 30 tell the stories of different individuals as well as institutions, and their contributions to the struggle.

The last part consists of only one chapter. It looks at the significance of the ANC Cleansing Ceremony, which provides a final closure to the liberation struggle as it was waged from Swaziland.

Throughout the book, I have taken account of the manner in which people are addressed in isiZulu, in which names of people always have the prefix 'u'. However, whilst keeping in general to this formulation, where necessary the prefix is omitted.

Finally, it may be instructive to mention that the book is not only about the history of the ANC in Swaziland, nor is it simply a work of biography. It is an account of the life experiences of numerous individuals, each of whom was a vital piece in helping to complete a massive jigsaw, with its centrepiece a house and a woman who brought all these life experiences together. As a consequence, classifying the book proved rather tricky, even though a final decision was reached to classify it as an historical account.

However, while the larger historical events form the background, uMagogo and her family remain the human drama in the foreground. They define the life of the struggle at a particular point in time and in a particular place, revealing in their personal triumph and tragedy the larger hopes and sufferings of all the freedom fighters in southern Africa in those tumultuous years.

Siphelman gebor 29 Sept 1913
Theefulos Tatau gebor   Feb 1916 –.
            nge sikntu i nyanga ya ye ili' ka

Johanna gebor 22 Sulyi 1918

Sibeti gebor 27 Dec   1922

Salmon gebore 5 Agost 1925

Telephe gibor 1 Aperl 1927

gebor kwabantwana. ababili
Augst   die 20. 1933
A magantwabo gu
Joel masilela. No
    Jonnas masilela
Baselue E gomeblom

The serendipitous discovery of this handwritten note confirmed the date of Buthongo's birth as 5 August 1925. However, uButhongo himself insists he was born in 1924. The note was made by a teacher who kept records for families in the Middelburg area.

PART I

Origins

I the undersigned
Solomon Mongo Masilela of
P O Box 137 Manzini having this
day entered into a Deed of Sale
for the purchase of portion 43
Trelawny Park Township
understand and agree that the
sale to me is conditional to
the non-payment by the former
Purchaser Solly Mahlangu to the
Township Authorities of the amount
overdue by him on or before
the 15th instant, and that
should he in fact pay this
amount then the sale to
me will be null and void and
the deposit of R200. paid by
me will be refunded.

Signed at Manzini this 3rd
day of September 1966.

Witnesses: — J. T. Masilela

for Trelawny Park
Township
D Williams

1. T C Elaine
2. S S Vilakazi

"You have worked very hard on the property, you have paid off my debt . . . it is now yours, just keep it." Solly Mahlangu's words to uButhongo were a stroke of good fortune for the Masilela family.

CHAPTER I

Origins and Life at Number 43
Trelawney Park

Number 43, Trelawney Park has been our home over the past forty years, from the time uButhongo arrived in Swaziland in 1965.

Many people have argued that the house qualifies for a place in the annals of South Africa's liberation history. Aware of the temptation of self-praise, I have been reluctant to accept this idea, let alone internalise it. Over time, however, I have grown to agree with it, and to develop a deep appreciation of my family's history. Whether this view will gain general acceptance is difficult to determine. Perhaps it would be best simply to tell the story of Number 43 and leave the reader to judge.

Number 43 started from humble beginnings, both of structure and intent. Like any other home, it was developed for the purpose of raising a family, of strengthening family bonds, of offering a decent education for the children and a healthy lifestyle. That at least, is what its architects, my parents uButhongo and uMagogo, had in mind.

Building the structure that became home and fortress

When uButhongo arrived at Number 43 in 1965 he did not have enough money to construct a permanent house. Instead, he could only afford to build a makeshift structure out of corrugated iron that had been used and reused many times. As a result, the walls and roof had many gaping holes reflecting old scars left by nails over years of repeated use. One could stand outside the house, peep through these openings and literally see everything inside the house.

Because of the porous nature of the building, it was quite common to find a snake or two in the house, and my brother, uTodd, developed the habit of catching them.

Without a doubt, this was a step backward from what uButhongo had established before leaving South Africa. He had built a large house at Number 466, in Mofolo North, Soweto. Even by today's standards, the Soweto house, a standard three-bedroom structure, was modern and comfortable. On his departure he sold the place to his nephew, uBhomo, to fund his long and uncertain journey to Swaziland.

While makeshift, the new house at Number 43 was fairly large, with decent partitions, allowing uButhongo and uMagogo the privacy of a bedroom, plus a kitchen and a spacious sitting area. By night, the nine children used the kitchen and sitting area as bedrooms.

In summer, the house offered all the warmth required by any family. However, in winter it would be bitterly cold, with temperatures periodically around zero, and we would cluster around a Welcome Dover coal stove for warmth. In the middle of winter, it was typical that no water would come out of taps in houses along the uMzimnene river, including Number 43, owing to the frigid temperatures. This meant that on occasion we would be forced to go to school without having had a wash.

Some of our friends from well-to-do families mocked the state of our house, causing us a lot of misery. It did not end there. Our poverty showed not only in the house that we lived in but also in the clothes we wore, which were mostly tattered and torn. While we relied on home-stitched clothes, these friends bought theirs through expensive and prestigious mail-order houses such as Kays, then very much in vogue. Anything with a label that read 'Made in the USA' was the product to buy. To us, this was a luxury, far out of reach. But the family was content with what we had.

In our first year at Number 43, life was extremely difficult. To earn money, our parents had temporarily remained in South Africa. Left without parental support, the children often went hungry. The situation only improved, albeit marginally, after uButhongo and uMagogo returned permanently to join their family in Swaziland.

Construction team

By now, uButhongo had decided to build a permanent structure that would afford better comfort, safety and privacy, laying the foundation for Number 43 as it stands today.

The construction of the new house called for hard labour on the part of every member of the family, young and old. Weekends and early mornings, before the children set off for school, were dedicated to construction. The allocation of tasks was strictly regimented, and productivity was extremely high.

No labour was employed from outside the family – simply because uButhongo could not afford it. All the blocks used for the construction were made on site. They were solid blocks that took a lot of packing space, which meant clearing and levelling the entire yard by hand, shovel by shovel. By the end of the project, uButhongo did not owe a cent to a bank or anybody else, since the construction was funded directly from his own pocket. It still baffles me, how he afforded all this on the meagre salary he earned as a bricklayer.

It took slightly more than five years to build the house. In its final form it comprised four bedrooms, a lounge, dining room, kitchen, bathroom and toilet. We moved from the makeshift to the permanent structure in 1972. When occupied for the first time, the house had no electricity, no cupboards, no tiles or carpets (these were a luxury) and no ceiling. Nevertheless, it was quite habitable for a modest family and a significant improvement from the makeshift structure – worthy of celebration.

To this day, the house has never been altered from its original design. The paint configuration on the outside has been kept the same – cream walls and light green window frames, doorframes and fascia boards. The only major change was the fitting of burglar bars in 2000, after the family was held up at gunpoint. That was the first burglary in 35 years. It shook the family – for the first time we felt vulnerable.

Indeed, over the years this house at Number 43 has raised three living generations.

Meanwhile, the makeshift structure was kept and rented out for a while, side by side with other similar structures, before it was destroyed to make way for a fowl run. At any one time, there would be at least four different families living on the property as tenants, an arrangement which continues today.

Life in the kitchen

My central image of life at Number 43 is that of the old man and old lady sitting in the kitchen, merrily chatting away for hours on end. This is a departure from common tradition, where people spend most of their time in the family or living room. At Number 43, that part of the house commonly used for cooking is instead used for a much wider range of activities, from eating and drinking, to storytelling and praying. It is also used as a place to reminisce. This tradition of spending time in the kitchen is probably what has kept the family as closely knit as it is today.

Being a large family, we might have been expected to use the living room for relaxation rather than the hot kitchen. Instead, the living and dining rooms, which are very large relative to the kitchen, were reserved for guests, whom we grew up calling 'strangers', a term I would later in life discard from my vocabulary after learning how inappropriate it was. But thinking about it a little deeper, it was the best way to describe some of the people who visited Number 43, as we shall learn later in the book.

While possessing the features of a regular homestead, Number 43 was also an important meeting place and a haven for many people, friends, acquaintances and operatives of uMkhonto WeSizwe (MK) the military wing of the ANC. Likewise, the kitchen was the main part of the house for these meetings.

Besides the family, there were almost always people residing in the house, sometimes on an almost permanent basis. A few are worth mentioning here, even though their stories are not told in this book. The first is uBilly Mabiletsa, familiarly known as 'uTa Billy', who spent over ten years at Number 43, died there and was buried by the family and the ANC in 1994. The others are uVictor Greenhead, uPhilip Nkomo, uChippa Ndabandaba and uVusi 'Jwi' Kunene. All were *de facto* part of the family. Indeed, uPhilip and uChippa even put

6

their sweat in the construction of the main building. Another important person in my early development was a half-brother, uDumisani Masilela. We grew up together and went to the same school, but by the height of the political activities, he had moved to stay in Ngwane Park. He was never really exposed to my experiences and is amazed when he hears the depth of the stories being told today.

* * *

All and sundry enjoyed meals around the same table. It was common for uMagogo to prepare food for as many as twenty people at any one time. It remains a mystery to me how my parents afforded this kind of expenditure, given their meagre income. None of this hospitality was sponsored. Unlike others, the Masilela family has never received an allowance from the ANC, or any other organisation for that matter.

Mealtimes at Number 43 were always eventful and remain truly memorable, particularly to those of us who were children at the time. Like at boarding school, mealtimes were announced by a resounding call to assemble at the kitchen. However, unlike at a boarding school, this call was not a bell, but a unique Masilela call, "Under age!" The person responsible for dishing out would stand at the door leading to the kitchen and shout out the words at the top of his or her voice, "Uunnderrrrr – aaaaaaaage!" In the blink of an eye, every young one would scuttle from every corner of the yard and the street to join the queue for a plate of food, which was always delicious even though simple pap, gravy and a piece of meat if we were lucky. Mind you, this did not exclude neighbours and friends who were visiting at the time of the meal. They also had a claim. At times, when resources were low, two to three children would share a plate, just to ensure that the food got around to all present. Nobody complained.

Just to give an indication of the likely number of children who would constitute the 'under-age' of the time, a rough count was done and we came up with the following: Dombolo Masilela, Sizwe Hlongwana, Zozo Hlongwana, Oupa Hlongwana, Ranthobeng Matlala, Peter Mekoa, Stanley Nkadimeng, Bongani Makhubu, Ntombi Makhubu, Sibusiso Makhubu, Khwahla Brown, Pitjie Brown, Beverly

'Bheveli' Brown, Molly Cunha, Dumisani Masilela, Linda Masilela, Bhekani Masilela, David Ngozo and many more.

All these people were part of the larger family in the house and many remain close to Number 43 to this day. However, to keep to the underlying aim of this book, attention is focused on those who were related to Number 43 for political purposes.

Trelawney Park in historical perspective

Number 43 is situated in Trelawney Park, one of the middle to upper income suburbs of Manzini, the industrial capital of Swaziland. A *Times of Swaziland* reporter once described it as a 'posh house', writing after arms had been found there during a raid by Swazi police. The name Trelawney Park was inherited from a Krugersdorp-based estate agent who managed the township on behalf of Mr Sydney Williams, through Bambi Stewarts in Manzini. The name was originally spelt as 'Trelawny', without the second 'e'. It is not clear whether the change was deliberate or crept in through evolution.

Manzini is the largest city in Swaziland, located in the central middle-veld of the country. It is Swaziland's convergence point for commerce and customs, race and beliefs. The city is always buzzing with people from all parts of the country and from the neighbouring countries, in particular Mozambique, making it the perfect place to launch a guerilla armed struggle.

The city is said to derive its name from a prominent chief, Manzini Motsa, whose homestead was on the banks of uMzimnene River, which divides Greater Manzini roughly in half. In our early days in Swaziland, the river was a source of water for Number 43.

In 1890, European settlers renamed the town Bremersdorp, after a settler trader, Arthur Bremer. Apparently irritated by this, as they should have been, Swazi authorities took their first chance subsequently to revert to the original name.

For a long time, many of the South African families who had migrated to Swaziland in search of tranquility and to escape from apartheid mostly lived in Trelawney Park or Coates Valley, a slightly more up-market suburb on the east of Manzini. One South African who was known to many who stayed and did business in Trelawney Park was uDr Jivho. Others included uProfessor Sam Guma, father to the current Deputy Governor of the South African Reserve Bank, uXolile Guma; uChicks Nkosi; uTom Nhleko, father to uPhuthuma Nhleko, the current CEO of MTN; uGwamanda and many more.

It would be remiss of me not to single out uTom Nhleko and his wife, uDorah, whom we respectfully addressed as 'Mrs Nhleko'. I have always referred to uTom Nhleko as 'Dad'. In this book, though, he is simply called uTom. I grew up under the hand of the Nhlekos, together with their daughter, uMathabo. This was a family that against all odds remained loyal to the Masilelas, even when other families openly pronounced censure on us.

On one occasion, uMathabo found herself in the crossfire of a raid and ended up at the Manzini Police Station. Her crime was simply that of being a friend of the Masilelas and on that particular occasion, of having visited Number 43. Her mother had sent her to pick up something from uMagogo. Because of the erratic nature of the Swazi police, young as she was, she was mistaken for a collaborator.

Relating her experience in the hands of the Swazi police, uMathabo highlighted the bravery of uMagogo in dealing with the situation. She remembered one key phrase repeated by uMagogo, "Hhey, angazi lutho mina . . . Hhabantwa bami laba . . .", (Hey, I know nothing . . . these are my children . . .) when questioned about ANC operatives. Simple as the strategy was, it kept her out of trouble and saved her from incarceration. This chimes with Mrs Nhleko's own memory of uMagogo. She recalls the Swazi police arguing, "Angeke utfole lutfo kulo Msushwana lona . . .". (You are never going to get any information from this little MoSotho . . .)

Despite all this exposure and risk, the Nhleko family continued their friendship with the Masilelas. uMrs Nhleko is still surprised that "there are families today, both in Swaziland and in South Africa, who claim to be ANC veterans, yet in those days they openly refused to identify, let alone assist, the Masilela family." She recalls uSos Mokgokong saying, "This is a very brave and strong woman. If there is anyone to be recognised for their political work, she is the one."

9

She reinforced this observation when she said, "Lekhaya ngiya lazi. Bekuyi khaya le ANC. Bengithi umangifikile ngizovakasha, bengihlala ngichucha njalo. Ngoba kwaku se khaya, bengingeke ngibaleke. Uma kukhona abantu abafuna ukwazi ngalo, babobuza kimi." (I know this house. It was the house of the ANC. Whenever I visited, I would always shiver. But because it was home, I could never stay away. If there are any people who want to know about it, they should ask me.)

UMrs Nhleko was the key link with Number 43. She got to know the Masilela family before uTom did, after being introduced to uMagogo by uSos Mokgokong. On arrival in Swaziland, uTom worked in Tshaneni, but had a property in Trelawney Park. Because uMrs Nhleko was then unemployed, she would frequently visit Manzini. Every time she was in the town, she would call at Number 43 and on many occasions used the house to receive her own relatives from South Africa. That is how the relationship was cultivated. On her advice, uTom contracted uButhongo to build the house in which they lived for the greater part of their time in Swaziland.

During the first South African democratic elections, South Africans who were resident in Swaziland went to vote at the Somhlolo National Stadium. As was to be expected, uMrs Nhleko was at uMagogo's side on Election Day. As she recalls, "Only a handful of South Africans went to vote. Most of them probably stayed away for fear of being persecuted by the Swazi police . . . This did not deter uMakgomo and myself." She vividly remembers the comments of some Swazi police observing the election process, as she and uMagogo were approaching the booths, "Ye wena Make Masilela, usasekhona kantsi la?!" (Hey you, Mrs. Masilela, are you still here?), to which uMagogo defiantly responded, "Nifuna ngiyephi kanti?" (Where do you want me to go?) At that point, uMrs Nhleko became extremely uncomfortable, fearing that they might be victimised or even arrested. As time showed, that did not happen. By then, attitudes had changed significantly in Swaziland.

I had a more direct and personal relationship with uTom. He was like a father and mentor to me, reflected in the way I addressed him.

Together with the late Mr Isaac Fortune, we established the Trelawney Park Ratepayers and Residents Association (TRARA), which gave birth to the Manzini Ratepayers Association. These were important historical instruments for the improvement of local government in Manzini, which in a short space of time reverberated across the country. UTom was Chairman of the TRARA and the political brain behind the Manzini Ratepayers Association, while I was the Secretary for both until I left Swaziland in 1998.

The Gwamandas, on the other hand, owned a house that would later become a pre-eminent ANC residence in Swaziland, under the command of Ntate John Nkadimeng. He was one of the most important residents of Trelawney Park, in the period 1976 to 1982. Because of its colour and the nature of the work that took place there, it became known as the 'White House', both within and outside ANC circles. This period saw a rapid increase in the activities there, following the Soweto student uprisings. Because the two properties literally shared a street, with Number 43 closer to the entrance to the suburb, even those who would have little or nothing to do with Number 43 ended up being familiar with its strategic importance.

For a time, the ANC attempted a rationing programme for ANC families and operatives living in Swaziland. Two distribution points were set up: one at Mabele Heights, a block of flats owned by another prominent South African, Robert Ntshingila, in the Manzini city centre, the other at Number 43. (It is important to mention that Mabele Heights was another key ANC house at that time.) The rations were stored in the garage at the back of the house. This operation did not go on for very long owing to various difficulties, including the inefficiency of the system, a high propensity for corruption and theft, as well as the security risk it posed, not only for Number 43 but also for those operating underground.

When the rationing programme stopped, one of those responsible for its coordination, uReggie Mhlongo, ended up renting the garage for residential purposes. During his stay there, a strong bond developed between the Masilela and Mhlongo families, which continues to this day. He stayed there until he left Swaziland.

Encounters with security police

Owing to our political activities, some overt but mostly covert, Number 43 became a playground for the police. Joint forces of the Swazi police and the South African security forces raided the house many times. The period from 1982 to 1989 saw the highest frequency of these raids. In order to raise doubts in the minds of the police on what was actually happening there, the house was turned temporarily into a shebeen. While this was a wonderful alibi, it did not sit well with the family. It was decided to jettison it and face the risks and consequences head-on. Whilst it was easy for those members of the family who were not resident at Number 43 to reach this decision, it was not so for those who were exposed to the wrath of the Swazi police on a daily basis. However, the risk and exposure had to be taken. At the time, family members remaining in the house were uButhongo, uMagogo, uGranny, uJoana and myself. The rest had left to stay on their own or had left the country to get away from persecution.

* * *

Only much later did we notice a pattern in the raids. While they seemed to occur on a fairly *ad hoc* basis, as one would expect, it became apparent that some of them were closely linked to month-ends and to the closure of UNISWA.

It transpired that the Swazi police had information that funds for operations launched from Swaziland and for the upkeep of operatives transiting Swaziland were delivered and collected at Number 43. The month-end raids were seemingly staged to intercept such transactions. The money would be confiscated, and no one ever knew what happened to it. All we knew was that on the occasions when the police were lucky enough to stumble over the money, they would promptly terminate the raid, with no questions asked. Owing to good intelligence on the ground, these confiscations were quite rare. However, on those occasions when no money was found, they could spend an entire afternoon or even a whole day on the premises, lingering around on the pretence that they were waiting for operatives who might unsuspectingly drop by.

The raids that coincided with the closure of UNISWA also coincided with my return home. Because it was safer and more neutral ground, many of the activities I was engaged in took place on campus. These mainly involved harbouring operatives and distributing political literature. It is my theory that the security branch hoped I would bring incriminating information home with me from campus. This never happened, apart from large volumes of political literature, which were confiscated. Fortunately for me, none of this was incriminating, at least not in their eyes.

A number of books stand out when I recall the literature that was confiscated, and that I would like to replace. These included one on the life and activities of Che Guevara, a book by uPeter Magubane and uZinzi Mandela entitled *South Africa Through the Lens*, and many more. I am pleased that I still have a book that I treasured, *Brothers in Blood*, which they missed. Through a friendly printer in Manzini, called Inter-Agencies, I had the book rebound with a plain maroon cover, which concealed its contents. Unfortunately, I could not afford to do the same with all of them.

It is difficult to talk about activities at Number 43 without referring to UNISWA. The university was an important recruitment, training, and hiding ground for the ANC. I would belatedly learn that many students who were active in politics had one kind of relationship or another with Number 43.

The raids were stepped up in the period from November 1983 to January 1984, for a totally different reason. An intense search had been launched to capture uNkosinathi Maseko, a brother-in-law who lived with us. At this time, we were raided almost every second or third day. On several occasions I was picked up as a result of mistaken identity. It had been said that uNkosinathi and I looked alike, with the result that the police were fed with wrong tip-offs about uNkosinathi being at Number 43.

In one of the raids, which triggered a trend, the Swazi police had a helicopter back-up from the South African security forces. It was later revealed that the back-up had been called on information that uNkosinathi had arrived with a team of operatives fully laden with arms.

This, of course, was completely false. It was the end of the calendar year at UNISWA and I was returning home for Christmas, which meant I had to bring all my belongings with me. A half-brother, uThemba Masilela, and a friend helped me with transport, leaving soon after dropping me off. By the time the raid was staged, I was on my own.

Until now, the raids had never really bothered me. My only concern had been that they would involve more people than just my family. All those who rented rooms at the back would inevitably be dragged into the parade. This must have been extremely inconveniencing and irritating to them, but at no point did I hear any of them complain or threaten to vacate because of the raids. Instead we had a lot of sympathy from these people.

* * *

This was the first raid that really shook me. On this particular day, I had decided to take a nap before going about my chores. A sudden commotion rudely shook me out of my sleep. When I ran outside I was completely disoriented and confused. A part of me thought it was a dream, another part was convinced that it was real.

A huge fear engulfed me. I had never been so petrified in my life. Not having experienced battle, I had never heard the deafening sounds of a helicopter propeller a mere two metres above my head, accompanied by fierce gunfire as the police fired into the air, shouting with the deliberate aim of intimidating and disorienting us. They ordered everyone to walk out with their hands in the air. As they put it in si-Swati, "Tandl' etulu!" (Hands in the air!) – a phrase which earned the Swazi police the title of 'Bo Tandl' etulu' in ANC circles. I was fearful that the house was being bombed and that this time around we would be shot.

In the event, none of that happened. Instead we submitted, as we had always done, to the anger of the police, because none of the people they had been hoping to find in the house were there. After the display of power, abuse and intimidation, we were frog-marched, close to twenty people in all, to the amusement of neighbours and onlookers, across town to the Manzini Police Station. This was a walk of about three or four kilometres, during which an army of policemen with guns escorted the entire family of at least two generations, together with their tenants. The only person who was left at home was my sister, uGranny, who was paraplegic.

We were kept at the Manzini Police Station for a day, before being released. During this time, uMagogo was tortured. This was neither the first nor the last of her experiences with torture. None of this was covered in the newspapers, nor did we press any charges.

For some unexplained reason, in all the arrests that I have gone through, at no stage was I tortured. To this day, this remains a big mystery to me.

Under the shelter of the mango tree

A mango tree that anchors the southeast corner of Number 43 bears its own interesting history. With this in mind, I prevailed on uMagogo never to cut it down. Previously, the front of Number 43 was populated with a wide variety of trees, ranging from mango and guava to avocado. All the other trees have been felled, but not the mango tree.

While it provided wonderful shade for family and friends, it was also used for other interesting purposes. Comrades used it on several occasions to hide from the police when raids were staged. The same police, in turn, used it during many of their camps at Number 43 to ambush those who dropped by unsuspectingly. It also served as a sentry post in the post-August 1986 period, following the kidnap of uGlory September, when security at Number 43 was stepped up significantly, with 24-hour armed surveillance.

On one occasion, when the whole family had been rounded up and detained, it was shared under very interesting circumstances. It was used as an overnight shelter by relatives, among whom were uBaningi Masilela, visiting from South Africa. Finding that the house was barricaded, and having no access and no other place to go, they parked their car under the tree. While trying to settle down to sleep, they observed unfamiliar movements above them. It turned out there were armed police who had perched in the tree, laying an ambush for operatives. Surprisingly, they did not bother the relatives, presumably because they were seen to be innocent.

It was under the same tree that the first interview for this book was conducted and its title conceived.

A relationship paradox

Three senior special branch officers in Swaziland consistently led these raids, namely Irvin Simelane, James Vilakati and Jeremiah Msibi. From time to time, a squad from the Mbabane security branch would join in the raids.

Much later, we learned that uIrvin Simelane was an uncle of my wife, uNonhlanhla. I did not know about this until the funeral of my father-in-law, in May 1992. We had never met uIrvin in a social setting and had never communicated in a civil fashion before that day. At the funeral, he recognised my family and unexpectedly walked over to greet us, addressing us as boS'bali, meaning in-laws. We were baffled, confused and angered by this gesture, which we found rather provocative. On enquiry after the funeral, my wife revealed the relationship to me.

She told me that during our courtship she had had to battle a strong wave of disapproval from her family. They saw our relationship as extremely dangerous, with the potential of bringing pain to them and even death to uNonhlanhla. They argued that she was "courting a terrorist". She learned to brush aside their disapproval, live with it, but carefully contain it so that it did not reach my ears.

I learned all this many years later, and by then the security situation had changed significantly, both in Swaziland and South Africa, so we could joke and laugh about it. Nevertheless, the revelation surprised me a great deal. What surprised me even more was her ability to deal with such a difficult situation on her own, keeping the information so close to her chest. I was deeply touched by this commitment to our relationship. Happily, when we finally married on 25 October 1990, our decision had the approval of both families. With hindsight, I look back on this as a Romeo and Juliet type of relationship.

UJames Vilakati was a more interesting character. While his colleagues embarked on their duty with hate and a desire for vengeance, he was friendlier and attempted on various occasions to engage on a friendly note and be more civil. He was a typical 'good cop'. However, his overtures were met with contempt and suspicion from the Masilela family.

He would later be close to a friend and work colleague of uNonhlanhla, between 1995 and 1998. It was only at this point that I came to appreciate his sincerity, to the extent that he offered to hand back the literature that had been confiscated during the various raids. For some reason, I never pursued the offer, which I came to regret.

I met up with him again at the Swazi High Commission in London in August 2003, where he was working as the security attaché. When I raised the issue of the literature he simply smiled and said, "Hhhawu Masilela, mngan' wami, bengingafisa ku kusita. Mane nje, sengahamba sikhatsi lesidze ekhaya. Ngeke ngisati kutsi tikuphi letincwadzi." (Masilela my friend, I wish I could help you. Unfortunately I have been out of the system for much too long, I would not even know where any of that material is kept.) My later attempt to pursue the matter directly with the Manzini police, where he had worked, proved equally futile. I simply dumped the idea.

Christmas at Number 43
Christmas has always been one of the most revered dates on our family almanac. It can be paralleled to the annual pilgrimage to Mecca for the Muslims. It has always been tradition that, irrespective of where one was in the world, this journey had to be taken at this time of the year. It continues to be an important pilgrimage for those of us who have left Swaziland. Christmas was seen by many of our comrades and friends as an opportunity to come to Number 43 to reminisce and renew. For the rest of the year we would be scattered across the world.

The house remains a hive of activity and a stopover for a great many people from all parts of the world.

Parallels with Liliesleaf Farm

Trying to equate Number 43 with Liliesleaf Farm is for me a complex yet natural exercise. Its complexity arises out of the potential conflict and debate it is likely to raise, given the disparate value judgments and beliefs on this subject. In drawing this parallel, however, one can identify both similarities and dissimilarities that are important and relevant to the theme of this book.

The logic of equating these two places is premised upon their historical significance to the struggle waged against white apartheid rule in South Africa. Both were seen and used as pivotal bases for the launching of onslaughts of a political or military nature against the government of the day. This is one critical similarity. A related similarity is that, while Liliesleaf housed the high command of the ANC of that time, Number 43 was the *de facto* operational base of the ANC high command in Swaziland.

However, while there is no doubt there were significant similarities between these two properties, there were also important differences. Firstly, while both made invaluable contributions to the achievement of independence in South Africa, they did so at different times in the liberation struggle and from different, albeit neighbouring countries. A further difference is that, while Liliesleaf Farm had political significance, Number 43 had a major practical significance, owing to the number of military operations launched from there. Thirdly, while the highest command of the ANC, including uMadiba, operated from Liliesleaf Farm, the same cannot be said of Number 43. Nevertheless, those who operated from Number 43 and the operations undertaken from there were significant enough to warrant the same recognition. Finally, a notable difference is that Liliesleaf farm ended up as the scene of one of the biggest disasters in the ANC's liberation struggle, where the entire leadership was arrested. Number 43, on the other hand, operated above ground for close to forty years, yet lived to witness independence without undergoing a change in character.

Liliesleaf was on a medium-sized property in Rivonia, some 20 kilometres north of Johannesburg. UMadiba moved into the house in October 1961. Two years later, on 11 July 1963, it was raided, bringing to an end its role as the ANC headquarters. It had served as a safe house, from which military plans to overthrow the government of the day were hatched, as well as serving as a fortress for the ANC.

For its contribution to the liberation of South Africa, and its significance to the Rivonia Trial, Liliesleaf Farm has been declared a national monument. At the time of writing, Number 43 was presented to the Manzini City Council as part of an exercise to identify historical sites in the Manzini Urban Area. I serendipitously stumbled into the Council's initiative after approaching the offices to access their documentation centre. When I presented the work I was doing to the PRO, she was excited about the hypothesis I had developed and the historic importance of a property, which was just around the corner but had not yet been considered for the project of the City Council. She immediately requested that I provide her with more information in the form of a précis of the book. This I immediately did.

This is how Number 43 was born. The rest of the book will show how its character changed over the years and how those associated with it grew with the changes. There is no doubt that it gains its historical importance, side by side with many other houses that are not discussed in this book. What sets it apart is the warmth of the relationships among the many and varied people who passed through it, as well as the close attachment they had to the person behind the house – thus earning its title, kwaMagogo.

CHAPTER 2

Magogo

At the heart of the Masilela family, and of the liberation struggle as it was waged from Swaziland, as well as my own personal success, is a humble woman, greatly deserving of recognition, who herself would never acknowledge this view. She was born Rebecca Makgomo Kekana, but later in life came to be known simply as uMagogo, a title bestowed on her to show respect and admiration for the position she held among South Africans in exile. Even her children ended up calling her uMagogo, instead of uMama. Interestingly, even people of her own age would come to call her uMagogo.

UMagogo is my mother, but because of her abundant love and care for people in general, many friends and comrades have seen her as their mother as well. As a direct consequence of that, I have always viewed her as a shared asset. I write about her here not as my mother, but as this unifying character for many who sought the security of a family in exile.

I cannot think of anyone who has gone through the Masilela homestead and has left without a feeling of warm appreciation and admiration for the old lady. She has been a pillar not only for the family but also for the comrades and other activists who were based in Swaziland or transiting, in particular during the period of the 1970s through to the 1990s.

Politically innocent

Ironically, uMagogo was not herself a political person, though she had great wisdom and an amazing ability to envision the world many years ahead of all of us, out-performing many political commissars of both the ANC and PAC.

The relationship between the ANC and PAC in Swaziland is of particular importance in the context of Number 43. Owing to a lack of political maturity on the part of some individuals, there was an under-lying animosity between the two political parties. Some would argue that this was due to the philosophical differences between them. Others asserted that it was purely a function of the competition for power, recognition and membership, with each party wanting to claim political and military victories. Clearly, it was a combination of the two views.

These differences notwithstanding, kwaMagogo was a neutral venue for both parties. For many years, it acted as the melting pot for politi-cal debate and education. This can only be attributable to the open-ness with which uMagogo accepted everybody who came by, with no prejudice against anyone's inclination.

Throughout most of my high school life, I spent whole evenings in long and sometimes uncomfortable political debates. Indeed, it would be more correct to say I simply sat in on these debates, given that I spent most of my time quietly listening to what I found to be intellectually interesting people, and never really engaged in the argu-ments. This quiet demeanour attracted the wrath of my elder broth-ers, uTodd and uLucky. They would say, "Uthuleleni, sikhuluma? Usenz' iy'lima wena Elias!" (Why are you quiet when we are talking? You make us look like fools!) Unfortunately, that was my nature, which I could not change.

What I found interesting was the way some people got carried away during these debates, and became extremely emotional, with embar-rassingly little content or principle in their arguments. The only time I would involve myself was when I felt that a debate was no longer productive and bordered on triviality. It would be my self-imposed task to bring people back on track and focus them on specific out-comes. This role earned me the title of 'Professor', which was not in any way a reflection of my intellectual dexterity. My involvement in the discussions mainly happened in the period 1979 to 1983, after which I spent less and less time at Number 43, since I attended uni-versity from 1982 until 1986. In my first year, I lived off-campus and came in from home every day.

These debates, with their widely diverging views, made me understand how complex the South African struggle was and, even more, how challenging the governance of the country would be, post-independence. I often wondered if we had the capacity and depth to meet people's expectations. The things that I worried about then are a reality today in South Africa.

An interesting origin

No description of uMagogo would be complete if done in isolation from her family history. Her disposition and vision are defined by this history, not only because it is appealing but also because it is graced with a royal heritage and dignity.

UMagogo was born on 12 December 1928, in Hammanskraal, north of Pretoria, previously Farm 396, Leeuwkraal. This is an Afrikaans name for 'a kraal of lions'. It was later renamed Kekanastad, Majaneng. The Chief of the Ndebele at the time, Abraham Jambo Kekana, facilitated the purchase of Leeuwkraal on behalf of the Ndebele people, hence the change of name.

UMakgomo was the daughter of Abraham Jambo Kekana and Batseba Magogodi Mkhonwana. Abraham acted as Chief and advisor of the Ndebele people on a number of occasions until his death on 6 June 1964, of an unknown ailment. He did this with dignity, integrity and respect for his role. At no point did he nurse any ambition to hold the responsibility on a permanent basis. For this reason he was loved and respected by the Ndebele people.

His was a complex history. Understanding it is essential not only to record the wisdom passed on to uMakgomo, but to clarify the family tree, which was consolidated by the Nhlapo Commission, sitting at the time of writing this book.

The first time he assumed the role of acting Chief, uAbraham took over the reins from his grandfather, Seroto Karl Kekana. UKarl had four wives, Mahlangu, Mabhena, Skhosana, and Masango. UMahlangu bore one boy child, who was named Jan. The rest of the wives had several children each. UJan was anointed as the next chief by virtue of being the only son and only child of his mother. This created a huge amount of animosity, resulting in his half-brothers attempting

22

to kill him by burying him alive. To the dismay both of his brothers and the rest of the family, he survived. The elders implemented their decision to make him Chief.

Unlike his father, uJan had one wife, Maria Makgoboketsha, and they had eight children. The eldest child was Nathaniel, followed by Karl, Abraham, Jan, Johannes, Tyson, Rebecca Makgomo, and Riba. As the first son, uNathaniel was heir to the crown, but instead he went to Kimberley to work in the diamond mines. He disappeared without a trace, and to this day no one knows what happened to him. His son Hosiah was next in line to be the chief, but could not assume that responsibility, since he was still too young. Instead uKarl took over the throne.

He also had one wife, and was blessed with three children. When he died, none of the children was old enough to take over the reins. To remedy this, the elders appointed uAbraham Jambo Kekana to act as Chief once again. When one of the boys, Dingaan, came of age he took over and uAbraham Jambo stayed on as his principal adviser.

UDingaan had four children, Karl, Hans, Segoputso and Annah. His reign was cut short when he died of poisoning in 1951, for which his wife was believed to have been responsible. In his will, he had indicated that his preference was for Hans or Karl to take over the crown. This was revealed by the Native Commissioner of the time, who read the will at a public gathering. Unfortunately, both were still too young, so uAbraham Jambo was yet again appointed to act as Chief. The decision by the elders was a reflection of the trust the Ndebele people had in his leadership skills, integrity, and willingness to serve without pursuing his own selfish interests.

In his wisdom, uAbraham sent uKarl to Kilnerton High School in Pretoria to study. He argued that leadership without education, in the light of white rule, was untenable and compromised the black people. While in Pretoria, uKarl joined the Boy Scout movement. His mother and mother's uncle, Madikologa, visited him quite frequently. It is believed that, during one of their visits, they gave him some medicine in the form of the root of a plant for him to keep as a good omen. Subsequently, his health turned and deteriorated. It is believed this was as a result of the medicine from his mother's uncle, and that he instructed his Scoutmaster to communicate this to uAbraham.

When he died, the Kilnerton Boy Scout movement delivered his corpse to uAbraham. Karl's message was then given to Abraham, in the presence of the elders of the tribe. This created an extremely volatile situation, with the people baying for Madikologa's blood. The police had to intervene to quell the fires.

When Hans came of age he took over the throne. As was an established tradition, uAbraham had hoped to continue in his advisory role, as he had done with uDingaan, but uHans would not hear of it. It is said that he lived a fast life of cars and alcohol. He died in a car accident in December 1962, while driving from Pietersburg (now Polokwane, in the Limpopo province). Since this period, the traditional leadership of the Ndebele people in Majaneng has not been a stable and certain one.

★ ★ ★

Such was the life and leadership of Abraham Jambo Kekana. He left a legacy that has not been equalled. He also imparted skills to uMagogo which could not have been taught in any academic institution. Commenting about her background and character, a friend of uMagogo, Mrs Eva Gluckman of Johannesburg, described her: "The woman is very special. It shows that she is not a commoner and, like her father, who spent his life serving the people, she has served with a big heart".

A meeting made in heaven

UMakgomo met Solomon Buthongo Masilela, often called 'Thongo', soon after the Second World War, when he returned from the front in 1945. Both uMakgomo and uButhongo attended the Lutheran Church in Majaneng, where they met and started dating. They courted for close to five years, finally marrying in August 1951.

At the time they met, uButhongo was on a building apprenticeship programme, to develop what is now Themba location, in Hammanskraal. He had trained as a bricklayer, as part of the demobilisation programme of the South African army. He was later known in Swaziland as 'uMahlabahlaba', for his hawkishness in the supervision of his building squad. He always insisted that members of his family be part of the squad. This included the girls, who were never spared from these building chores.

During his stay in Hammanskraal, uButhongo fell in love not only with uMakgomo but with the place as well. He approached his father-in-law, uAbraham, who was acting as chief at that time, with a request to be allocated a piece of land, on which he could build a house for his mother and siblings.

UButhongo had earlier lost his father, who had lived and worked for many years on land belonging to a white farmer, on a sharecropping arrangement. This man had a farm in Middelburg and another in Bethal, where the labourers spent most of their time. As was to be expected, the family was expelled from the farm, as they were no longer of use to the farmer. That meant they did not have a place to stay and would end up on the streets if an alternative home could not be found.

Buthongo's father was buried on the farm in Middelburg, but for many years uButhongo has had no access to the grave, which sorely pains him. On several occasions, he made failed attempts to have the body exhumed in order to give it a burial at a place he could access.

The death notwithstanding, I feel my father's family was finally liberated from the bondage of the 'Bethal effect'. News reports in the late 1940s carried chilling revelations about the atrocities on Bethal farms. Labourers were cursed, beaten and locked in their compounds overnight. Their clothes were taken from them and savage dogs guarded them to make sure they did not try to escape. Routine forms of discipline included savage whippings, cutting their feet with hoes to immobilise them, as well as chaining the workers together at night.

While the father was labouring under these conditions, the family was oblivious of the atrocities. To save his family the embarrassment, he kept his degrading experiences to himself. UButhongo only came to hear about them much later, after he returned from the army, through the press and farm boycotts led by the ANC. He was distressed about the discovery, but could do nothing about it. He was even more upset that he had never had the opportunity of discussing these issues with his father.

When Themba location was completed in 1953, uButhongo moved back to Johannesburg. He and uMagogo set up home in Soweto, next to the Nancefield (pronounced as 'Nicefill' by people then) train station. Nancefield is one of the older locations in Soweto, started with the resettlement of the African population following an outbreak of bubonic plague in 1904. Many locations were razed to the ground to contain the plague. It later became Pimville, the heartbeat of Soweto.

By then the couple had two children, uSwazi and uTodd. Both were born at Littleflower Clinic in Lady Selbourne, just outside Pretoria. Coincidentally, uTodd, who died in 2003, was buried in a cemetery adjacent to the clinic where he was born.

In those days, it was common for people to give birth at home, but Magogo's father insisted the delivery of the two babies be performed in hospital. Her mother, uBatseba, had passed away in May 1945, meaning there would be no one to oversee the procedure and attend to the newborns, or their mother.

The couple's arrival in Johannesburg coincided with the tearing down of Sophiatown. As part of this development, they moved from Nancefield to S'godiphola, Mofolo North.

With the introduction of Bantu education in 1953, uButhongo began to think of emigrating. In 1958, he became exposed to the Swazi education system when he provided transport services to people travelling between Johannesburg and Manzini. The result was a conscious decision to emigrate to Swaziland, where he hoped to give his children access to a superior, or at least slightly better, education. With hindsight, this decision turned out to be an extremely beneficial one for the whole family and even, however insignificant it might be, for the development of South Africa.

The decision to emigrate was also influenced by a number of people, including several Swazi politicians who frequented South Africa for consultations with the ANC on developments relating to Swaziland's independence. Among them were Douglas Lukhele, who rose to be one of the most accomplished advocates in Swaziland; Ambrose Zwane, a medical doctor, founder and leader of the Ngwane National Liberation Congress (NNLC); a certain Prince Charles (this was his name, and has no connection with the Prince of Wales); and a certain McDonald.

UButhongo came to know these people through an old family friend and mentor from Swaziland, uMaboya Masilela. UMaboya also introduced him to uMlondolozi Masilela, who played a crucial role in Buthongo's settlement in Swaziland and the acquisition of Khonta status. This is a slightly lower version of citizenship in Swaziland, which can be likened to permanent residence. It is acquired through the traditional chieftainship system. A further person instrumental in the decision was uMaduna, father to the former Minister of Justice in South Africa, Penuel Maduna.

To fund the move to Swaziland, uButhongo sold his house, Number 466 in Mofolo North, to his nephew, uBhomo Masilela. In January 1965, he and uMagogo started the journey to Swaziland. By then they had eight children.

According to their original plans, they were to have embarked on the journey in 1964, but had to postpone because of the death of uAbraham. He died less than two months after the birth of their eighth child, uElias, on 27 April 1964. Coincidentally, this would later be an important date for South Africans, Freedom Day, as it represents the attainment of independence and black rule in this country. I must admit I feel special to have a birthday that coincides with one of the most important dates on South Africa's calendar.

Such was the origin of the partnership of uButhongo and uMakgomo, which ushered them into the most challenging forty years of their lives, during which they raised their children, searched for a livelihood in various places and in two different countries, and found themselves at the crossroads of one of the most documented revolutions of our time.

CHAPTER 3

Buthongo

My father, Solomon Buthongo Masilela, has a family history as interesting and challenging as that of uMagogo. The only difference is that he does not boast the heritage of royalty that uMagogo enjoys. The name Buthongo means 'sleep' in isiZulu, which is a contradiction to the man's character, because he never sleeps. We have always wondered how he ended up with the name.

According to uButhongo, he was born on 5 August 1924, in Ngobi, Middelburg, to Moraka Daniel Masilela and Sarah naMngwane. He was one of a family of eleven – uElias, uAlfred, uJoana, uNamdlangu, uBetty, uButhongo, uPhillip, uWilhemina, uJoel and uJonas, the latter two being twins. One child, Losaniya, was lost early after birth to an unknown illness.

Interestingly, his identity document gives a different date of birth. It shows that he was born on 5 August 1925. It is not clear whether this was an error at the time of registration or a result of the generally observed arrogance of government officials of the time. This tendency resulted in many people assuming incorrect personal details, which they had to live with for the rest of their lives.

Given that most births took place at home, few formal birth certificates were issued. To try and remedy this gap, a teacher by the name of uMabhena helped the family document the dates of birth and death of all the siblings. This assistance was extended to the rest of the community, as most, if not all, black parents were not formally educated. He was also instrumental in building the first primary school in the area.

He kept a book where he wrote all these dates and provided the families with a similar record to keep for themselves. While researching for this book, I spent much time and effort, including meetings, telephone calls, visits as well as physical searches, trying to locate this document. All these efforts came to naught. Then one day in September 2006, as uBetty (whom we call 'uKgare') was rearranging things in her house in Mamelodi, a "rotten piece of paper", as she put it, "iphepha loku bola" (fell from among the rest of the stuff). She did not know what it was and almost crumpled it and threw it away. When she read it, she had the surprise of her life. There it was . . . the very document that uMabhena kept for the family. It had all the names and dates of birth of the family, from 1913 to 1933. I was immediately called to come and pick it up. Ironically, the date of birth against the name of uButhongo coincides with the one on his identity document. Even though he insists on his version, the document remains invaluable.

UButhongo attended school at Berlin School in Rietvlei. He was still at school when his father, Moraka, died on 7 September 1939, four days after Britain and France declared war on Germany.

Forced to the battle front

Due to financial difficulties, uButhongo could not continue with his studies beyond Standard 1. This period coincided with a serious crisis brought about by a devastating drought that almost decimated the family. The coincidence of the death of the breadwinner and the outbreak of a drought brought untold hardship to the family. The piece of land they tilled became dry and virtually unusable. Because there were no prospects of uButhongo finding a job to feed the family, he was forced to join the army in 1942. This quickly became the way to go for most young healthy boys and men like him. He went to register and was enlisted in Germiston.

By the time he joined the army, most of his siblings had left Ngobi and were scattered across Pretoria in search of a better livelihood. As a soldier, uButhongo earned £1.10s a month, part of which he would remit to the family back home. This gave them money for sustenance. His mother used to collect the money from the offices of the Commissioner in Middleburg every month.

The recruits underwent training for about six months, after which they were sent to Springs. This was a distribution point for soldiers who were to be posted to the front. It was here that uButhongo learnt how to drive and obtained his heavy-duty driver's license. They were subsequently sent to a camp in Durban, called Snell Parade (then Natal command headquarters). UButhongo spent little time there, as he was soon transferred.

In 1943 his unit was sent to the Wadi Garawi Camp in Egypt, where he worked as a driver distributing supplies. He was part of a large convoy operating at the front. At the end of the war, they were all returned to Wadi Garawi, after which they were sent back home. When they arrived in Durban, they were bundled into a train back to Germiston, where the whole experience had started.

Around August of that year he boarded a train that took him back home to Middelburg. On arrival, he was confronted with the greatest disappointment and setback of his life. He discovered that the money the family had been receiving on a monthly basis had cost them a seven-head herd of cattle. The Commissioner of the area had argued that, since the family was receiving an income from the army, they were not entitled to keep any cattle. As a consequence, the herd was confiscated. As if the confiscation were not bad enough, the family was later also evicted from the farm KwaNangoqwana shortly after uButhongo returned.

With no income and no savings in the form of cattle, the poverty that had faced the family before uButhongo joined the army was back to haunt them. He was forced to travel to Johannesburg in December 1945 to look for employment. Whilst searching he found refuge in Orlando East at the home of a friend, whom he only remembers as uMnela, who had been with him in the army. This was a critical time for him and finding a job was an urgent matter, as he had to bring his mother and some of his siblings to Johannesburg. He gave consideration to the fact that he could not place an undue burden on his friend for an extended period of time.

The job search proved to be a gruelling experience. At all the places of possible employment, there were people employed merely to sit at the front gate as gate keepers, with stamp pads that had big block letters reading 'No Job'. When confronted with a job seeker, without a word and with well-practiced swiftness, they would simply stamp these words on a piece of paper. It would then be handed to the job seeker as the only form of communication he would receive. The possibility of getting through the gates to talk to someone in authority was nil.

After a tiring search, uButhongo eventually found a job as a night watchman at the Trade Fair grounds in Milner Park, sometime in 1946. This job earned him about £7.10s a month, an improvement on what he earned in the army. After all the effort of finding a job, he worked for only three months. He had to leave the job to join a demobilisation programme where he was given training in bricklaying. This was a well-reasoned decision, as he saw it as a temporary reduction in his earnings in favour of a long-term professional gain.

This training lasted six months. As part of his internship he was posted to Hammanskraal, in a team that would build Themba location in 1947. It was at this point that he brought his mother and siblings to join him in Hammanskraal. With the help of friends, he built a house there for his family. This was a task for Saturdays, after work and Sundays. Working weekends was to be the norm in the family for years to come, a good lesson in the value of hard work.

When the Themba project was winding down, uButhongo had a fight with his white supervisor and was forced to resign, resulting in him rejoining the ranks of the unemployed. The search for another job started in earnest, but since Hammanskraal could not offer good opportunities, he was forced to go back to Johannesburg. When he finally found work, he stayed with his half brother, uLucas (pronounced Lukas) Tshakane, at 3417 Mlamlankunzi. He was very fortunate in that uLucas introduced him to a friend of his who ran a construction company. After working with him for a while and establishing contacts, uButhongo went it alone.

At that point he brought uMagogo and the children to Johannesburg to join him. Before he could find them a place of their own, they stayed with uLucas. After a while, they moved briefly to KwaMamoletsana and then to Nancefield. When Mofolo North was established, uButhongo found a plot there and built a house out of his own pocket.

By now the political environment in South Africa was worsening and was no longer conducive to a family and the proper upbringing of children. In addition, the cost of living in Johannesburg was becoming untenable. UButhongo, therefore, decided to relocate to Swaziland, in search of a better quality education and a good family life.

Settling down

UButhongo had started visiting Swaziland in 1958. In 1962, he took uMagogo along to view the place and to satisfy themselves that Swaziland was the kind of environment they wanted to live in. While there, they spent their first night at the residence of Dr Ambrose Zwane. They proceeded to eNkambeni, to the east of Swaziland, where they stayed with a Masilela family, that of uSam Masilela, the second black Tax Commissioner in Swaziland.

A follow-up trip was undertaken in 1963. This time, however, they did not stay long, as the timing of the trip coincided with the introduction of border controls between Swaziland and South Africa. It was during this visit that they finally made the decision to move, leaving a deposit with Peter Forbes (known as 'Mabhodweni' by locals), a real estate developer, for a vacant plot in an undeveloped Ngwane Park Township.

A certain Solly Mahlangu, who became a close family friend and later a benefactor, was hired to assist in transporting their belongings to Swaziland. On the morning after their arrival, they went to Peter Forbes, hoping to be shown the plot that uButhongo had paid for two years earlier, only to discover that the subdivisions had not been done. Forbes suggested they move temporarily into a huge, decrepit Dutch farmhouse, which had not been occupied for many years and could well have been a hideout for criminals.

This turn of events left uButhongo in shock and disgust. The 'great trek' in search of a better life had instead landed them in misery. He was confused as to what to do with his belongings and the children. He felt as if he were in the 'Gramadoelas', an Afrikaans word for 'in the middle of nowhere'.

USolly saved the day by offering uButhongo temporary refuge on his property at Number 43, Trelawney Park, which was not far from Ngwane Park, but much closer to the centre of Manzini. This gesture was warmly welcomed. On their arrival at Number 43, which was still bush, they set about clearing the place and erected a makeshift structure to see them through the first few months. This structure ended up being the family's principal dwelling for the next five years. It served them well, providing the warmth they needed. This was in spite of the gaping holes, which allowed the vagaries of the weather to be felt at the slightest change.

Search for schools

By now, uButhongo and uMagogo had eight children. The youngest was barely a year old. The daunting task of finding schools started in earnest. This could not have been carried out successfully without the assistance of several concerned and helpful South Africans then living in Manzini. With the assistance of Mrs Mabuza, places for uSwazi and uGranny at the Nazarene School were secured fairly quickly. Mr Habedi used his weight to find places for uTodd and uLucky at the Salesian Boys' School. Both through this assistance and the fact that the Habedis were from the same area as uMagogo in Makapanstad, a close relationship developed between the two families. Further, Mrs Mokgokong and Mrs Mhlanga assisted in getting uGrace and uThandi places at the St Theresa's Girls' School. This assistance too spelled the beginning of a long-term relationship between the families.

His mission had been accomplished, but uButhongo still had to go back to South Africa to continue with his work. Keeping the children in school was the next challenge. With uButhongo away, the rest of the family at Number 43 again faced hunger and hardship. On many occasions the family went to bed without a meal. At some point, water services were cut off. The Mabuzas allowed us to collect water from their outside tap, but the offer did not last, as uMagogo could not pay the token fee they asked. In desperation, we resorted to water from the bilharzia-infested uMzinene River. A kind Mr Hitchings came to the family's rescue. He allowed the family access to water from his property until services were reconnected at Number 43.

The family is together again

Owing to financial constraints, distance and the difficulty of travelling between South Africa and Swaziland, uButhongo hardly ever visited. He was, however, forced to move permanently to Swaziland when Angel was born in May 1966, owing to complications that uMagogo developed at birth. She went into a coma during the delivery. Given the magnitude of the problem, uButhongo decided to quit South Africa, opting to work in Swaziland where he would be close to his family, albeit for a much lower salary.

He secured a job at the Public Works Department in Manzini. In this post, he earned about R60 per month. Given such a salary, meagre even by the standards of those days, the compelling objective of educating his children meant cutting out any form of luxury, even in its narrowest definition. For example, there was never anything like birthday or Christmas celebrations. (This tradition has carried through to the way in which I run my own family today. My children never get any birthday or Christmas presents.)

In order to supplement his income, uButhongo built more makeshift structures that he rented out. These were made of reused corrugated iron, which he bought from his employer. To this day, uButhongo is grateful to uSolly, who allowed him to use the property as he pleased and never charged him a cent for its use. The income from this enterprise made a great difference to the family's welfare and lifestyle. It is probably stretching it to talk of a lifestyle, but it did enable the family to shift away from the brink of dismal poverty.

This hard-earned comfort was soon to be expunged. A few months later the landlord, Mr S.B. Williams, known to the locals as 'Helemisi', arrived with a demand for payment of the balance for the property, failing which the family would be evicted. Williams had built a house, just north of Trelawney Park, in a suburb that would later be named after him – 'kaHelemisi'. He was one of the first District Commissioners in Manzini and one of two well-trusted white advisers to King Sobhuza II. At the time of writing, his house was being considered by the local authority as one of the historical sites in Manzini.

Williams argued that uSolly was not servicing his bond. While all this was happening, uButhongo was in South Africa. UMagogo pleaded with Williams to allow them time to find uSolly or take over the servicing of the bond. On uButhongo's return, he was told what had happened and the options that uMagogo had suggested to Williams. None of these resonated with him. Instead uButhongo insisted that they immediately move to Ngwane Park and occupy his property there, and allow Number 43 to be attached. Owing to its proximity to the town centre and to schools, uMagogo insisted on keeping Number 43. After a long, tortuous debate, an agreement was reached that they would take over the bond on behalf of uSolly. On his return, he would have to refund uButhongo for the transaction and any other related costs. This was done. Months later, on completion of the bond, and when it became clear that uSolly was not returning, uButhongo took title of the property. By way of a letter signed on the 3 September 1966, he entered into a conditional Deed of Sale with Williams for the purchase of Number 43. For this agreement to come into force, he paid a deposit of R200.

This debate would probably not have been settled in the manner it was if it had not been for the intervention of a neighbour, Mr Buthelezi, a South African residing in Trelawney Park at the time. UButhelezi was a shrewd businessman, with a good deal of foresight. As soon as he heard about uButhongo's predicament, instead of seeing a liability he saw an opportunity. He firmly supported the idea of servicing Solly's debt in full, giving uButhongo control over the property.

USolly had disappeared for a long time and was no longer visiting or communicating. By the time the bond was fully paid, uButhongo had had no contact with him and did not know where he was. Williams came with a further demand against uSolly, which uButhongo was forced to take over as well. He was becoming justifiably weary of this trend, not knowing when these demands would end, and facing the dilemma of whether to remain on the property or move. Fortunately, this was the last of such surprises.

A bold decision and a big handout

In the meantime, he considered building a decent, permanent home on Number 43, to replace the makeshift structure. This was a bold step, since it would be taken without consulting or getting approval from the rightful owner of the property, uSolly. Nevertheless, he went ahead to implement his plan. Because the construction was funded out of his pocket and was undertaken during his free time and weekends, it was not ready until around 1971. Even at that stage, the house was barely habitable. There was no water or electricity, the walls were not painted and the floors were not tiled. But it was still a significant improvement on the previous corrugated structure, and brought the family a notable increase in respect and dignity. All this happened within a period of about five years.

A year or so after the completion of the house, out of the blue, uSolly showed up for a visit with his wife. He could not believe his eyes. At first he thought he was at the wrong address. The last time he had seen the place it had been partially bush. Now he was presented with a big, completed house. Surprisingly, when the various events and decisions were communicated to him, he was nonchalant about the whole matter. He just said to uButhongo, "You have worked very hard on the property, you have paid off my debt . . . it is now yours, just keep it." There was no exchange of any money, as a result of this decision. The family was elated, and uButhongo was filled with relief and pleasure at the manner in which the matter was concluded. UMagogo was honoured for her bold risk in taking over the liability attached to the property. After all these years, it had paid off.

When uSolly left after that visit, we heard nothing more from him until January 1993, when he suddenly appeared at Number 43 to invite the family to Siyabuswa, in Mpumalanga, for an official function on the sixteenth of the same month. He was celebrating his appointment to the position of Minister of Police.

That is how Number 43 was founded and came into the hands of the Masilela family.

PART II
The Role Played by My Family

11ᵗʰ *March 1967*

re: TOWN RATES TO 31ST MARCH, 1967 - TRELAWNY PARK
TOWNSHIP

ı our letter dated 18th November, 1966 Purchasers were
notified of the values placed on the various portions at the interim
valuation and informed that in cases where they exceeded the amount
of the purchase price objections would be lodged.

The result of the objections was disappointing but
portion 61 was reduced from R900 to R850, Portion 64 was reduced from
R 2000 to R1800 and Portion 86 was reduced from R1800 to R1400.

We further endeavoured to protect the interests of
Purchasers from the increase of valuations by requesting the Town
Management Board, in cases where Purchasers were still paying by
instalments, that assessments should be made on the original site
value. This was refused, as also representations that the dating
back of the assessments at the higher value to 1st January, 1966 was
inequitable being 3 months of the previous financial year for which
rates had already been paid and receipts issued.

The assessments are therefore for the period of 15 months
from 1st January, 1966 to 31st March, 1967 and portion _43_ pur-
chased by you is assessed as: Land R _45.00_, Buildings R _1.25_
Total R _46.25_ An amount of R ___ can be deducted for payments for
the three months of the previous year and subsequent payments, if
any. Total deductions in your case are therefore R _____ leaving
a balance payable of R _____ .

Your present rates run from date of Purchase
by you to 31.3.67 and is calculated at R21.63

The Estate being primarily liable as at 15th March, 1966
has already paid an amount based on last year's valuation and will
now pay the increased amounts but in terms of the Deed of Sale and
the provisions of the Law, Purchasers are required to refund.

Payment of R _21.63_ is therefore requested before
31st March, 1967 and amounts not paid by that date is liable for
interest at the rate of 7% p.a.

The delay in submitting these particulars is regretted
but is owing to circumstances beyond our control.

S.T. Masilela Esq.   Yours faithfully,

In this 1967 letter, uButhongo disputes the rating of the house by the municipality.
Taking ownership of Number 43 marked the beginning of a long tradition of activism in
the Masilela family, which led to the author establishing the first two ratepayers asso-
ciations in Swaziland (one for Trelawney Park, the other for Manzini) in the late 1980s.

CHAPTER 4

Prelude

UButhongo and uMakgomo were blessed with nine children: uSwazi (1949), uTodd (1951), uThandi (1953), uGrace (1956), uGranny (1957), uLucky (1958), uJoana (1962), uElias (1964) and uAngel (1966). At the time of writing, there were 27 grandchildren and 11 great-grand-children.

As children born into this family, we never really had the luxury of making a conscious choice as to whether or not we entered politics. It came as a given. From an early age, we found ourselves deeply immersed in it. I have often asked myself the question, "Would I have ever entered politics and would I have been actively involved had I been born into a different family?" This is clearly a difficult question to answer.

We, however, had the option of making the decision whether to align ourselves with the ANC or the PAC. At that time, those were the only two credible choices. Indeed, in Swaziland they were the only available choices, since the Black Consciousness Movement (BCM) never really had any notable form of representation in that country.

Owing to the default alignment of our parents with the ANC and its prominence both inside and outside South Africa, most of us ended up in the ANC. A factor in this may have been the sheer organisational superiority and recruitment drive of the ANC compared to the PAC. This notwithstanding, uLucky and uGrace went a separate route and joined the PAC. However, uGrace, whose political alignment was never obvious to me while she was in Swaziland, would later switch to the ANC.

These differences sometimes made it awkward in dealing with uLucky. This became more intense as my views became stronger and I was more willing and better able to express them freely and confidently. To a degree, the tension continues to this day. As brothers, though, we are able to separate political differences from our underlying family bond, as we have in the past. Most of our debates nowadays are much more intellectual and academic, compared to their character prior to 1994.

One of my biggest emotional challenges over these ideological differences came when I visited the United States for the first time in December 1989. During this visit, I was to meet uLucky and uAngel in Washington, DC, where they were based at the time. Part of my trepidation came from my ignorance of how uLucky had developed ideologically since he had left Swaziland ten years earlier. I had never really engaged with him in my maturity. I was concerned that with the passage of time we might have drifted further apart ideologically. I was resolved not to engage in endless debates that would leave me with regret at having met him again. Hitherto we had never agreed and some of our discussions had been heated and emotional. Were it not for the fact that he was my brother, I probably would not have looked him up.

My fears were to be confirmed. Throughout my stay in Washington, members of the PAC, exiled in the US, surrounded me. The visit coincided with the release of uMadiba in February 1990. Indeed, throughout our discussions, we disagreed on the appropriateness of his release. They argued that the ANC and uMadiba had undermined the struggle by going for a settlement with the Afrikaner government. In their view, anything less than civil war and a military takeover of government was tantamount to selling out. Of course I could not agree with this view. A further speculative view, which was repeatedly emphasised but which I refused to debate, was that "uMadiba was being set up to fail, just like Toivo Ja Toivo".

Despite these tensions, the experience was not as bad as I had anticipated. The visit was extremely worthwhile and an eye-opener on dealing with opposing political views, particularly as a new era dawned in South Africa.

Different roles for different siblings

Each of us in the family became involved in the struggle at different levels and with varying intensities. This part of the book looks at the contributions of each sibling. Unfortunately, not all are still alive to tell their own histories. Heavy reliance is placed on the knowledge base of third persons in weaving the missing stories together. This has been carefully done, so as to avoid any parody and under-representation. The latter, however, is an unavoidable error.

Four of my siblings are no longer with us, namely uGrace (24 April 1990); uAngel (6 May 1999); uGranny (21June 1999); and uTodd (24 March 2003). Their stories are abbreviated compared to those of the other siblings, resulting in a possible underplaying of their respective contributions. After going through the process, I was amazed by the level of ignorance we had about each other as a family. It was ironic to note that friends and other third parties often knew more about us than we did ourselves.

Following in this section of the book is a brief account of each member of the family. The experiences of each are unique and deserve their individual recognition.

Overcoming physical inhibitions

One member who was adored both within and without the family was uGranny, whose contributions were astounding, despite her physical condition. She had an amazing level of bravery and energy.

UGranny was a paraplegic following a polio attack as a child. She relied on crutches to get around. This meant she periodically had to undergo treatment, with physiotherapy and refitting of her boots at the Baragwanath Hospital in Johannesburg, now the Chris Hani Baragwanath Hospital. She was the only member of the family who could enter South Africa post-1976, following the blacklisting of the family by South Africa. It was during these medical visits that she undertook her clandestine operations.

She worked as a courier, and among her many tasks she was responsible for ferrying letters between operatives in Swaziland and their families in South Africa, as well as propaganda material. She was instrumental in distributing campaign materials in locations such as Soweto, Atteridgeville and Mamelodi, where we had relatives. These included campaign posters, write-ups and lapel pins, including those protesting against the hanging of uSolomon Mahlangu and uJames Mange, among others. She would stuff toothpaste boxes with these letters and pamphlets. These in turn would be concealed in her boots.

During one of these missions she arrived at a place in Kliptown in the middle of the night, to find there was no one at home. At that time of night, she had no way of getting to any of our relatives, as the taxi in which she travelled had dropped her off and left. However, by a stroke of luck, a priest rescued her and sheltered her for the night. When she returned the following morning to the house she had gone to the previous night, she found people at home. To her dismay, she was kicked out like a dog. The occupants told her they had had enough trouble with the police and never again wanted to deal with terrorists. While being rejected in this manner affected her gravely, it was her only negative experience of this kind.

This experience and risks that uGranny took, are just a glimpse of the broader risks that the rest of the family was exposed to. The rest of the section will provide an indication of the extent and impact of this exposure.

CHAPTER 5

The Pioneer

Swazi Wilhelmina Masilela

The eldest in the family is uSwazi. She is an important figure for us, as she has become the pillar for those of us who have resettled in South Africa. She has assumed the role of uMagogo.

Our paternal grandmother, maMajampela, in Hammanskraal, raised her. Later, she went to live with Magogo's elder sister, uAnnah Moeketsi, whom we called Mmamogolo Annah, further simplified in day-to-day speech to 'Gol' Annah'. They lived in Lady Selbourne, from which they were forcibly removed in the late 1950s and early 1960s, to be resettled in Vlakfontein, now Mamelodi, a location that later became important for its resistance against apartheid. Some people were moved to Atteridgeville and Saulsville, while others were dumped in Winterveld and Garankuwa. Lady Selbourne gave way to a white suburb called Suiderberg.

Her house, 7381 Mamelodi, became our second home. Whenever we visited South Africa, during the years when this was possible, that is where we would go. Unfortunately, the house became a source of dissension among the Kekana family on the death of uGol' Annah in July 1994. UMagogo, as Gol' Annah's only surviving sibling, found herself at the centre of a fierce family feud that involved cousins and grandchildren – one that destroyed the strong bond we had all treasured as a family. When all this was happening, uSwazi was staying in the house, but as a result of the feud was forced to leave, moving to Nellmapius, where she still lives today. Much against the will of uMagogo, the house was sold off, ending a very painful chapter.

USwazi studied in Hammanskraal up until Standard 4 at a school run by the Lutheran Mission. Because of lack of resources, classes were held under a tree on the premises of the parish, next to the chapel. She went on to Enkolweni Primary School in Johannesburg

43

to do her Standard 5. In 1965, when the family moved to Swaziland, she enrolled at the Nazarene High School in Manzini to study for her Standard 6 and later went to St Theresa's Girls' School in Manzini, where she completed her high school education in 1969.

She was introduced to the struggle in 1978 by uGebhuza (Siphiwe Nyanda), who was a commander in Swaziland and later became commander of the South African armed forces. His story and relationship with Number 43 are discussed in Chapter 13.

Her responsibilities

In her early days, uSwazi was tasked with harbouring operatives who were underground and in transit though Swaziland. At the time, she was staying at Mobeni Kuyehlela flats in Mbabane. The first batch of people she dealt with arrived in 1978 and included 'uSeptember', 'uKelly', 'uFannie Motebang' and 'uCassius', all of whom are discussed elsewhere in the book. These were people with whom I spent much of my time and who afforded me an extensive political and military guidance. They later became instrumental in most of the major operations launched from Swaziland and as a result became a focus of interest for the Swazi and South African security forces.

It was not long before they attracted raids from the Swazi police. On one occasion uSwazi was arrested together with uZweli Nyanda, a brother to uGebhuza, and was called upon to account for the people kept in hiding, either by her or other operatives. This marked the beginning of the police turning a hawkish eye towards her house. Owing to the frequency of the raids, she was forced to change residence. She moved to Zakhele, a suburb in Manzini, which later became a target for attack by the South African security forces. Her stint in Zakhele was short, on the back of ANC intelligence, which indicated that her house was one of those targeted for bomb attacks.

First bomb attack in Manzini

Early in June 1980 we received the first warning that several houses in Manzini were targeted. Ironically, at no stage was Number 43 on the list of high-risk spots. Indeed, on 4 June a house adjacent to the one where uSwazi stayed was bombed. The attack was seen as a retaliation for the Sasol 1 attack, a few months earlier. The Sasol attack was described as 'marking a new stage in guerilla warfare' and was estimated to have cost the government R6.8 million.

A certain Jackie Moreke was suspected of being implicated, directly or indirectly, in the Zakhele blast. He was seen, or at least his car was seen, in the vicinity shortly before the bomb went off. UMoreke was a teacher at the Salesian High at the time. He left Swaziland and later died in South Africa.

Incidentally, Oliver Tambo had predicted such an attack. He made a prophetic statement in Dar es Salaam just before the Zakhele onslaught. He said that he expected South Africa's response to the Sasol attacks to be raids against neighbouring states: "There is no African country bordering on South Africa which can be said to have helped the ANC do what it is doing . . . unfortunately, no matter how little involved the countries neighbouring South Africa may be, South Africa will harass them."' (*Times of Swaziland* (TOS), 5 June, 1980.)

This retaliation significantly increased the security risk faced by uSwazi and the rest of the family. On the night of 16 June she joined a group of comrades at a function held at Ntate Baartman's place in Sithwethweni, just outside Manzini in the vicinity of Zakhele, to celebrate the 1976 Soweto student uprising. As part of the security alertness, she was instructed to keep her surroundings spotlessly clean and the yard well swept. In that way, we would easily be able to pick up if there had been any unwanted guests to the house.

Sure enough, on her return from the celebration, she detected several footprints in the garden and on the well-polished stoep, indicating that there had been unwelcome guests. Only intruders could have gotten that far, given that the gate was locked. She knew she would have to be doubly vigilant until the following day, when alternative security arrangements could be made.

She stayed up waiting for developments, to find her worst fears turned into reality. Just after midnight she heard dogs barking viciously. Looking out, she saw the silhouette of a mysterious person standing watch at one corner of the yard. Without giving it much thought, she immediately jumped out of the house through a back window. Her escape did not go unnoticed, and she was pursued all the way to Trelawney Park, a distance of about three kilometres. However, while she covered this distance on foot, her pursuers were driving and she eluded them by using back routes, which the car could not follow. She finally reached the safety of Trelawney Park after 3am. To this day, she does not know who her pursuers were.

As originally planned, the following day she hastily moved houses and went to stay in Matsapha, Mobeni flats.

Untiring pursuits

USwazi's pursuers, however, did not give up. In 1985 she was tormented by endless telephone calls from the South African security police. They knew she was in contact with members of the ANC high command, people such as uPaul Dikeledi, uGebhuza and uSeptember. They hoped to get information about these people and their whereabouts in order to eliminate them.

The callers proposed a meeting with uSwazi. To stave them off while at the same time learning their identities, a decision was taken at the highest level of the ANC in Swaziland that the meeting be allowed to take place. Certain precautions had to be taken for her safety. These included notifying the Swazi police of the meeting and requesting an escort. The meeting was finally set up and took place at the Royal Swazi Spa in Ezulwini valley.

When she arrived at the Spa, three white men, who introduced themselves as Naas (later identified as a rugby player), De Bruyn and Nel, received her. It turned out that some of these names were fictitious. The main objective of the meeting was to propose that she join the ranks of the Askari, a clandestine arm of the South African security police.

The Askaris were the killing machines of the death squads. Jacques Pauw, in his book, *In the Heart of the Whore*, describes them as "typically ANC and PAC defectors who had been captured, 'turned' and drafted into the South African security police. Of course, there were those who came directly from the police force. They would go around, under the leadership of the white South African police, locations and neighboring countries acting on information that the security police had, or provided by the same Askaris, seeking out, capturing, maiming and killing their former colleagues. The majority ended up at Vlakplaas (a secret police farm just to the west of Pretoria, used as a place to torture and murder people captured mainly from neighbouring states). Ill-discipline, bad training if at all, heavy drinking and dagga smoking as well as low motivation characterised them. On various occasions they have been reported to have assaulted each other, even in public places, such as shebeens."

During the meeting, her hosts indicated that they wanted uSwazi to lead them to several people, specifically naming uGebhuza, uViva, uPaul, uSatane, uMatewu, uTodd and uGrace. The latter two, of course, were her siblings. Including them on the list reflected the insensitive, crooked and immoral nature of the people working for the security forces at the time. Before the meeting, uGebhuza had advised that if she were asked about certain people in the movement, she should not deny knowing them, as doing so would put her in danger, but should deny knowing their whereabouts. This worked, to the extent that her interrogators calmed down and behaved like reasonable human beings.

During the meeting, uSwazi became cheeky and led them on in pursuit of their goal. She enquired as to how much money they would pay her if she joined the ranks of the Askaris. She was told it would be about R500 per person apprehended, to which she reacted with a pretense of awe. Immediately, as if to show that resources were not a problem, she was promised a car, but responded by saying that she did not drive. She was then offered a motorbike or a bicycle. None of these were accepted as offers. Of course, a deal was the aim of the enquiry. When they parted, she promised to think about their offer.

A few weeks later, a second meeting was arranged for the same venue. This time, the Swazi police refused to give her an escort as they had for the earlier meeting. This was reported to the then Commissioner of Police, Sandile Mdziniso. To everyone's dismay, when he

47

was approached, he already knew about the impending meeting. This confirmed our old suspicions about the links between the South African security forces and the Swazi police.

Security link between the South African and Swazi police

We had long been suspicious of the Swazi police. We appreciated their responsibility to maintain peace and stability in Swaziland, but found this difficult to reconcile with the precision with which the South African security police undertook their operations inside the country. It seemed they were always ahead of us with their intelligence. We had always suspected there was a hand responsible for this in Swaziland. Askaris were a key variable in the equation that spelt the success of the South African death squads, under the command first of Dirk Coetzee and later of Eugene de Kock, but increasingly we were growing convinced that another element was at work.

One incident that raised our eyebrows happened in 1981 when Joe Pillay, a senior member of MK, was kidnapped from St Joseph's Mission, on the outskirts of Manzini. After an eyewitness identified the registration number of the car involved, the kidnappers were arrested by the Swazi police but were later released, never to be seen again. It turned out that support for the kidnappers, suspected to have been led by Dirk Coetzee, came from the highest level in the Swazi government.

Jacques Pauw has revealed that Dirk Coetzee was a guest of honour at the tenth independence anniversary of Swaziland and eightieth birthday of King Sobhuza II: "He enjoyed special recognition from the King and the royal family. At the start and end of each hunting season, the King's secretary, Martin Mdziniso, brought to the border post a gift of a blue wildebeest and four impala for Coetzee. When his superiors learned about these gifts, they begged Coetzee to arrange some venison for them as well. This led to some poaching of the benevolent King's game" (Jacques Pauw, p. 39).

This action further reveals how immoral members of the South African security forces could be. They would dine with you during the day and betray you at night. There was no way that uSwazi, or anybody else for that matter, could enter into a mutually beneficial and lasting agreement with this kind of people.

Dirk Coetzee himself learnt this fact the hard way in the late 1980s. He had been commander of the South African police death squad, operating from Vlakplaas, responsible for a wave of terror in the period 1977 to 1981, murdering many political and security opponents, in operations carried out in countries bordering South Africa. For all this, he was awarded a police medal for outstanding service, only to be later sidelined by his apartheid bosses. He would seek refuge in the ANC, and, to the surprise of many, was accepted into their ranks.

Of course, uSwazi had to make a clean break during this second meeting, which naturally infuriated her pursuers. She began receiving more frequent telephone calls, coupled with threats of physical harm. The callers now included black people. According to our information at the time, the mission had been elevated to a new level of violence, so these threats concerned us gravely. Raids by the Swazi police at Number 43 were escalated. In one of these, uStanley Bhembe, Head of the Security in Manzini, threatened to bomb Number 43 himself if we did not cooperate.

A number of events around that time scared us to the bone. One major turning point came with the signing of the Nkomati Accord, between South Africa and Mozambique, in 1984. As people were retreating from Mozambique, many mistakes were made. This was a massive operation that had to be undertaken in a short space of time and coincided with the intensification of cross-border raids. The consequence was many unjustified deaths. Several of the people I stayed with lost their lives during the period.

Three people were gunned down in a house in Mbabane in June 1986. In the same year, a former bodyguard of Oliver Tambo was abducted in Mbabane and later killed. A close comrade, uTheophilus 'Viva' Dlodlo, was ambushed and killed in a car, together with three other people, in May 1987, as related in chapter 18. The survivors pointed at uSeptember as the main culprit. In July of the same year, uCassius Make and uPaul Dikeledi, both senior officials in the ANC, were ambushed and killed, together with a woman from Mozambique. These events worried us deeply, not only as a family but also as an organisation. There was a growing feeling that a big internal security weakness was developing, or that the enemy was growing more sophisticated.

USwazi has had one of the longest and most challenging experiences in the family. However, she also enjoyed among the lowest levels of direct intimidation and arrests by the Swazi police, owing to the fact that at the height of the tide she had left Number 43 to stay on her own. She was thus spared the frequent onslaughts. However, this did not in any way diminish the extent of her exposure.

CHAPTER 6

The House of Todd

Busisiwe Glory Masilela

Together with uGrace, uTodd was one of the most active members of the family. He worked closely with people such as uGebhuza, uSeptember, uSatane, uJabu Omude, uPaul Dikeledi and many other prominent members of the ANC operating from Swaziland. He is cited directly and indirectly in a number of places in the TRC documentation. In particular, he is cited in the confessions made in connection with the assassination of uViva.

I would have liked to present his story, but am simply unable to do so, given that we worked at different levels and deliberately avoided common operations. I have, therefore, left this account principally to my sister-in-law, uBusisiwe, whom we familiarily refer to as uSis' Busi. This is how she recalls the life of uTodd.

"Throughout his life, Todd's house was open to all kinds of people, regardless of who they were or where they came from. Despite the fact that his house was supposed to be a place to raise his family, he strongly believed that he should share whatever he had with those who were less privileged and who happened to visit his house, without asking for anything in return.

"However, those who were welcomed in the household would sometimes spread the word around and soon the house would be full of strangers. I sometimes feel that his interest in newcomers was enhanced by the fact that he was a teacher whose natural instinct was to work with people. Coupled with his flair for reading, his love of music, and of course his bottle, this allowed him to connect easily with a wide range of people from all walks of life. He thrived on good conversation, initiating robust discussions that often led to fruitful developments. His interest in bringing people together earned him many friends from far and wide.

"This made uTodd someone who could be trusted and counted upon, especially in relation to the liberation struggle. At this time, many young people were leaving South Africa, where they were persecuted by the apartheid regime, and crossing over into neighbouring states such as Swaziland, Lesotho and Botswana. Because most of them were not sure of exactly what they wanted to do, uTodd undertook to give them guidance. He would help them settle into their new environment and support them in whatever moves they deemed necessary. This was not an easy task as some of these young boys and girls were wounded both emotionally and physically. Often it would take time to get them talking and cooperating.

"The influx of those seeking asylum in Swaziland, especially of the youth, was unpredictable and at times erratic. Sometimes a large contingent would arrive, making it difficult to provide accommodation under one roof. The main determinants were events in South Africa, the unrest, demonstrations, detentions, and torture, as well as the general fear for one's life. This called for radical measures to accommodate the newcomers. UTodd made arrangements with those among his friends he trusted, so that most of his friends' houses were referred to as 'safe houses'. Dotted around the town and in the surrounding countryside, these were places where refugees could stay without fear. Among the many who supported the struggle by offering shelter for cadres were uBheka Dlamini, uVictor Fakudze, and uMafrisco Mhlongo."

Retracing their steps

"Some of the young people who passed through Todd's house left for military training in different parts of Africa and beyond. Generally, the understanding, when these soldiers left, was that one would never meet them again, as the future was unpredictable. The assumption was that death was never far away.

"Others went for many years and pursued different kinds of training, which required them to come back to South Africa to infiltrate the enemy. These men and women occasionally retraced their steps back to Todd's house. They would come back through Swaziland en route to South Africa to carry out their missions. When this happened, it was always a wonderful experience that would generate great excitement and celebration. Unfortunately, such incidents of people reuniting after many years of separation were few and far between.

"One such personality whom uTodd knew well was uTheophilus 'Viva' Dlodlo. He was a regular visitor to the house. He would move between Swaziland and South Africa, using Todd's house as a springboard for his work as a combat soldier. UTodd and uViva grew close, to such an extent that uTodd introduced him to members of his family. Viva's mother and sister came to visit him, and a few years later, when uViva married, the celebrations took place at Todd's house."

Several of the comrades I talked to hold uTodd in high esteem and cherish warm memories of their relationship with him. They consider him one of the key ANC strategists who operated from Swaziland and a person both trustworthy and highly dependable. Such was the life of uTodd 'Majikiza', as we would call him when we were in high spirits.

CHAPTER 7

The Prodigal Daughter

Thandi Elizabeth Masilela

UThandi was always a 'prodigal-type' child. During her high school days, she was known as 'Fanta' among her friends, because of her exceptionally bright complexion and bubbly character. However, the latter trait seems only to have been displayed to non-members of the family. At home, she was seen as 'itshobolo', meaning 'a mean woman'.

Among all the siblings, uThandi spent the least time at home with the rest of the family. To this day, she prefers to live an isolated life – at least, isolated from the family. It is ironic, therefore, that outside of the family she is seen as 'a people's person'.

She was born on 23 April 1953, in Nancefield, Soweto. She attended primary school at the Vuyo Community School in Mofolo North before the family moved to Swaziland. There she went to the Nazarene High School but was expelled during Form III, not for political reasons but for being naughty. She was forced to work for a year at the Punch Bowl Café in Manzini to raise money for the following year's tuition. She completed her high school education at Evelyn Baring High School in Nhlangano in 1972.

Her first job after high school was with Barclays Bank in Nhlangano. This was short-lived, as she fell foul of a manager who was hostile towards South Africans and who forced her to resign. She found another job with the George Hotel, now Tum's New George, in the centre of Manzini. It was here in 1974 that her political career began.

While working for the hotel as a receptionist and guest relations officer, she came in contact with uThabo Mbeki and uJacob Zuma, to whom she was introduced by a family friend, uMandla 'Stokes' Sithole. Known as Bra Stokes because of his streetwise character and fatherly status in the community, uSithole would feature prominently in many political activities in Swaziland.

UThabo Mbeki and uJacob Zuma frequented the hotel, where they would spend hours at the Rex Bar hatching the downfall of the apartheid regime. In those days, hotels in Swaziland would typically have two bars, one for the blacks (masquerading as a bar for low-income earners) and another for the whites. The Rex Bar was one of those open to the high end of the market. However, unlike in South Africa, the colour distinction was not pronounced, which meant that those with the means could enter the bar without any restriction – hence the patronage of the two ANC chief strategists.

Ironically, ten years later, the same hotel would be used as a key meeting point for Askaris and the South African security forces, who combed Swaziland in search of ANC operatives and sympathisers.

Among uThandi's first responsibilities was to provide communication services for these two ANC leaders, sending and receiving telexes to and from the ANC headquarters in Lusaka, Zambia. Her position in the hotel gave her the necessary neutrality as well as the appropriate facilities. These, however, had to be used behind the back of her inquisitive white manager, Mrs Booza, whose husband owned a similar and very popular hotel in Pretoria, also called the Rex Bar.

After a while, uThandi became aware of a growing interest in her from the Swazi police. On one occasion, one of the CIDs, a certain Dlamini, offered to walk her home from work, a distance of four or five kilometres. The offer was unexpected, and she immediately sensed that something was amiss. True to her suspicions, the policeman did not engage in normal social conversation but instead plied her with questions about uThabo Mbeki and uJacob Zuma, wanting to know what they did, where they lived and where they obtained the money to spend at the Rex Bar every day. She pleaded ignorance to all these, but could see that the policeman was not convinced.

Shortly after this incident, she received an urgent summons from Mrs Mabizela, the wife of uStan Mabizela, to meet her at her place of employment, the Standard Bank in Manzini. UThandi arrived, to be told that uThabo had been arrested. UBra Stokes confirmed the arrest. While talking to Mrs Mabizela, she noticed that the same policeman, Dlamini, was loitering around nearby, monitoring their discussion.

A surge of panic followed Thabo's arrest. Word quickly spread that more people were being watched and more arrests were to follow. At the end of the working day, uThandi was picked up by uBra Stokes and Ntate George Monare. They suggested that, as she was one of those under surveillance, she should leave Swaziland as soon as possible. The family respected Ntate Monare's judgement.

The Monares were among the early arrivals in Swaziland. The two families celebrated New Year's Eve together every single year, with the hosting of the celebration alternating between the two venues, Ngwane Park, where the Monares lived, and Number 43, Trelawney Park.

UThandi immediately went into hiding at the house of Bra Stokes, before being smuggled out of the country. She left with two other people, Solly Makwakwa and Mandla Simelane. UBafana Duma, who later lost a limb in a parcel bomb blast in Manzini, ferried them into Mozambique. On arrival, they spent their first night at a large, elegant house called kaMkhulu, just across the border. The next morning uThandi was booked into a hotel, where she spent a further two nights, before journeying on to Dar-es-Salaam.

When asked how she felt about this crisis in her life, she says that by now she had resigned herself to joining the struggle, adding: "My parents gave their approval for me to join the fighting ranks of the ANC. They also realised that my life was in danger."

On arrival in Dar-es-Salaam, she was taken to a block of flats called ANC House. There she met all the ANC people she had known through Number 43, among them Ntate Mashego, uLindi Sisulu and uAlfred Nzo. She was given work in the ANC office, before being asked to choose between military or academic training. She chose the latter, and in September 1976 left for Bulgaria.

For the first nine months in Bulgaria, she pursued studies in language, and then enrolled in the Friedrich Engels Technikon for a degree in economics. This was followed by an internship with the Bank of Bulgaria. After a year, she signed up with the Karl Marx Institute of Economics for a Masters Degree. She returned to Tanzania in 1987. Despite her left leaning as a result of her decade in the Soviet bloc, she and I have never had major disagreements on matters of economic principle, given that I am an economist trained in the other extreme.

Mystery letter

Throughout her years in exile, uThandi barely communicated with her family. This did not come as a surprise, since such silence was typical of her. At the same time, we were not greatly concerned, as we received information about her health and welfare through comrades who went in and out of Bulgaria.

This changed when she met a certain Bethuel Ndlovu from Swaziland, who was in Bulgaria for a conference. For the first time, she felt a desire to write home. She gave uNdlovu a letter, asking him to deliver it to uMagogo. Instead, he reported his meeting with uThandi to the Manzini Police Station and handed her letter to the police. UMagogo was later paid a visit by the Manzini Special Branch and interrogated about the letter. On discovering what had happened, uThandi decided to stop communicating, however much she missed home and family.

In February 2005, two months into writing this book, I was sitting in a restaurant in Mbabane with my wife and a Swazi friend, uVusi 'VVO' Mabilisa. Suddenly, Bethuel Ndlovu walked in and sat at a table across from us. I could not contain my curiosity. I told my companions I was going to ask the man his version of the story behind this mysterious letter. They objected, fearing a confrontation. However, I was determined, so I brushed aside their protests.

I boldly invited myself to uNdlovu's table and sat down. I introduced myself and explained why I had approached him and how important his input would be for the objectivity of the book. He seemed to sense what I was going to ask him, as he spent a great deal of time trying to evade the issue, telling me how wonderful uThandi was and how excited he had been when they met in Bulgaria. When I finally managed to put my question to him, he denied every aspect of the version of the story I knew about the letter. He insisted he had delivered it to

uMagogo, and claimed he knew nothing about the police involvement. Realising that there was no way I could reconcile and conclude
the investigation, I thanked him for his time and returned to my table.

This encounter left me more confused than before. I related this
experience to both uMagogo and uThandi, who were equally baffled.
Even allowing for the passage of time, I did not believe uMagogo
could have confused events to the extent of the inconsistency in the
stories. Like many questions we have as a family, this is one of those
that will remain unanswered.

Deep nostalgia

Contrary to what we believed, uThandi says she deeply missed home
and family. The homesickness was often unbearable, but she trained
herself to ignore it. She tried to manage her emotions by thinking the
worst, reminding herself of the low likelihood of a political change in
South Africa. As a result, she did not expect to find anyone alive, including her parents, when she returned. She used this thought to cut
her memory ties with the people she had left behind and to make a
life for herself that excluded her family.

On her return to Tanzania, uThandi went to Mazimbu where she
worked at the ANC Treasury. Within a year she was transferred to
Dar-es-Salaam, where she was seconded to the Norwegian People
Aid. Following training in clearing and forwarding with a Swedish
company, she worked at the harbour, where she was responsible for
clearing goods for all the liberation movements based in Tanzania.
She was further trained in modern techniques of conference organisation, before resuming work at the ANC Treasury, where she stayed
until her return to South Africa in 1991.

In 1992, uThandi enrolled at the University of Cape Town for a
bridging course in economics, followed by an internship with the
Development Bank of South Africa. She worked at the Western Cape
Development Forum until the first democratic elections, after which
the firm closed down. She then returned to Pretoria where she waited
for her first permanent job, as all people do in the South African
labour market, a post that only materialised in 2002.

At the time of writing this book she was well settled in the same neighbourhood as uLucky. But despite the fact that they are half a kilometre apart, they hardly ever meet. This recalls the characteristic that defined her in her youth, one that continues to define her today.

CHAPTER 8

Destined to be a Freedom Fighter

Grace Khabakazi Masilela

No one in the family knows the details of the activities in which uGrace was involved outside Swaziland. Even after she returned, her work was strictly clandestine. She was the only member of the family trained in military combat. She worked in Gebhuza's machinery and had a friend and confidante in uSindiswa Olive Mthembu, who later became part of the Number 43 family. She was known to us simply as uSindi, but was later given the nickname 'Syndicate' by uMagogo. This happened when she was first introduced to Number 43 by uCassius and uKelly. UMagogo, in her usual jovial spirits, on hearing the name Sindi, burst out with "Dumela, Syndicate!" (Greetings, Syndicate!) The name stuck.

Brave and confidential

Of all those who knew uGrace, uSindi was the closest to her. Much of this chapter is based on her memories of her experiences with uGrace.

She describes uGrace as a brave combatant, who combined calculation with an iron discipline. This was maintained with her children as well as with her comrades. A teetotaler and a non-smoker, she seldom showed emotion. In moments of crisis, she would remain straight-faced and rarely showed any stress signals, apart from a tendency to twiddle her fingers.

She loved her family, and no amount of risk could separate her from her children. On her return to Swaziland, her youngest child, uMatitila (Kgositsile), was always on her back wherever she went, making them a familiar sight in Manzini. She did not drive, nor did she bother to learn. She was content to leave this to her husband and brothers. I always played the chauffeur. She happily did the journey from Woodmasters, where she lived, to Fairview, Trelawney Park,

Ngwane Park, Zakhele or Coates Valley on foot. These places are on average three kilometres from Number 43, forming a circle with the house as its hub.

Further traits were independence and caution. She never relied on her comrades for protection. Often she used Kgositsile as a decoy. The child became a cover on several occasions when she crossed into South Africa. Despite the closeness of their friendship, uSindi has never seen the passport that she used to cross the border, nor did she ever learn what operative name she used in South Africa. Even at the most critical point of her life, when her husband, uDan 'Little Dan' Leepiloe, was arrested entering South Africa, she kept the information to herself. Neither uSindi nor her commander, uGebhuza, were told until much later.

The family had always noticed this secretive side to her character. For instance, when she left Swaziland, we were merely told that she was travelling to Botswana with Manzini Wanderers, one of Swaziland's leading football clubs in the premier league. She had once been crowned Miss Wanderers, and enjoyed a special relationship with the club. I walked with her to the Ritz Café in Manzini where they were to board the bus to ferry them to Botswana. When the club returned, however, she was not part of the group. UMagogo asked uWelcome Mazibuko, one of the club officials who was also a neighbour and a family friend, where she was. To our surprise, he had no information about uGrace. All he knew was that she had decided to remain in Gaborone with friends and had indicated that she would find her own way back to Swaziland.

Of course this did not happen. The first the family learned of her whereabouts was when she wrote to uMagogo from Dar-es-Salaam, directing her to find a letter in her wardrobe. The message, which she had left before departing, bade us farewell, saying simply that she was following in her father's footsteps. It is not clear what this meant.

Liberation, religion paradox

Those who trained with her say uGrace was a tough soldier. She underwent her military training in Libya. While there, she was forced to convert to Islam. The Libyan government set this as a condition for giving training to PAC combatants. Those receiving the training had no say in the matter. However, on completion of their training they were not recalled to Tanzania as expected. Instead, for no clear reason, they were forced to repeat the course. This led to a revolt among the trainees, who were anxious to return to Tanzania and thence to the front. Their revolt coincided with a broader mutiny within the PAC, resulting in a number of people being sold out by their own organisation. The revolt put them at odds with the leadership.

When they finally returned to Tanzania, they discovered that the PAC had no passage to South Africa. The group was grounded in a camp, with no immediate hope of proceeding. The situation further deteriorated, reaching a crisis when the Tanzanian Red Beret, acting on information that the group had an alliance with the Tanzanian opposition, attacked the camp. Several people were killed. UGrace herself escaped with a bullet wound in the thigh.

It was then that she made the decision to cross over to the ANC. This led to hostile and acrimonious relations, with further threats on her life. She was forced to leave Tanzania to operate from Mozambique.

During her time in both Tanzania and Mozambique, uGrace was given many critical responsibilities in the ANC. She was among the survivors of the Matola raid in Mozambique in January 1981. Regrettably, we were unable to glean any details about this event. The closest person to her regarding this raid was uDan, but his state of health did not allow us to take the discussion any further.

While uGrace lived a life of mystery, the biggest mystery to the family was her death in April 1990, after fifty years of good health. It was preceded by an unexplained mental disturbance, which after many months of professional help, took her life, leaving the family in a state I could never begin to describe. The closest we came to finding a source for her state of mental health was in the experiences she underwent both in Libya and Tanzania, as well as her escape in Matola.

Family tragedies

UGrace was the first to die in the family. What made it worse is that it seemed to have opened the floodgates. In a period of slightly more than ten years, the family experienced the loss of three other members.

For me, the biggest blow came with the death of uAngel in a car accident. I was affected not only by her loss but also by the circumstances around it. At the time she died, her daughter uMpinti (Mabel), together with other nieces, were at my place in Pretoria on a visit. They had arrived a few days earlier but I had to curtail their visit to make the trip to Swaziland. What I could not tell them, though, was that uAngel had died. I made up some reason for the journey, one that I cannot remember now. More challenging still was that I had to keep them feeling that nothing was wrong until we got to Swaziland, which meant containing my grief from the day I learnt about the accident. This was extremely difficult. I remember making frequent retreats to the bedroom in the middle of discussions, to cry in private, only emerging after I had fully recovered, all in an attempt to conceal from the children what was going on.

The next challenge was undertaking the journey to Swaziland. The closer we came to the reality, the more difficult it was to contain our emotions. We did the whole four-hour journey in a tense silence, feeling that the slightest mistake would have caused us to crack. We went through the border without an incident but by then we were emotionally exhausted.

The final test came when we drove into Number 43. We were the last to arrive, and the place was already teeming with people, cars lining the driveway and the street. The question I had dreaded popped out of my son. This was the first word from any of them, since our departure from Pretoria. He wanted to know why there were so many people at Number 43, but there was no answer. Only a cold silence filled the car. As if sensing something, as soon as the car stopped, without waiting for the doors to unlock, the children bolted out and headed for Magogo's bedroom, where everyone was gathered.

By the time we walked into the bedroom, all my siblings, apart from uAngel, were there. It did not take long for uMpinti to realise that something to do with her mother had brought us to Number 43 and was the reason for cutting their visit short. When her eyes met those of uMagogo, her worst fear was confirmed. I will never forget the shock in her eyes, and the hysteria that followed. I was still not sure I had done the right thing in not telling her and in leaving her to make the discovery for herself. Finally, all the emotion I had bottled up for the previous two days and during the drive to Swaziland exploded. Overwhelmed with grief, I cried like a baby.

To this day, I have still not recovered fully from this experience. I know too that the gap left by the loss of these members of the family will never be filled.

CHAPTER 9

Ideologically Different, Yet the Same

Lucky Lucas Masilela

In every family there is a special child. ULucky seems to hold that position in the Masilela family, owing to the circumstances around his birth. This has been much talked about in the family, for four reasons. Firstly, he was born on Christmas Day, which coincides with our family day. Secondly, the birth took place at home, contrary to a long family tradition started by our maternal grandfather, who insisted that the first birth take place in a hospital environment. Thirdly, when he emerged, he was covered by the caul (called 'i-veil' by Africans). This was seen as a good omen, hence the name Lucky. And fourthly, uMagogo was struck by lightning while carrying him. Both survived unscathed.

He was born in 1958 in Mofolo North, at House 466. As a child, he saw little beyond the immediate dusty street to the house. He remembers walking several times to the shops at eKhwezi, and recalls one particular incident from his childhood: "We played on a rubbish dump, which formed a playground for us. During this period a bottle cut through my foot, which has left an indelible scar both in my foot and my mind.

"I envied my elder brother and sisters going to school. I never even attended kindergarten. House 466 was my kindergarten. Our pastime as young boys was watching street fights, which were frequent. There would be yelling from mothers and sisters when these fights broke out. The next event I remember was when we were bundled into the old man's car for Swaziland. All we were told was that we were going to attend school there."

Importance of religion

Early in our stay in Swaziland, our parents were confronted with a challenge they had not anticipated. In those days, religion was a major determining factor in which school a child would go to. Because the Masilela family was non-Catholic, it was difficult to secure a place at the Salesian School or any other Catholic school. As a result, uLucky was pressured to convert to Catholicism, much against the wishes of the family. This would be the trend for most of the other siblings. During the week, we were under the guardianship of the Roman Catholics but on weekends went back to being Lutheran.

Children at Roman Catholic schools were expected to have what were considered 'appropriate' names. For instance, a boy named Dodge Mahlalela was forced to adopt the name Nicholas. Fortunately, uLucky did not have to change his name, as Lucas, a name he would drop later in life, was considered saintly enough.

Living in the shadow of role models

He regrets ever having gone to high school, arguing that, "When I arrived at high school, I lost my identity. Instead of being known in my own right, I was addressed as 'intwana kaTodd'", which is isiZulu for 'Todd's younger brother'. He acknowledges, though, that this had its own benefits, since it protected him from bullies and allowed him to focus on academics and sports. He dropped football, however, after being kicked by an older boy, Express Dlamini, who objected to being dribbled.

What also stands out is his enjoyment of the teaching styles of some teachers at high school, people such as uRosette Nziba and uStan Mabizela, who encouraged him in public debate. As he recalls: "One of my highlights was carrying the school to win a debate against St Theresa's Girls' School, which was a huge achievement for Salesian. Later, reading about the Black American struggle, and in particular the Black Panthers, influenced me. I became involved in informal discussions with some of my fellow students, basing my views on Black Consciousness."

These debates gained added significance during the 1978 celebrations of Africa Day, a politically charged event in Swaziland because of uncertainty over its legality. The festivities entailed poetry recitals, music, dance and drama. In this particular year, they also included a play entitled *uZwelonke*, in which uLucky starred and which would later be banned in Swaziland for its revolutionary tone.

Through these activities, he became exposed to people such as uPitika Ntuli, uCharles Ziyane and uBika Maseko. These were members of the PAC who stayed in a house diagonally behind Number 43. Owned by a family based in South Africa, the Masetloas, it would become the main receiving point for PAC members exiled in Swaziland.

Being of Ndebele origin, uPitika became a very close family friend. He was the shining star among the boys in Lucky's circle, assuming the multiple roles of poet, politician, and teacher. He enjoyed the writings of Amilcar Cabral, Karl Marx and Lenin, as well as African and Swazi political writers. At that time, there was a close link with the leader of the NNLC, Dr Ambrose Zwane.

They were exposed to the principles and policies of the ANC and PAC side by side with those of Black Consciousness. Questions on who an African was and on land ownership formed the core of the teachings. Bishop Zwane, Bishop of the Roman Catholic Church in Swaziland, provided a definitive conception of Black Consciousness, one that guided this debate both in Swaziland and South Africa.

While the majority of the participants were South Africans, there was a sprinkling of Swazis, people such as uCharles Ziyane. When the 1976 riots broke out, the groundswell sucked them in. They took the chance to mobilise and do more focused work for the PAC in Swaziland. They helped in receiving students and escorting them beyond Swaziland. Most were sheltered at key houses around Manzini, including those of the Simelanes, Mkhwanazis and Moabis, all of which were in Fairview.

As the numbers rapidly grew, a safe house had to be established, hence the use of the house behind Number 43. The ANC and PAC competed aggressively for membership, but the numbers grew much faster than the two organizations could handle. This led to a camp being set up by the Swazi authorities at Mdutshane.

Among the interesting personalities who joined the PAC was a certain Nxumalo, supposedly a nephew to Mangosuthu Gatsha Buthelezi. By a mysterious chain of circumstances, while serving his articles with a law firm in Mbabane, he appeared in Manzini in the latter part of 1977 running a fine disco called Las Vegas. For the next two years it was the pre-eminent social rendezvous in Swaziland, especially for the young. It received an unusual stamp of approval from two major schools in Manzini, Salesian High School (an all-boys' school) and St. Michaels High (an all-girls' school).

Some of the proceeds from this business were used to fund the Bethal 18 trialists and their families. It is not clear how the Swazi authorities got to learn about this connection, but the disco was raided in January 1979 and shut down as a direct consequence.

At the time of the raid, uLucky was in South Africa. He returned to find panic among his colleagues in Swaziland. Over and above the issue of the disco, the PAC high command in Tanzania claimed the PAC structures in Swaziland were plotting a coup and as a result declared them illegitimate. Many were arrested, while others were deported from Swaziland to England and other parts of Europe. Overnight all those involved with Las Vegas vanished. We were left with the job of clearing the place. Some of the furniture ended up at Number 43.

Fleeing Swaziland

Intelligence sources warned of further arrests. Heading the list were uLemmy Zondo, uVictor and uNkosana Mkhize, uDominic Zulu, uBenedict Ntshingila and uLucky. To escape arrest, all except uBenedict fled to Mozambique. On the night of their departure, the group assembled at Number 43 to be picked up by a certain Boy Motsa who ran a taxi company in Manzini. However, the reason for the trip was not revealed to uBoy Motsa. He was simply told they were going to Siteki.

ULucky says, "The only person I told about my departure was uTodd. Even a close girlfriend of mine did not know about my plans. UBoy Motsa would later come back to break the news to her."

It was a rainy night. After being dropped off on the border at Lomahasha, they walked through the dark into Mozambique. There, they stumbled into a military roadblock. Excited about the prospect of a warm, comradely reception, noting the common cause between Frelimo and the South African struggle, they gladly handed themselves over. Instead of the expected welcome, to their dismay, they were detained at the border and later sent to a nearby police station. In the morning they were taken back to the custody of the border police.

While there, Simon 'Douglas' Mhlongo, a son of uReggie Mhlongo who stayed at Number 43, arrived from Maputo, asking, "Where is this POQO group?" and making an attempt to lure them to the ANC. When this overture was rejected, he disappeared as swiftly as he had come. Later on, the group was bundled into a truck and driven towards Maputo. Their hopes were high that they were being taken to the Polana Hotel. Instead, a further surprise came when they were locked up in a prison in Machava.

They were welcomed in the usual manner in which newcomers are received in prison. By now, it was clear that they had walked into a nightmare. It was a regular Third World prison cell. There was no paper in the toilet, and the place was infested with fleas, which explained why most of the inmates sat naked, scratching at their bodies.

They stayed in the prison for three nights, which felt like weeks. On the third morning, just as they were becoming inured to their condition, their names were called. ULucky missed his name, since it was read out in an unintelligible Portuguese accent, and was almost left behind. Realising that the rest of his group had already been set free, he protested loudly and succeeded in having himself released.

They were taken to the Mavhalane transit camp, not far from Heroes Acre (Eduardo Mondlane monument). There, they were served only one meal a day, at midday. Whilst there, they were visited by uJacob Zuma, who asked if they were still determined to join the PAC or whether they would consider joining the ANC. When they held to their position, he told them he could not help them, but wished them luck.

They were called upon to perform odd tasks in the camp, including offloading bales of clothing from trucks. They helped themselves to some items, which they later sold. Finally, in April they were flown on one-way tickets to Tanzania. No travel documents were issued.

Instead, they were given a 'Gia de Marcha', a document similar to a deportation order. They had no passports and there was no one to receive them at the other end. They were abandoned at Dar-es-Salaam airport to be a meal for mosquitoes. It was not until the evening of the next day that they were rescued by a Mr Mantshontsho, a PAC representative in Tanzania. He took them to a PAC residence, where they met familiar faces and were finally welcomed into the exiled PAC community.

Caught in the crossfire

The split in the PAC, which had caused the havoc in Swaziland, resurfaced. The division was between the followers of Potlako Leballo and those who supported TM Ntantala, who operated extensively in Swaziland. The conflict worsened as the Ntantala faction was 'derecognised', degraded to the status of ordinary refugees, and no longer accepted as members of a liberation movement. This resulted in the residences being divided by support group. During the infighting a senior official, uDavid Sibeko, was killed.

The group from Swaziland was sidelined on the grounds that they were anti-Potlako Leballo and pro-TM Ntantala. They were forced to join the Ntantala camp, from which the All African People's Revolution Party (AAPRP) was eventually formed. UMkhwanazi, who was also with AAPRP but based in England, journeyed to Tanzania in an attempt to bring the opposing forces together, but his intervention came to nothing.

The government of Tanzania refused to recognise the AAPRP and their status changed to that of refugees. To avoid further conflict, the group was moved to Tabora, away from Dar-es-Salaam. The de-recognition of the AAPRP meant they had to resort to farming to survive. Life in Tabora was harsh, and morale reached a low point. The crisis was only resolved with the release of Phokela from prison. He succeeded in uniting the PAC factions, with the result that those in Tabora were brought back into the PAC fold, and were returned to the PAC camps in Mbeya and Bagamoyo.

ULucky, meanwhile, had remained in Dar-es-Salaam to coordinate training. The return to the PAC saw him in the Bagamoyo camp. He was employed in a newsroom for about six months, working with a man named Mazambane. The newsroom work extended into hosting a weekly cultural programme on Radio Tanzania.

(In 1981, uLucky secured a place at Dar-es-Salaam Technical College, where he took a certificate course in telecommunications. He was subsequently awarded a Phelps–Stokes scholarship to the United States, which opened a new chapter in his life. On arrival in Washington, DC, for orientation, his group were exposed to a new wave of South Africans. Ironically, the people they met there were sceptical of those coming directly from South Africa. He enrolled at Hampton University in Virginia, where he took Applied Physics and Electronic Engineering.)

Meeting with uGrace in exile

Returning from Bagamoyo, uLucky met uGrace while she was still in the PAC. She later crossed the floor to the ANC and met the man she married, uDan. ULucky recalls the wedding ceremony, which took place at Morogoro, with fondness. At that time uDan was the Head of Security of the ANC in Dar-es-Salaam.

One of the benefits for uLucky of having uGrace around was that, given her strategic position in the ANC, she had access to essential supplies. In particular, he cherished a mosquito net and bed sheets given to him by uGrace. Before that, his only bedding had been a sponge mattress and an old narrow grey blanket, which we call 'ungacambongolo'. Using this blanket meant he had to sleep dead straight, otherwise part of his body would have been an anopheles meal. The blanket had not seen water in months as wringing it caused further loosening of its stitches, which were already quite precarious. UGrace would later facilitate passage for uLucky through Mozambique to visit Swaziland.

What uMagogo knew

According to uMagogo, uLucky left a letter in her bedroom, which she found a day later. When he left the country he was working for the Swaziland Water Board in Mbabane. A few days after his departure, his manager, a certain Mr Metz, came to enquire about his where-abouts, at which point the news was broken to him.

Soon after this visit, the parents of the boys that left with uLucky, the Zondos, Zulus and Mkhizes, came to demand their children from uMagogo. They claimed that uLucky was the ringleader and the key influence on their sons' departure, thus trying to make uMagogo accountable. This led to much bitterness and animosity among the families. Eventually, in a very uncharacteristic manner, uMagogo ran out of patience and lost her temper with the persistent enquiries.

However, the tension dissipated when the Swazi security police hauled all the families to Mbabane, to explain the whereabouts of their children. This provided some kind of bonding and a reminder of the reality of their common enemy.

First visit back home

Lucky's first visit home was just before the Nkomati Accord in 1984. While in Mozambique visiting uGrace, he was helped by ANC comrades to cross over into Swaziland. He hitchhiked from Lomahasha to Manzini, and arrived home at about eight o'clock in the evening. UTodd responded to his knock, but at first did not recognise him. Instead, our nephews uJoel and uJonas, who were about ten years old at the time, were the first to recognize him. After five years away from home, there was a great deal of excitement and emotion.

This is how uLucky summarises his short stay in Swaziland: "At that stage uTodd was teaching in Hlathikulu, and uNkosinathi was on the run. While I had never met uNkosinathi, apart from a picture of him in a newspaper, I could see he was a source of discussion and sorrow in the family. A day or two after my arrival at Number 43, the news of his assassination hit us. I left Swaziland on 7 January, 1984."

ULucky's return to Number 43 from exile was in August 1993.

CHAPTER 10

Life with a Freedom Fighter

Joana Namdlangu Masilela

Our relationships with ANC operatives varied widely, depending on circumstances. Some of these were defined by social rather than political factors. UJoana was one of the family members who extended these boundaries when she was courted by uNkosinathi Maseko. Her relationship with him would later completely redefine the way Swazi officials perceived the family.

UJoana was born on 26 October 1962, in Johannesburg, and went to school at St Theresa's Girls School in Manzini. Since she left school, she has worked for the Swaziland government. A family friend, uSis' Tsali Malaza, was instrumental in finding her the job, as she did with uLucky.

Like most of the other siblings, uJoana cannot say precisely how or when she became involved in the work of the ANC. As she puts it, "It is not very clear when I really started becoming involved. I just found myself entangled during the period when Number 43 was extensively used as a key meeting point by the ANC and PAC.

"At first, I was very reluctant to come close to the process. I deliberately kept away from the tempting discussions and events that were used to politicise people. But once I was inside, I could not disentangle myself."

She recalls that a close family friend, uThabisile Nxumalo, introduced her to some of the activities in 1980. This coincided with a point in the political life of the Masilelas when the whole family was rounded up and kept for a day or two at the Manzini Police Station.

In the same year, she met uNkosinathi Maseko, one of the operatives who frequented Number 43. He would later father her daughter, uSibongile, born on 13 August 1983. Towards the end of 1983, he ran into trouble with the police and rapidly became the most wanted person in Swaziland, hitting the headlines almost every day. He found himself on the run not for political activities but for completely different reasons. A common friend, uDumisa Dlamini, who is discussed in Chapter 23, revealed to me the full details behind these events, at the time of writing this book.

Up until then, uJoana had no details about how uNkosinathi found himself in trouble, apart from what we read in the press. The same applies to his family. I had the unenviable task of relating the events to the Maseko family in Mamelodi. This was not because uJoana did not enquire, but because all attempts at uncovering the truth were met with silence. As she put it, "UNkosinathi would avoid any discussion. Instead, when confronted, he would just stand up and walk away." This same reaction was noticed with his uncle ahead of the Pretoria Church street bomb blast, as described in Chapter 22. While this information was important for uJoana and her relationship with uNkosinathi, it was also dangerous, as it would have made her vulnerable.

Since it was known that she was the mother of Nkosinathi's child, she was detained for questioning on 23 December 1983. She was kept in solitary confinement at the Malkerns Police Station until after Christmas. Whilst she was in custody, we did not know where she was. On her release, she was deeply disturbed by a report from uGranny to the effect that uNkosinathi would come to Number 43 every night to check on the baby, but would not reveal where he was staying. By the time she was released uNkosinathi had fled the country, so she had no opportunity of seeing or talking to him before he left.

The next news she heard about uNkosinathi was about his death in Mamelodi. This is how she relates the events: "One morning, on my way to work, I heard over the radio that someone had been killed in Pretoria. I did not suspect anything from this report. But as soon as I arrived at the office, I got a call from uTodd who told me that the person who had been killed was uNkosinathi.

"I so much wanted to communicate with my in-laws but could not, as their house phone was bugged. We relied on friends and public phones for news. At that time, cellphone technology did not exist.

Luckily, a close family friend also named Joana, uJoana Magwaza, some-how made contact with the Masekos in Pretoria." (We refer to UJoana Masilela as uJoana from this point on.)

The events following the death of uNkosinathi are troubling to re-late. By the time of the funeral, those on both sides of the border had gone through untold grief and suffering. When uNkosinathi was buried, uJoana could not go to the funeral. She only saw the grave for the first time long afterwards.

Long journey to the funeral

Once the arrangements had been made, it was decided that uSibongile should be at the funeral. Neither uJoana nor any member of the Masi-lela family could attend. This meant sending uSibongile across the bor-der with someone not known to the South African security police. The child was then only about four months old. We knew that every-one attending the funeral would be closely watched. Nkosinathi's fa-ther, whom we refer to as uBab' Maseko, had earlier warned uJoana not to be at the ceremony, as she was being expected by the security police.

So it was uJoana Magwaza who played a key part in our plan, both through her courage and her strategic position. Because uSibongile could not cross the border under either a Maseko or Masilela surname, as such, a fake birth certificate was produced for her, under the name 'Nomsa Yengwayo', which means 'fooled kindness'. USibongile, as 'Nomsa Yengwayo' then took Joana Magwaza's name, and travelled under this alias as her child.

Joana Magwaza's role did not end there. It was a daunting task for her to take uSibongile to Mamelodi to be part of uNkosinathi's fu-neral. Unfortunately, her involvement led to tensions in the Masilela family. It was decided that she should be accompanied by uGranny, the only family member who could still cross the border legitimate-ly. In order not to expose too many people, they had to use public transport.

However, when they arrived at Oshoek border post, uGranny was denied entry into South Africa for the first time. After being threat-ened with arrest, she returned to Manzini in tears. She was saved by her physical condition. This sudden change in attitude towards her was baffling and worried everybody. We suspected the worst.

UJoana Magwaza was now on her own with the baby. She could no longer go back, despite the fact that she was embarking on such a journey for the first time. She had never been to Mamelodi before and did not know what to expect. Fortunately, during this entire ordeal another family friend, uPeggy Manyatsi, had been watching, and came to the rescue. She took them with her to Benoni, where she herself was headed. On arrival, they called uBab' Maseko who came to pick them up.

They spent two nights in Mamelodi. It would seem that the police, who were keeping a sharp eye on the proceedings, noticed that there was a baby who was probably from Swaziland, but could not identify the mother. It was clear that uJoana Magwaza could not be the mother, as the child was very light in complexion while she was very dark. It is said that the police asked the neighbours about the whereabouts of the mother of this mysterious baby. UJoana Magwaza herself was never confronted, as no one could link her, let alone relate her to the baby. Soon after the funeral, they were bundled into a kombi and returned to Swaziland without further incident.

About a year after the funeral, uBab' Maseko came to Swaziland to pick up uSibongile, fulfilling the wishes of uNkosinathi before he died. She was taken to Mamelodi, where she still lives. This decision to separate her from her daughter was hard for uJoana to accept, but she respected Nkosinathi's wish, as did the rest of the Masilela family.

That is the most uJoana can tell about her involvement with liberation. Not only did it touch her politically but it affected her emotionally as well.

PART III

Experience with Comrades

HOME NEWS

Visuanathan Pillay — alias Ivan.

Shadrack Ndaba — alias Paul Dikeledi.

Collingwood August — alias Maphumulo.

B A Mhlambo — alias Solly.

Zondi Roller Molape — alias Clement alias Selby.

Sidumo Theophilus Dlodlo — alias Viva.

Siphiwe Nyanda — alias Gebhuza.

Boniface Mziwakhe Ngwenya — alias Thami Zulu.

Letoshie Glory Sedibe — alias September.

Michael Modise.

D P Motsoaledi — alias Castus.

Mduduzi Cecil Sithole — alias Trevor Vilakazi.

Ephraim Ndondo Thusi — alias Mike Ngozi.

Keith Mokoape.

Nelson Hlongwane — alias Nsizwa

Wilson Welile Twala — alias Chief

Reavell Rhodes Nkondo — alias Ricky.

In 1984, the Swazi Prime Minister Prince Bhekimpi called on Swazis to be "vigilant to help flush out ANC bands currently roving all over the country. The country is now infested with foreign crimnals, wherever they come from" (*TOS*, 8 April 1984). The period following the signing of the Nkomati Accord marked the apex of the efforts to flush out the ANC from Swaziland. The strategy briskly shifted from generalities to specifically identifying people who were seen as undesirable. The clipping shown above, found in Magogo's wardrobe, is a rarity; efforts to get a better-quality copy from the Swazi National Archives, the University of Swaziland, the *Swazi Observer* and the *Times of Swaziland* failed.

CHAPTER 11

Prelude

The Masilela family drew in people from all walks of life. Among them were operatives of MK. Many saw the latter as comrades, but to me they were much more than that – they were brothers and sisters.

I had a complex yet fascinating relationship with many of these people. The brotherhood grew from a need to engender a deep level of trust and dependency. As a consequence, we kept close, but were also very cautious with one another. The relationship was made complex by the fact that, while we had to trust and be dependent on each other, there was an asymmetry in the sharing of information.

The operatives had to know everything about me, but I could only have limited knowledge of them. The only data I was given about an operative was his or her name or alias and, where relevant, the name of the operation.

This inherent asymmetry was there for strategic reasons. It was important to preserve the security of operatives. I had to know very little, so that should I be caught and tortured I would be unable to reveal identities and other sensitive information. I would later appreciate this deliberate ignorance, after the kidnap and subsequent desertion of uGlory September (discussed in Chapter 16).

Over the years, I interacted with a myriad of individuals, holding various responsibilities in the movement, many of whom I no longer remember. I sometimes find myself in embarrassing situations when I meet these comrades and they remind me of the work we did together or events we shared. Often, I can recall the event, but am unable to remember the individual. My only excuse is that I have been exposed to a large number of people, some of whom I saw only for brief moments and never again. In this way, I justify not remembering them, but it does remain embarrassing.

I met many if not all the comrades as they passed through kwaMagogo heading for a mission in South Africa, when leaving to go deeper into exile, or when I ferried them from the Mozambican border to their next destination or mission.

Only with the passage of time, growing trust and the comfort in information sharing was I able to delve into the detailed backgrounds of particular individuals. Writing this book has given me a unique opportunity to research, investigate and come to know some of these people in detail. In certain cases, I was able to visit their homes and meet their relatives, something I would never have dreamed of in the past. This was a reversal of roles and a wonderful opportunity to reminisce.

In this part of the book, I look at experiences with certain individuals who influenced my life and that of the Masilela family, as well as the way in which I viewed the struggle at the time. This coverage is by no means comprehensive. The choice of individuals was governed to an extent by their availability and the practicality of the interview. While most were in Gauteng, for some of the interviews and data collection I made trips to Limpopo and Swaziland.

Most of the activists who went through Swaziland had a relationship with Number 43 in one form or another. This escalated after June 1976 when the flood of exiles into the country peaked. At this time, the PAC was forced by circumstances to rent a house diagonally behind Number 43, owned by another South African, a Mr Masetloa. Meanwhile, Ntate John Nkadimeng established the White House, which became the leading safe house for the ANC. For a long time, the ANC used Number 43 as a base and a bridge with the White House.

Critical phases in Swaziland's political landscape
The background against which these events unfolded was both a delicate and a dynamic one, calling for a high degree of adaptability on the part of those with whom we worked.

Certain distinct phases of the political dynamics in Swaziland can be identified. The manner in which one divides up the period may vary, depending on one's objective. For the purposes of this book, three unique phases are relevant. These were the 'Sobhuza era', a period of relative political and social stability; the 'Liqoqo era', marked by the most chaotic governance in the history of Swaziland; and the 'Mswati era', which brought back relative calm. Each of these periods presented its own set of challenges to the ANC in general and Number 43 in particular.

The Sobhuza era covered the period from colonial rule until the death of King Sobhuza II in August 1982. A high level of cooperation between the ANC and the Swazi authorities generally distinguished it. Whilst technically underground, the ANC was given full recognition and was allowed to carry on its activities almost unrestricted.

However, political tensions started showing by the late 1970s. In 1977, the only nationwide student class boycott in Swaziland was staged. As a result, many extramural activities were removed from the country's education almanac. The boycott was unprecedented and came as a huge surprise to the Swazi authorities. In denial of the realities in the country, it was blamed on the mass influx of South African students fleeing persecution. All subsequent forms of political instability in Swaziland would be blamed on the political process in South Africa and the resultant refugees in Swaziland.

The relationship was further soured with the ANC's decision to step up its armed struggle in 1979, a year which was declared the 'Year of the Spear', in commemoration of the battle of Isandhlwana. This declaration was part of Oliver Tambo's New Year's message of that year, and was reiterated in his New Year message of 1980, which in turn was declared the 'Year of the Charter' marking the 25th anniversary of the adoption of the Freedom Charter.

Amid the tension and fear for our lives, these messages were a key inspiration to us. Oliver Tambo, whom we simply addressed as uOR, was President of the ANC and commander of its armed forces, as well as a beacon of hope for many of us. The whole MK fraternity would clamour to lay their hands on the annual messages, which would be distributed both in audio and written form. No matter how low our spirits, uOR always had inspirational words to help us focus beyond the immediate risks, pressures and disillusionments. I was lucky in that I never had to race for these publications, as many people did. Because Number 43 was at the crossroads, I would be amongst the first to receive them, as I was responsible for their distribution to cadres in Swaziland.

A further turning point came in February 1982 with the signing of a clandestine non-aggression pact between Swaziland and South Africa. Contrary to its intention, this swung the doors wide open and brought harsh onslaughts by the South African security forces. They staged cross-border raids into the neighbouring states. By the time King Sobhuza died, there had been two bomb attacks in Swaziland, a number of kidnappings and attempted kidnappings, as well as several arrests by the Swazi police.

★ ★ ★

Of the three phases, the Liqoqo era was the shortest but the most notorious, not only for the ANC but also for the Swazi society in general. The country went through four years of unprecedented instability and intimidation, with profound social, political and economic effects. The Liqoqo ruled the country with a high level of autocracy and disruptiveness. It was also characterised by pillage and corruption.

When it was established, the Liqoqo assumed the status of Supreme Council of State, but was downgraded to Council of State after two of its key members, Prince Mfanasibili and Dr George Msibi, who had ruled the country with an iron fist, were removed. The period was brought to an end, to the jubilation of the Swazi nation, by the coronation of King Mswati III and the dissolution of the Liqoqo in April 1986.

★ ★ ★

Meanwhile, March 1984 had seen the signing of the Nkomati Accord between the governments of South Africa and Mozambique. The accord was a weird marriage of opposite ideologies, in an attempt to forge peace between two feuding countries. Mozambique, on the one hand, sought to reestablish an economic lifeline with its larger neighbour, while South Africa, on the other, aimed at coercing Mozambique into refusing sanctuary to the ANC.

The Nkomati Accord resulted in a complete change of direction for the struggle, as waged from Swaziland and Mozambique. People had to be moved out of Mozambique in a hasty and unplanned manner. As a result, Swaziland was flooded with operatives, raising the risk to unprecedented levels and putting enormous strain on the underground system.

To the surprise of many, the ANC greeted the Nkomati Accord with sympathy and understanding. Samora Machel's strategy was seen as allowing Mozambique to buy time and breathing space from the dominant and aggressive South African regime, Mozambique being almost defenceless against its powerful neighbour. The ANC adopted a policy of non-condemnation of the Mozambique government, noting the pressure that country was suffering from South Africa.

In his defence to the Frontline States, Samora Machel argued that, as a region, there was no strategy for the liberation of South Africa. Countries adopted uncoordinated stances and approaches. The ANC was tasked with developing this strategy. From this was to grow the Harare Declaration of 1989, setting the terms of a negotiated settlement for South Africa.

In the meantime, the military struggle continued in the changed political context. The ANC was forced to make strategic choices to adjust to the new status quo, at least militarily. One of the options was to retreat to Tanzania and Zambia. However, the high command of the ANC did not find this appealing, seeing it as a backward step. Instead, the decision was taken to enter South Africa and establish an operational platform within the country.

Hordes of people had to be routed through Swaziland, on their way to South Africa. Given the scale and poor preparedness for this operation, many operatives had to wait in Swaziland for long periods, pending further instructions. This significantly exposed everyone who harboured them.

Operations of historical and emotional importance

I have always seen myself as apolitical. In spite of this, I found myself deeply involved in many risky, clandestine but important operations, either directly or indirectly. My responsibilities included ferrying people from the Swazi border with Mozambique to safe houses in the country, assisting in establishing a network of safe houses, managing the safekeeping of materials used for operations, and liaising with those who would further ferry the units and equipment into South Africa.

The establishment of safe houses was greatly facilitated by uNonhlanhla, later to become my wife, who worked for one of the larger estate agencies in Manzini, VJR Estate Agencies. With her manager, Lulu Mdwara, she made sure that we found houses at short notice. They also alerted us if any shady enquiries were made about a house occupied by operatives. This would give us sufficient time to evacuate the place.

Unfortunately, it was not always possible to pick up the signals in time. As a result, many of our comrades were arrested, maimed and some even killed. One of these cases was the attack in 1983 on a house in Moneni, just outside Manzini, where uZwelakhe Nyanda and uKeith McFadden lost their lives, a story we come back to later in the book. Incidentally, uGrace had secured this particular house through VJR.

Other cases that showed the enemy was penetrating the ranks of the ANC were the ambush and assassination of uViva Theophilus Dlodlo in Mbabane on 22 May 1987, near the Swaziland College of Technology; of uPaul Dikeledi, uCassius Make and Eliza Tsinini along the Lobamba road on 9 July 1987; the attack on uJabu 'Omude or J-Cabs' Shoke at a flat in Mbabane; and many more. Many people link these tragedies to the kidnap and subsequent desertion of uGlory September in August 1986. Some of these cases are discussed elsewhere in the book.

These events showed that the South African security forces were developing a tight grip over the operations of the ANC in Swaziland and breaking down what we thought was a solid wall of security.

Essential military routes

Picking people up from the border with Mozambique would typically take place at night, between eight o'clock and midnight. Occasionally, it would be done in broad daylight, particularly over weekends when the border patrol was off. There were three basic pick-up points along the border. These were the 'Luthuli highway', just before entering a small border town, called Lomahasha on the Swaziland side and Namaacha on the Mozambican side, 'Morogoro', and a third one called 'eS'kolweni'. The latter was named for its proximity to a school, Lomahasha Central. Years later, I would discover that this pick-up point was just a few metres from my wife's homestead. Since this discovery, every visit to my in-laws in Lomahasha brings back nostalgic memories of my struggle days. Each trip feels like a pilgrimage.

Lomahasha is now a comfortable 104-kilometre drive from Manzini, on a well-paved road. In those days, the drive was a gruelling one. For about half the journey, the road was badly kept gravel. While it takes just under an hour to do today, in those days it took two hours, unless one was racing away from the Swazi police. Many accidents took place along the rough stretch of the journey.

I remember being involved in two car chases with Swazi police and soldiers who had spotted us at the pick-up points. In both cases, we decided not to jeopardise our operations by stopping to be arrested. That naturally raised the risk of being involved in dirty skirmishes. We thought it a risk worth taking and, in both cases, it worked in our favour.

Since most of these pick-ups took place on weekdays, I would often have to leave home for school in the morning, not to return until the early hours of the following morning. At first, this was a source of concern for uMagogo. She worried that the operations would disrupt my academic work, especially after the missions intensified in the early 1980s. This coincided with the completion of my high school education, a time that is critical for anyone's future.

Swazi authorities declare war on the ANC

The process became yet tougher and riskier when the Swazi authorities declared that ANC operations were no longer desirable on Swazi soil. Security was stepped up at the borders to prevent operatives illegally entering Swazi territory. There was a nationwide awareness blitz, aimed at the Swazi population, to help the police flush out what they termed 'emaphebula s'khuni', which means terrorists in siSwati. Announcements were made on radio, television and in print media, urging Swazis to report any unfamiliar faces to the police. This propaganda campaign had begun in the 1970s but was intensified in the 1980s.

Newspapers carried aggressive and uncompromising statements from the Swazi authorities, with headlines such as, 'Refugees are Welcome, but We Won't Be Used, Says PM' (*TOS*, 16 November 1981); 'Beware of Communists' (*TOS*, 20 August 1982); 'Bill to End Arms Menace' (*TOS*, 30 November 1982); 'What's Up in Manzini' (*TOS*, 25 November 1983); 'Flush Out this Scourge' (*TOS*, 17 April 1984); 'ANC Must Get Out' (*TOS*, 16 April 1984); and 'Red Alert' (*TOS*, 27 November 1984).

One Prime Minister of the time, Prince Bhekimpi, made a call for the nation to be "vigilant to help flush out ANC bands currently roving all over the country. The country is now infested with foreign criminals, wherever they come from." These pronouncements followed several confrontations between the Swazi police and army, on the one hand, and ANC operatives in Swaziland, on the other. A number of policemen were killed and injured in the skirmishes. In response, the police issued a public warning that read:

PLEASE BEWARE OF STRANGERS

i. Do you know the people living next door?
ii. Is the home next door too quiet during the day and becomes alive only late at night?
iii. Is the home next door frequently visited by strangers, either driving or walking, who avoid contact with you?
iv. Is the house next door changing occupants too often, especially transient males without wives and children?
v. Do strangers hang around the back streets and unlit corners in your locality?

Please do worry yourself when you see suspicious characters
in your area.

REPORT ALL SUCH INCIDENTS

(TOS, 18 April 1984)

Contrary to its aim, this was helpful information for us. We responded
by populating some of the houses with my nephews and nieces, to
make them look like regular households. Alas, this did not always
work.

The police blitz proved effective, both in rural and urban areas, and
resulted in many of our comrades being arrested and deported. Fortunately, very few were handed over to the South African security.
There was no place to hide, except at Number 43.

I recall moving people to what we thought was a remote and safe
farm in the vicinity of Big Bend, in the east of the country, about 70
kilometres from Manzini. It did not take long for the people to be
flushed out. They were arrested on the night of their arrival on the
farm. To this day, we do not know how the police learned about the
transfer.

Strategic plans and key operations

From time to time, I found myself involved in strategic discussions
and putting together some of the logistics of the operations. These
included the gunning down of the notorious cop in Soweto, Detective-
Sergeant Chapi Hlubi (June 1978); the Sasol 1 attack (1980); the Voortrekker military base attack (1981); the Tonga army outpost attack
(1982); the Hectorspruit blast (1982); and the Pretoria Church Street
bomb blast (1983).

In several of these, my wind-up wristwatch, which I wear to this
day, was used because it glowed in the dark. I remember 'uFannie'
saying, "Professor, it is not only its ability to glow in the dark that fascinates me, it is also the fact that it ticks. It will keep us awake whilst
we wait for the final onslaught." We laughed, partly in response to
the joke but mainly because it helped to relieve the tension.

Gunning down of Hlubi

The gunning down of Hlubi was one of the most daring missions. It was a one-man operation, with no go-betweens and no DLB (an acronym for dead letter box, a place where arms and other materials are kept for collection by operatives). UJabu Masina, who was a frequenter of Number 43, carried out the execution.

UJabu and I were not close at the time, and our relationship only firmed during the writing of this book. When we met for the interview, it was the first time since 1978. I did not recognise him at first, nor he me. In his mind, he still carried a picture of the high school student he had left in Swaziland. Also, with the passage of time, uJabu has notably accumulated a few more kilos.

For the operation, he entered the Transvaal with a fake passport using public transport. However, he can no longer remember the name he used on the passport. The operation was not carried out the first time around. UHlubi no longer stayed at his house, owing to the hostile reputation he had earned for himself among Soweto residents through his work. That meant searching for him well beyond the vicinity of his house. UJabu was forced to return to Swaziland after fourteen days of trying to track down his target. At that time, those entering South Africa were given a maximum of fourteen days in the country. Concerned about the expiry of this period, he was forced to abandon the operation.

Worse still, when he returned to Swaziland, he was mocked by his commander, who refused to accept that the target could not be located and joked, "ungen'we yi nyoni!" – meaning that he had developed cold feet. Given this frustration, uJabu pushed himself to launch the mission again, about two weeks later. This time he was successful, but not without another round of patient searching. It was not until day thirteen, 25 June 1978, that he struck.

His gun failed him at the critical moment, and almost cost him his life. It jammed after firing one bullet, wounding his target. Like a wounded animal, uHlubi retaliated, firing several shots, which rang across the location. Hlubi's house was next to the Moroka Police Station, which meant the sound of gunfire alerted the police and brought back-up from other parts of Soweto. UJabu was forced to flee for his life. A massive search was launched for him, lasting throughout the night. He hid himself at a friend's place in Soweto until the commotion died down. He learnt from news reports the following day that uHlubi had died in hospital of his wound.

A similar operation that remains vivid in my mind involved a comrade who was armed with a pistol and an AK47. Wearing overalls and masquerading as a farm worker, he carried little money and rode a bicycle from Number 43 to the point of his operation and back. We joked before the mission about the overalls and whether he would pass as a farm labourer. One of us commented that if the residents of Liliesleaf succeeded in fooling the boers, this should be much easier. At no point did we question his ability to pedal the long distance, since he was a physically fit fellow. After the operation, he dropped the bicycle off at Number 43. What happened to it, I do not remember. It just disappeared.

Voortrekkerhoogte

My main responsibility in the Voortrekker attack was the safekeeping of a camera and other materials used for reconnaissance before the operation. I had a similar responsibility with the Hectorspruit mission, where I was also responsible for the materials and for the safe car, a red Pulsar, used to cross into South Africa. Unfortunately, the car had to be destroyed along the border after the operation. It was spotted just before the operation and we were afraid that if it crossed back into Swaziland, it would lead the South African security police to Number 43. In both operations, I was involved with the teams that were dispatched and received.

During informal discussions of the attack on the Voortrekker military base, it was proposed in passing that the Voortrekker Monument and the Union Buildings be included among the targets. I held out against enlarging the scope beyond the army base, on the grounds that these were important historic landmarks, from which the economy would benefit in the future. I had not seen either of these structures, so I combined my passion for economics with a little self-interest.

I would later visit the Voortrekker Monument on 16 December 1998, in my first year after returning to South Africa. I took guests I was hosting from Swaziland to visit the Monument. Little did I realise the historical significance of the date for the Afrikaners. We only learned about this on our way out, when a *Sunday Times* reporter, noticing that we were the only blacks in a sea of white faces, asked about the treatment we had received. Four days later we were in the Sunday newspaper, described as having strayed without incident into the sacred territory of the Afrikaner. This was hailed as a hopeful sign of change in South Africa.

Pretoria Church Street bomb blast

The Pretoria Church Street bomb blast was significantly different from the other operations. It marked a major departure from the philosophy that underlay the ANC armed struggle, attracting widespread criticism both from domestic and international commentators. The reason for this outcry was that nineteen innocent people ('soft targets', as they were termed) died in the explosion and a further 217 were injured.

It was constantly impressed upon operatives that in guerilla warfare "the people are your bushes and forest". It was a fundamental principle that the trust of the people be preserved. Thus it was imperative to avoid involving soft targets in a mission.

However, enemy personnel, government stooges, collaborators and those who had been turned were clubbed together with the rest of the targets marked by the ANC. These included strategic roads, railway lines, other forms of communication, power stations, police stations, military camps and other similar structures.

To this day, I cannot forget the emotions of this operation. For the first time, we knew that the operatives involved might not survive the mission. Among them was a relative, uEzekiel Maseko, who was an uncle to our brother-in-law, uNkosinathi. I met uEzekiel for the first and last time just before they embarked on the operation.

Many years later, I discovered that he was the father of a colleague, uPhumzile Maseko, in the South African National Treasury. I did not know this until after four years in the Treasury. UPhumzile invited me to the unveiling of her father's tombstone in Mamelodi, on 20 May 2003. Before the day, I wondered who her father could have been, but thought it inappropriate to ask her. I arrived at the homestead, where I learnt for the first time whose tombstone would be unveiled. I revealed my identity to Phumzile's family and the extent to which I had known uEzekiel. Since then, uPhumzile and I have developed a special relationship.

Operations were structured very precisely, particularly in their timing. In most instances, we knew exactly when the strike would be carried out and when the team would return to base. If an operation were to take off from Number 43, my bedroom would be used as the place for rumination. Today, this room is kept locked to preserve its historical importance. It is only opened to guests.

In almost all cases, the missions went according to plan. The night before an operation would be filled with anxiety and fear that something might go wrong and we would fall foul of the South African security forces. Nerves were always on edge. There would be little conversation. The only sound would be that of quiet background music from old vinyl LPs. This music was essential therapy to calm our nerves.

Marauding Death Squads and Askaris

The fear reached a crisis point in the mid-1980s, when the South African security forces rattled the security in the ANC and tore into the heart of its operations. Several people were kidnapped, others defected to the enemy, and the Askari operations spread like a plague, resulting in several cross-border raids into Swaziland, Lesotho, Botswana and Mozambique. These fears were heightened by the capture and later defection of uGlory September, known to us as 'uSbata' (lion, or show of great respect for a person), together with uXolile 'Humphrey' Mkhwananzi.

Throughout this period, we lived on a day-to-day basis. Every new day that dawned was celebrated and we rejoiced to be alive. There were occasions when Number 43 was under 24-hour armed surveillance. This was a trying time for the family. There were times when there were not enough people to provide this service. As a consequence I was conscripted into the team. This meant balancing my time between schoolwork and functioning as a sentry.

There would typically be two evening shifts, of two people each. The first team would start around 10pm and break at around 2am. The other team would take over until 6am. Experience showed these were the most likely times for an attack. One person would be in the house, watching through the lounge and dining room windows, while the other would be at the old mango tree at the front corner of the yard. These two would alternate throughout their shift. We remained on alert for several months, but nothing amiss happened. It remained a mystery why there was no incident in this period, until a revelation in June 2006 by a police officer who had worked closely with Eugene de Kock (see Chapter 16).

The rest of this section relates the stories of the various individuals and families who were associated with Number 43, the operations in which they were involved, and the impact these had on their lives, as well as ours.

CHAPTER 12

Soft Leadership

John Kgoana Nkadimeng

Among the senior members of the ANC based in Swaziland in the period from 1976 to 1982 was John Kgoana Nkadimeng, known to those close to him simply as Ntate Nkadimeng. 'Ntate' is seSotho for father, but is also used as a mark of respect for any elderly male figure. To me, the title 'Ntate' was not simply a figure of speech. John Nkadimeng was a true father figure during those times of hardship. When I made the proposal to interview him, to my surprise and delight he jumped at the idea. He was one of the few I approached who made themselves immediately available.

Ntate Nkadimeng is an old hand in the ANC. He first served the ANC under the leadership of Chief Albert Luthuli. Following the 1953 elections in Queenstown, he was co-opted onto the National Executive Committee (NEC). Together with Advocate Duma Nokwe, he became one of its youngest members. He continued as a member of the NEC from 1976 to 1980, only this time in exile.

Both in this period and in later years, he held key positions in the ANC. He served on the Revolutionary Council, with a brief to develop internal structures, create publicity for the ANC, and wage the armed struggle. He was later responsible for the regional structures of MK operations, chaired the Maputo Senior Organ, and served on the Secretariat of the Maputo Senior Organ Political Committee.

My excitement at the prospect of our interview was momentarily dampened when he was forced to cancel our first appointment. President Mbeki had summoned him at short notice to Cape Town. He was to be recognised in the State of the Nation Address, tabled in Parliament on 11 February 2005, as one of those who had made an outstanding contribution to the struggle and the liberation of South Africa.

This is what the President had to say in his address about Ntate Nkadimeng: "Also among us is John Nkadimeng, a volunteer himself and founder-leader of the South African Congress of Trade Unions (SACTU), which was formed fifty years ago. Through their efforts, which we acknowledge in this Chamber today, John Nkadimeng, Chris Dlamini and their colleagues ensured that we could today say with pride that South Africa belongs to all the working people of our country." Also acknowledged by the President was Madoda Nsibande, whom Ntate Nkadimeng singles out as the founding Deputy President of SACTU, saying that he owes his trade union achievements to him.

Our first interview took place soon thereafter, on 13 February. Prior to this, I had not met Ntate Nkadimeng since he left Swaziland in 1982, aside from hearing about him on news broadcasts and on one or two occasions catching sight of him driving along the N1 between Pretoria and Johannesburg. When I first called to request an interview, I had been concerned about whether he would recognise me or recall who I was. He surprised me by remembering me immediately. When I told him about my meeting with uMadiba, a few weeks earlier, he quipped, "However, my memory does not compare to that of uMadiba."

He attached at least as much urgency to compiling this book as I did. Since his return from exile, he had considered writing the story of the ANC in Swaziland, but had never found the time to actualise his thoughts. Further, given the complexity of the subject, he did not know how to describe his experiences in a way that would not cause embarrassment to those around him and in the ANC, but would promote a new knowledge about the struggle as it was waged from Swaziland and contribute to the sharing of a deeply felt history.

He emphasised, however, that the story of Number 43 could never be complete without being told side-by-side with that of the 'White House'. A few blocks from Number 43, this was Ntate Nkadimeng's base and the focus of ANC operations in Swaziland during his time there.

* * *

Ntate Nkadimeng was born in the Sekhukhuniland village of Manganeng. As often happened at the time, birth records were vague:

"Because my family was uneducated, I do not know when I was born. The only indication I have about my birth date is that I was born on the 12 June 1927, as it is the date written in my identity document. This could well be wrong." This made him 78 years old at the time of the interview.

He is today the only survivor of a family of five, three boys and two girls. His father died while he was still a toddler, leaving him with no clear memory of him: "All I remember of him is that he suffered from an unknown ailment which he developed while working in the mines of Johannesburg. He was later retrenched due to his illness." Almost certainly, he died of silicosis from working underground.

As a result of losing his father at such an early age, he grew up under the guardianship of his uncle, Kgoshi Sepeke Nkadimeng, in Mangameng. His mother had moved him to escape his half brothers who threatened to kill him because of a family feud, adding a further incentive for entrusting him to his uncle.

He attended school up until Standard 6, which he completed in 1944. On leaving school, he moved to Germiston, where he found work in a hat factory, in Siemet Street in Doornfontein. While there, he studied part time, taking night classes in Albert Street in Johannesburg. He continued with this up to Junior Certificate.

A mentor and good friend

In 1952, Ntate Nkadimeng became exposed to politics for the first time, when Flag Boshielo recruited him to the ANC. According to him, Flag was one of the 'famous generals of the ANC, a well seasoned politician and an outstanding revolutionary'.

Before this, Flag had worked for the *Guardian* newspaper. For the first three months of their association, he used to deliver a copy of the daily paper to Ntate Nkadimeng: "He would direct me to read the leader articles by the editor and insisted that I analyse and discuss these with him." This provided him with a steep political learning curve, which became valuable later in his political life.

Though Flag never reached Standard 7, his intellectual capacity for politics fascinated Ntate Nkadimeng. He carried on a running debate with the ANC leadership about combatants 'rotting' in the camps, arguing that he would rather die at home than in the camps at the hands of people who differed with him.

Flag died in battle while returning to South Africa from training in the 1960s. His body was never found. At this point in the interview, Ntate Nkadimeng broke down and wept. I was reminded of how strong were the bonds between comrades in exile. These relationships were not just part of a political process: they were the key to survival.

Work in the underground

When President Mbeki recognised Ntate Nkadimeng in the 2005 State of the Nation Address, among other topics he referred to was the defiance campaign of 1952. Ntate Nkadimeng was among the first batch of defiers to enter No. 4, 'the big prison', as he calls it: "We were taken to Marshall Square – this was long before John Vorster Square was built. We were kept behind bars for about three months. The security police lodged a serious charge against us – that of 'Sabotage against the State' – but this was subsequently dropped.

"While in custody, we were tortured. To this day I carry the scars of that incarceration. My left ear was damaged, which permanently impaired my hearing."

He is modest about his role in South Africa's labour movement. He does not acknowledge that he was the founder member of SACTU: "Prior to the defiance campaign, I founded a trade union movement in the tobacco industry. I was made a shop steward in a factory. When Flag was banned in 1953, I became the Chairman of the Central Branch. In 1955, after the adoption of the Freedom Charter, I was arrested with 155 other people, and charged with high treason, together with the high council of the ANC. We were tried at the Drill Hall near the Alexandra bus rank in Johannesburg, before the hearing was shifted to Pretoria."

By then, Ntate Nkadimeng had established a fairly close relationship with uMadiba and other members of the High Command of the ANC. On one occasion, when uMadiba was underground, he had to receive him in his neighbourhood, Alexandra Township, for a meeting. UMadiba came on a bicycle disguised in a baSotho blanket and hat. He was met on the outskirts of Alexandra, along the main Pretoria road, and was taken to a house in 4th Avenue. The house served as their strategic and secret meeting place, as it had a basement. It still stands today.

He has much to relate on his experiences with the security police and the legal system at that time: "The first time I got arrested was long before the Rivonia trial, and this was for sabotage. The police had nothing against me, apart from suspicion. My mother-in-law, who stayed in Lady Selbourne, a place I operated in, was called to testify against me.

"She steadfastly refused to bear witness against a relative. She was a devout Christian who could not speak English. When asked to repeat the oath, she instead said, 'Modimo nthuse, ngwana oo ke mokgwenyana. Molato wa hae wa ho tla mo, ke eng?'" (God help me. This is my son-in-law. I do not know what crime he has committed by visiting this place.)

Nonetheless, he was sentenced to two years in Kroonstad. He comments: "This arrest, which was meant to be a spirit dampener, turned out to be a golden opportunity. It gave me the chance to educate prisoners about the struggle. However, on my release, a fellow inmate, an old man I had trusted and respected, gave me an address for his son in Brixton, asking me to visit him once I was outside. Unexpectedly, the police searched me on my way out and discovered the address. I learnt later that this was a set-up. I was rearrested, to the bitter disappointment of my wife, who was waiting for me outside the prison gate. I never emerged."

During this further incarceration, he was kept in Viljoensdrif. In a further attempt to break his spirit, he was kept with criminals. Luckily, he had literature with him. This, and the nature of his case, distinguished him from the rest of the prisoners. Contrary to the hopes of the security forces, he was treated well by his fellow inmates. When he was arraigned in court, he was given a fine. He was also issued with a banning order, restricting him to Orlando in Soweto. He was expected to report to the Orlando police station every Friday. One day he forgot to report because he was involved with hosting a party during a visit from his mother. For this omission, he was arrested once again.

After his release, he moved into a three-roomed house in Diepkloof. There he met a certain Masuku from Swaziland, who helped him put up a ceiling in his house. This meeting was opportune. By now, he was thoroughly tired of the harassment from the police, and decided to flee the country. UMasuku helped to facilitate his passage to Swaziland, and in 1976 he left South Africa with no intention of returning.

His Holiness

On arrival, uMasuku took him to the Salesian Boys' School, where he met uStan Mabizela, who in turn introduced him to Bishop Mandlenkosi Zwane, Bishop of the Roman Catholic Church in Swaziland. Bishop Zwane, known as 'Mbhishobhi' by the Swazis, was deeply involved in the liberation struggle, having been active in rehabilitation work for refugees from South Africa and Mozambique. During the Bethal terrorism trials in 1979, he testified in defence of South African black nationalists. This led to stiff entry restrictions to South Africa being imposed on him.

Bishop Zwane was the founder of the Council of Churches in Swaziland, and one of the few in the priesthood to embrace the Black Consciousness Movement. Much of his thinking could be explained by his education at St Peter's Seminary at Pevensey in Natal and later in Hammanskraal. He said about the movement: "Black Consciousness is the result of long suffering and oppression. Perhaps not so much physical oppression but denial of history, culture and in these two areas there has been an insistence that black people had no history, black people had no culture, and all that they read, all that they learnt, was European history, white man's culture and so they were expected to behave like the white man. So a reaction to this was to try and find themselves. That's what Black Consciousness is all about."

On 9 August 1980, he died in a mysterious car accident near Mbabane, after addressing an All Africa Council of Churches conference. Ntate Nkadimeng told me they had warned him against driving alone, particularly at night. They were worried about the attention he was attracting from both the Swazi and South African governments with his radical views. As a man of the cloth, he did not take their concerns to heart.

The birth of the White House

In Swaziland, Ntate Nkadimeng first stayed at Fairview, north of Number 43, at a safe house named 'Come Again'. UBafana Duma, known as 'uMdumane', working as a clerk at a law firm in Manzini, together with uMoses Mabhida, was responsible for the house. UThabo Mbeki and uJacob Zuma used it whilst in Swaziland. UJacob Zuma was familiarly known as JZ, a title reflecting his popularity in the ranks of the ANC and as a member of the senior organ in Mozambique. The name 'Come Again' originated with uThabo and uJZ, in a phrase they always used when bidding guests farewell. By the time Ntate Nkadimeng arrived in Swaziland, however, they had both left, having been deported by the Swazi authorities.

In his early days in Swaziland, Ntate Nkadimeng was very mobile, moving between residences. These included the residences of Ntate Monare, uStan Mabizela and uBra Stokes Sithole, as well as Come Again. The Transvaal machineries reported to him, which meant he had to consult with a number of the operatives working from Number 43, in particular uSeptember. Together with Ntate Mashego (another father figure to me who is no longer with us), they used the house as their prime meeting spot. Ntate Nkadimeng remembers it as, "An extremely warm place. On the basis of information collected there, I would develop my reports to Lusaka. Number 43 was like an engine room."

Come Again was used mainly by the Eastern Cape and Natal machineries. Due to the conflict of interest at the house and his growing responsibility for the Transvaal machinery, he decided to set up permanent camp elsewhere. This led to the establishment of the White House. UMrs Mabizela gave the name to it. She argued that since uThabo and uJZ had left Swaziland, Ntate Nkadimeng was developing a centre of power around the house and himself. He laughed it off, but the name stuck. The house is still called the White House by those who associated with it then. It later developed a Siamese twin-like relationship with Number 43. He emphasises that the story of Number 43 can only be fully understood side by side with that of the White House.

A further refuge of note was Ntate Monare's house in Ngwane Park. This is a residential area just outside Manzini, to the southwest of Trelawney Park. Because of its position, the Monares' place was one of the key strategic homes in Swaziland. It was out of town and therefore away from the hawkish eyes of the Swazi police. As a result, it was used mainly for harbouring operatives working underground.

Ntate Nkadimeng's first exposure to the Monare house was when he intervened in a feud between these operatives and the ANC leadership in Swaziland. He was asked by Ntate Baartman to assess the situation at the house. On arrival, he found the operatives preparing to stage a toyi-toyi, to protest that they were not being fed. They had already produced placards making demands, with inscriptions such as, 'Take us to Maputo, or else!'

To deal with this imminent mutiny, he had to draw on the assistance of other leaders, such as uMabhida, uStan Mabizela and uNzima. This turned out to be difficult since the leadership was divided on the legitimacy of the action. Whilst some felt they needed to take a stern line with the protesters, the trade unionist in Ntate Nkadimeng felt that their demands were legitimate. The latter view finally won the day and uBafana Duma was instructed to supply the food, much to the chagrin of some of the leadership.

Ngwane Park would be turned into a battleground in the 1980s, as operatives of MK were holed up in another safe house by a joint force of Swazi police and their trainers. At the time of writing, the house where this battle took place was being considered for inclusion in the list of historic sites in Manzini.

Ntate Nkadimeng was not alone in setting up the White House. Two other comrades, 'General' and Mahahe, assisted him. During his stay in Swaziland, uGeneral involved me in a motorcar operation across the Lomahasha border in 1981 that left me with the dubious pleasure of almost writing my Form V exams behind bars. This experience is related in chapter 28.

UGeneral was a fascinating character, about whom many stories are told. One is worth recounting here. In December 1981, he was the target of Dirk Coetzee's last death squad operation. Jacques Pauw writes in his book, based on interviews with Coetzee: "The plan was to bring him to South Africa, interrogate him about the ANC activities in Swaziland and dispose of him afterwards. Coetzee and Almond Nofomela sneaked into the house and waited for him in his bedroom. When their target suddenly walked into the room, pandemonium broke out." He used every muscle in his stubby body, plus his teeth, to fight off his assailants, who abruptly disappeared back into the night. He was the hero of the movement in Swaziland for many months to come.

The White House later hit the headlines following a failed assassination attempt on Ntate Nkadimeng. A bomb was found under his car. It has never been established who planted it and Ntate Nkadimeng does not want to speculate about the matter. The only comment he ventured was that, after giving an account of the attempt to an ANC NEC meeting in Lusaka, the Secretary General of the ANC, then uAdvocate Duma Nokwe, said: "You were only saved by the grace of our National Anthem, Nkosi Sikelela" (God guide us).

Setting of the sun

In Swazi tradition as well as other Nguni traditions, when the King dies, it is said that the sun has set. When it set in Swaziland, it did so not only for the Swazi nation but also for the ANC. The failed attempt on Ntate Nkadimeng was only the beginning of a wave of fear that engulfed Swaziland, following the death of King Sobhuza II in 1982. The ANC had looked on the King as their protector.

His death ushered in the coming to power of the Liqoqo, and hard times not only for the ANC but for the average Swazi as well. The mood and attitude of the Swazi authorities towards the ANC suddenly hardened, making it extremely difficult for the organisation to continue operating from the country. It was not very long before the White House was forced to shut down and Ntate Nkadimeng had to leave the country for Lusaka.

Since the White House was so close to Number 43, security and vigilance had to be stepped up there as well. Number 43 was left as the only nerve centre for the Transvaal machinery, and to some extent for other machineries.

The Amandla Group

Ntate Nkadimeng has eight children. Six of them settled in Swaziland, while the others left South Africa, going through Botswana and Mozambique. One of them, Veronica, joined the Amandla Group while in exile. I had never met her until my interview with Ntate Nkadimeng. Purely for her role in the Amandla Group, she stood out for me above the rest of the siblings.

The Amandla Group was the ANC's pre-eminent cultural group in exile, nurtured by people such as uJonas Gwangwa and uDennis Dipale. As a musician and composer himself, uOR was the patron of the group. He was instrumental in its formation and wrote some of the songs they performed. The spirit of the group had an important bonding effect among those in exile and strengthened their determination to fight, despite all the hardships they faced. In 1980 or 1981 they performed in Mozambique and attracted many of those exiled in neighbouring states. I was one of those who were sneaked into Mozambique for the show, by uFannie and uKelly.

The Amandla Group stage act was electrifying. I have yet to watch a performance as emotionally and politically charged as theirs. It was literally political training and conscientisation on stage. I often wonder why the ANC has never considered reproducing it after independence. I always compared it to Gibson Kente's 'How Long' and other similar ensembles, but none came close to the experience of the Amandla Group.

This is how Ntate Nkadimeng describes Veronica and her role in Amandla: "I went to watch her play in Mozambique. But I did not

TOP: UMagogo and uButhongo enjoying life, 29 April 2006. (Masilela Archives)

ABOVE: The only picture that shows the whole family, circa 1966–67. Standing behind the baby (author) is an old family friend, uBenedict Dlamini. (Masilela Archives)

TOP: The house in which uMagogo was born and raised in Majaneng, Hammanskraal. The house was built during the period 1915–1918. It was built of stone and boasts walls averaging 100cm in thickness – undated photo. (Masilela Archives)

ABOVE: The house that uButhongo built in Mofolo North, Soweto, and subsequently sold to uBhomo before he migrated to Swaziland in 1966. (Masilela Archives)

TOP: The back view of the main house at Number 43, soon after it was built, circa 1971–72, with uGrace standing at the door. (Masilela Archives)

ABOVE: A view of the front of the main house at Number 43, taken in December 2004. (Masilela Archives)

TOP: Flanked by his advisors, uAbraham Jambo Kekana, father of uMagogo, is shown seated during one of the periods when he acted as Chief – undated photo.
(Masilela Archives)

OPPOSITE TOP: This photo of uButhongo (standing on far left) was taken in August 1945, soon after his return from the Second World War. The man on the right is Solly Msiza, uButhongo's cousin; the man in the centre is unknown.
(Masilela Archives)

OPPOSITE BOTTOM: UButhongo and his siblings: seated on the left are uButhongo and his brother uPhilip; standing are sisters uWilhemina and uBetty – photo taken in 1997.
(Masilela Archives)

TOP: UMagogo and uButhongo soon after arriving at Number 43, circa 1965. In the background is Solly Mahlangu's truck, used to transport the family to Swaziland. On the ground, from left to right, are uTodd, uLucky and uBenedict Dlamini. (Masilela Archives)

ABOVE LEFT: Seated on the right is uMagogo with her sister, uMaria Mothoa, in the kitchen at Number 43, during one of many family gatherings and ceremonies – undated photo. (Masilela Archives)

ABOVE RIGHT: UJoana, uElias and uLucky playing on the dusty streets of Trelawney Park during the early days in Swaziland – circa 1968. (Masilela Archives)

TOP: USolly Mahlangu (wearing a cap in this photo) ferried the Masilela family to Swaziland in 1965 and later 'gave' Number 43 to the Masilela family – photo circa 1965. (Masilela Archives)

ABOVE: UGrace, uJoana, uLucky and uGranny at Number 466, Mofolo North, just before the migration to Swaziland – circa 1965. (Masilela Archives)

TOP: The kitchen at Number 43: facing the camera, from left to right, are uMagogo, uButhongo and uTaBilly – circa September 1985. (Masilela Archives)

ABOVE: The main passage of Number 43, with the telephone on the display cabinet at the far end, was a key point. This was where all calls, both devastating and pleasant, were received – 14 July 2006. (Masilela Archives)

TOP: Standing in the middle is uBhomo, who bought house 466 in Mofolo North. With him are uEdnah Mkhwanazi and uNorman Masilela – Hammanskraal, 9 August 2003. (Masilela Archives)

ABOVE: The early congregation of the Lutheran Church in Manzini, which originated at Number 43 – circa 1973. (Masilela Archives)

ABOVE: The White House was set up by Ntate John Nkadimeng and flourished from 1976 to 1982, when he was deported from Swaziland following the death of King Sobhuza II – photo taken 14 July 2006. (Masilela Archives)

OPPOSITE TOP: The mango tree anchoring the southeastern corner of the property at Number 43 was used by comrades, friends, family and the police. The first interview for this book, in December 2004, took place under this tree – photo taken 19 December 2004. (Masilela Archives)

OPPOSITE LEFT: The wardrobe in the author's bedroom that was used to store arms and ammunition destined for most of the operations launched from Number 43 – 14 July 2006. (Masilela Archives)

OPPOSITE RIGHT: The author holding uSibongile 'Bobo' just before the funeral of uNkosinathi – January 1984. (Masilela Archives)

TOP: UJoana with uJoana Magwaza and uMarie Maseko, in the kitchen at Number 43, after the death of uNkosinathi – circa 1984. (Masilela Archives).

ABOVE: Todd's house, from where uViva and five other people left, before three of them met their deaths on 22 May 1987 – photo taken 14 July 2006. (Masilela Archives)

TOP: The spot where uViva was assassinated, along Ncoboza road – 14 July 2006. (Masilela Archives)

ABOVE: Fr Larry McDonnell, Fr Patrick Fleming and Fr Patrick Ahern in front of the Salesian chapel – 11 June 2006. (Masilela Archives)

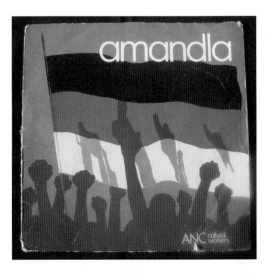

TOP: The power of liberation music: the Amandla Cultural Group provided the necessary motivation and a major source of inspiration to operatives in Swaziland and across the globe. This was the album that kept our spirits up.

ABOVE: This photo shows the recognition of uButhongo, on the occasion of Kelly's burial in Tohoyandou. Also in the picture, standing, are uPhilipos, one of the people who stayed and worked from Number 43, Minister Sydney Mufamadi and the King Vho-Thobela MPK Tshivase – 23 September 2006. (Masilela Archives)

TOP: UMagogo delivering her acceptance speech, at the Thulamaha-she stadium in Bushbuckridge, Mpumalanga, on the occasion of her recognition by the Premier of the province, Premier Thabang Ma-kwetla – 12 August 2006. (Masilela Archives)

ABOVE: UMagogo being recognised at the occasion of Kelly's reburial, in Tohoyandou, on 23 September 2006. On the left is Minister of Local Government, Sydney Mufamadi; on the right is Chief Vha-Musanda Vho-Takalani. (Masilela Archives)

TOP: UMagogo with iNkosikazi naMtsweni, in her capacity as MEC of Arts and Culture in Mpumalanga, during the celebration of the Age of Hope, on Women's Day, 9 August 2006, in a ceremony held at the Union Buildings in Pretoria. (Masilela Archives)

ABOVE: The author meets uMadiba at the Dochester Hotel in London, where he took the opportunity to ask his lifelong question. Picture taken by Trevor Manuel, SA Finance Minister – 5 February 2005. (Masilela Archives)

recognise her until they started performing. I watched them again in Angola at Kibashi camp. The performance in the camp was completely different from the stage act. I asked myself what might happen if they were to stage this act in the middle of Johannesburg at that time. Soweto would explode, man!"

I had countless sessions with Ntate Nkadimeng, most of which ended up not being interviews so much as lessons in history. During these I would stop writing, and simply follow the narrations with my heart. In particular, I was impressed by his amazing memory and recollection of events and people. After every visit to his home in Kew, I would walk away with at least two more names of people I had to interview, as well as information to help me close information gaps in interviews I had already had with people much younger than him. This book could easily have been written entirely on the basis of the information he provided. A lot more could be written about his rich life and warm family, as well as the depth of his relationship with and attachment to Number 43.

CHAPTER 13

A Lifetime Commander

Siphiwe 'Gebhuza' Nyanda

Siphiwe 'Gebhuza' Nyanda is described in many accounts as the ANC's most successful regional military commander. The name Gebhuza was bestowed on him by uMoses Mabhida. Even today, those who worked with him in exile know him simply as uGebhuza. The name Siphiwe has a more official ring to it. He had a number of other aliases in Swaziland, such as 'Kgole Tebogo' and 'Zakhele'. On several occasions, especially during the 1980s, he topped the list of wanted people in Swaziland.

He headed the Transvaal urban machinery from 1977, based mainly in Swaziland. He trained in the German Democratic Republic in advanced military tactics, and was a close confidant and partner of people like Mac Maharaj and Ronnie Kasrils. He came to prominence in the world outside the ranks of the ANC when Operation Vula became public, to the deep embarrassment and annoyance of the South African government. For me, his most outstanding achievement was commanding the G5 Operation. This operation reignited the firepower of the MK after years of inaction, largely by carrying out attacks on police stations.

The purpose of this chapter, however, is to describe his relationships with those comrades who operated in Swaziland, in particular those based at Number 43.

Unlike the rest of the comrades he worked with, uGebhuza was not a frequent visitor to the house. He always kept a low profile, taking a strictly business-like approach in his engagements with Number 43. I do not remember him spending a full day at the house, and I can count on one hand the times we had an extended discussion. The only vivid instance I can recall was the last night uSeptember spent at the house, just before his kidnapping. UGebhuza dropped by to consult briefly with uSeptember, leaving soon afterwards.

Given his demeanour, uGebhuza attracted much speculation about the sort of person he was. Clearly a well-respected leader, he was said to be brave, calculating and exceedingly security-conscious. We knew the house was under constant surveillance by both the Swazi and the South African security forces, which explained his limited exposure to the place.

When I came to interview him, he had recently retired as the Commander of the South African armed forces. With this in mind, the discussion necessarily had to deal with the broad generalities of his role and activities. He preferred that his colleagues and comrades, who are discussed elsewhere in the book, provide the details. Nevertheless, he made a significant statement about Number 43:

"Given that Liliesleaf was a national headquarters of the ANC, one of highly strategic and national importance, it cannot easily be paralleled. On the other hand, Number 43 was a haven mainly for people operating on the eastern front, like similar houses in Botswana and Zambia. It was at the centre of the ANC's military operations. From an operational viewpoint, however, it may be a complex exercise to try and compare the two properties."

Two houses in the region outside of Swaziland that came to mind when he made this statement are the Green House in Lusaka and the Terror Nest in Maputo.

Introduction to politics

UGebhuza was born in 1950 in Moroka, Soweto. He attended school at Nthabiseng Primary, in Orlando West, Thulasizwe Higher Primary, and Orlando West High School. In 1970, he enrolled with the University of Zululand (Ongoye). He had become involved in politics at school, with people such as uZwelakhe Sisulu, who were in the same group. However, there were no political vehicles for them until they reached university. The South African Students Organisation (SASO) had recently been launched under the leadership of people such as uSteve Biko and uWelile 'Satane' Nhlapo.

In 1971 he was expelled from university for protesting against the use of plastic mugs in the dining hall. He led a campaign that involved punching holes in the mugs, rendering them unusable, in the hope that more sensible ones would be provided. Naturally, this did not go down well with university officials. He found himself having to seek work. He began with menial jobs until he landed a post as a sports journalist for *The World* newspaper. This lasted from 1973 until he left South Africa on an ANC ticket.

It was not until 1974–75 in Swaziland that he formally joined the ANC. UTom and uTokyo Sexwale introduced him to the high command. His first responsibility was to recruit people from South Africa, a brief that called for frequent travel across the border. During this time, he received basic training in security awareness and survival tactics. In 1975, however, he was ordered by uThabo and uJZ to leave the country. They were concerned about the extent to which he was being exposed by his activities, which in turn would put at risk the entire cell he had developed.

Unlike most of those who went into exile, he had the chance to inform his parents about his planned departure. He recalls his father saying, "I hope it is not what I think." He never had the opportunity to ask him what his thought actually was, but could easily deduce it from the tone. On the same day, he crossed into Swaziland. While in Swaziland he stayed kwaDhlomo in Zakhele. He remained there only briefly, as he immediately proceeded to Mozambique.

He had various responsibilities in the ANC, among which was that of Commissar of the Transvaal Urban Machinery, before he assumed command following the death of uSelaelo Ramusi, who died of pneumonia in incarceration in Swaziland. The machinery would later become known as the 'Gebhuza Machinery'.

By all accounts, it was the most successful machinery in the urban areas, with few casualties. For a long time it was not infiltrated. This was an outstanding feature for the time, when Askaris were being bred like flies. However, it would later suffer serious casualties and losses following the kidnap of uSeptember and the signing of the Nkomati Accord, events which opened a huge security gap in the ANC operations in Swaziland.

His first encounter with Number 43 occurred quite early in his stay in Swaziland. He nostalgically recalls how healthy relationships with the Swazi authorities then were, still within the Sobhuza era. The ANC underground worked in a semi-clandestine way. It was then that he was introduced to uMagogo and came to know her.

Of all my siblings, he was closest to uSwazi and uGrace who operated directly with him. He knew uTodd but only from a distance and indirectly through people like uDikgang and uViva who worked with both uTodd and him. This changed significantly from the mid-1980's when uTodd became one of the key underground contacts in Swaziland.

As for all the other operatives, kwaMagogo was for uGebhuza a key meeting point. When uGrace was not on a mission, she would be at Number 43 during the day and only went back to her house, which they shared, at night. That meant he would have to visit Number 43 fairly regularly, even if only for short stints.

Trying times

Three events continue to ring clear in his memory. These were the abduction and defection of uSeptember, the murder of uViva, and the assassination of his brother uZweli.

Among all those I interviewed, he was the only one to say that September's behaviour did not come as a surprise. Everyone else recorded shock at the event. No one had expected uSeptember to defect, whatever the circumstances. According to uGebhuza, September's interests were never in military activity. He had observed that uSeptember undertook his responsibilities with obvious reluctance. He believes the problems began with the amalgamation of the machineries. This caused his own machinery, which was largely free of infiltration, to be exposed, making it difficult and sometimes impossible to screen people.

UGebhuza was close to uViva, uJabu and uNsizwa. He found Viva's death a great loss to the ANC. He remembers him as extremely intelligent and brave. When he was killed, uGebhuza was out of the country on mission, having left a mere two days before the assassination.

His most devastating experience, however, was learning of the death of his brother, uZwelakhe 'Zweli' Nyanda, on 22 November, 1983. It left the entire underground in shock and disarray. When uZweli died, he was again out of the country, in Bulawayo en route to Botswana on mission. He heard about the death over the radio, and as a result of the travelling he could not attend the funeral. But to pay tribute to his brother he wrote a speech, which was to be read by uAli Twala. For some reason, he was unable to do it. In his place, Ntate Monare, an old friend of uZweli from his early days in Swaziland, read the tribute.

It transpired later that the person responsible for Zweli's death had been until then a comrade and trusted confidant. In Gebhuza's words, "It was a classic betrayal. What angers me is that the person had the audacity to go to Ali Twala's place after Zweli's death. He was unrepentant." He would not elaborate about his feelings beyond this.

UZweli joined the ranks of the ANC in Swaziland, much later than uGebhuza, but was very active during the 1976 riots. In 1977, uGebhuza took him to Swaziland where he would later teach at a school in Nhlangano. While uZweli had no direct relationship with Number 43, he spent part of his stay in Swaziland kwaSwazi in Mobeni, Matsapha.

UGebhuza continues to be seen as the central figure in events as they relate to the history of the struggle in Swaziland. In June 2004, he was a member of the official South African delegation at the cleansing ceremony in Swaziland, which is discussed in Chapter 31. This was a major rebirth for those who had operated from there. It fittingly brought together friend and foe in a spirit of reconciliation, rebuilding and remembrance.

CHAPTER 14

Every Step of Growth
was Fully Earned

Jabu Shoke

Like uGebhuza, uJabu Shoke found himself constrained in the amount of detail he could provide for this book. This was partly because of his position in the South African National Defence Force, but also because of a task he had been entrusted with relating to ANC activities in Swaziland. At the time of the interview, he was the Chief of the army. He achieved this position after rising steadily through the ranks of the ANC. He prides himself in having been well grounded in military and political discipline, but notes that he was never among those high flyers of the movement who shot to glory in a short space of time. As he says, "Every step of my growth was fully earned."

Those close to him knew him as J-Cabs. To the Masilela family, he was uJabu Omude, meaning 'tall Jabu'. Like many other activists, he joined the ANC at the height of the student uprisings in 1976. In September of that year he joined MK and underwent military training in Angola. Following this, he was posted back to South Africa, working on missions run from Swaziland and Mozambique.

When he first arrived in Swaziland, uBafana Duma received him in Manzini. For the first few months, he had to stay underground, and therefore could not visit Number 43. But he knew about uMagogo long before he met her, through senior members of the ANC such as Ntate Nkadimeng. Even after he started frequenting Number 43, he made it a point never to spend a night. Given his mandate to operate in South Africa, too much exposure to Number 43 was deemed too risky. He recalls that the first time he spent a night there was at the wedding of uLucky, only in 1999.

When asked to compare Number 43 with Liliesleaf, he said: "The two could not be compared. Number 43 was a place where all cadres operating from Swaziland met and were warmly welcomed, in spite of the risk the Masilela family was exposing itself to. With the passage of time, it ceased to be a secret that the family was ANC, since their loyalty was not hidden.

"UMagogo was a living example of the expression 'Wathint'umfazi wathint'imbokodo' (You strike a woman you strike a rock). She played a critical role in influencing and moulding the political views of the family and some of the cadres. Despite the frequency of the raids, people never realised that the house was a nerve centre for all the work we did in Swaziland.

"While Liliesleaf was the ANC HQ in the country, Number 43 was a base outside South Africa. It was a home away from home for most South African exiles, both underground and above ground. The same cannot be said of Liliesleaf. Number 43 was not clandestine; it remained above ground even in the most dangerous of times. Despite this making it a huge security risk, the house continued to be the cornerstone for our work. There is ample evidence that many people were arrested as a result of the surveillance of Number 43. Ironically, however, this saved the house from attacks.

"From both political and strategic viewpoints, it would not have served the South African security to attack. Instead, both the Swazi and South African forces resorted to harassing the family members, with the aim of intimidating and weakening them. Of course, this tactic did not work. Instead, the reverse was achieved."

UJabu was close to uTodd, whom he considered not only a comrade and friend but a brother. After Todd's death, he adopted uLucky to close the gap that was left. He was also close to uSeptember, and does not believe he was originally an informer. Having said that, he emphasises that he had always been wary of his cowardice, which emerged at the most critical time, resulting in him turning informer. After 1993, uSeptember approached several people in the hope of rejoining the ANC. UJabu is unaware what happened to those advances.

Contrary to other views, he is convinced that uSeptember had nothing to do with the killing of uViva, maintaining that Eugene de Kock was responsible, whether directly or indirectly. At the time of the assassination, uJabu was also being targeted. He recalls that the death squad tortured uPriscilla, trying to squeeze out information about his whereabouts.

He was finally tracked down and attacked on 14 August 1988, at a flat in Thokoza in Mbabane, by a squad under the command of Eugene de Kock, as revealed in De Kock's submission to the TRC. He survived a ferocious fight, but was hospitalised with serious bullet wounds. While he was in hospital, uAngel, the youngest in the family, who was a nurse at the Mbabane government hospital, served as the link between uJabu and his family. She also mobilised the other nurses to cooperate.

To this day, he continues to sing the praises of uAngel. I guess this character of openly showing recognition of people around him has earned him respect from his colleagues. My own recent engagement with the SANDF has amply confirmed this.

CHAPTER 15

Young at Heart

Welile 'Satane' Nhlapo

The ANC circle has proven to be an extremely wide one. This is reflected in the frequency with which one stumbles into comrades,
sometimes in the least likely of places. My relationship with uWelile
Nhlapo, known to others and us close to him in Swaziland as 'uSatane', extended beyond the borders of Swaziland and as far afield as
Addis Ababa. In 1995, when I was studying at the Addis Ababa University (AAU), uSatane was posted as South Africa's Ambassador to
Ethiopia, the OAU and the Horn of Africa region.

My relationship with uSatane was a close one. He almost doubled
as a replacement brother to me, given his closeness to uTodd. Like
everybody else, he was fond of uMagogo, but with a slight touch of
sensitivity. His role in Swaziland was that of a political commissar
and intellectual. At the time I interviewed him, he was the President's
Special Envoy to the Great Lakes. This is a responsibility he carried
over from his ambassadorial days in Addis Ababa. This is how he
opened the discussion for this chapter.

"Part of the philosophy behind the operations of the ANC was to
try and curtail and/or sabotage the economic muscle of the apartheid
government. The thinking was also that of limiting such operations
to hard targets, hence the targeting of economic installations and
plants. It was important to guard against corrosion and to preserve
the credibility of the struggle, as well as to avoid attracting unneces-
sary terrorist-type criticism to the movement. We had earned our
stripes as responsible freedom fighters with a sound long-term vision.
We were not about to lose that.

"On the other hand, the survival strategy of the regime was to
invest in areas which would allow them to reduce their dependence
on the rest of the world. Oil was a key resource, developed with the

establishment of Sasol, and based on the country's abundant reserves of coal. Not surprisingly, it became one of the main strategic targets of the ANC onslaught against the government.

"The decision to target economic installations was grounded on both political and military logic. The view was that penetrating an area of high security would expose the regime as incapable of effectively defending itself. Hitting at the heart of its security would have a huge psychological impact on both black and white communities.

"It was important that we took cognizance of the distinction between hard and soft targets. A conscious effort was made to avoid loss of life at all cost, in order to preserve the credibility of the struggle. This fell within the broader scope of armed propaganda."

In spite of the care to avoid soft targets, there were incidents that resulted in the ANC finding itself accused of terrorism. One of these was the Pretoria Church Street bomb blast. The target was army personnel, but tragically there were unintended casualties. A major international debate followed this attack.

He continues: "There was a conscious decision to coordinate military strikes with activities organised by citizens on the ground. Orlando Police Station, Moroka Police Station, the gunning down of the notorious police officer Hlubi, sabotage of electricity installations and mine operations to limit the rural defense strategy of the regime, are cases in point."

When asked to select what he considered as flagship operations of the ANC, he responded: "Every operation was important in its own right. Everyone who contributed to the struggle, no matter how insignificant that contribution might have seemed, made a difference.

"The choice of operations was critical, given the apartheid regime's drive to undermine the ANC and its credibility, in particular by using the Askaris. It was a war of nerves. The official claiming of successful operations by the organisation was thus an essential part of the liberation struggle as well as a critical defense of the ANC's credibility. The example of the Silverton hostage drama is a case in point, as was the case of Solomon Mahlangu, which unfortunately resulted in his execution in 1979. This coincided with Unyaka we Sandlwana, the 'Year of the Spear'".

Path to ANC membership

I was intrigued when I made the discovery that his political life did not date as far back as I had imagined, given his position and influence in the ANC as well as his role in Swaziland. As he revealed, "In 1973, at the time when a lot of people were coming out of Robben Island, we got in contact with them. I had close contact with uJoyce Skhakhane and uSnuki Zikalala who supplied us with political materials and literature. In that year, I was placed under a 'miniskirt' banning order, a phrase given to a banning order that gave limited access to certain institutions such as schools and publishing houses, but allowed movement across magisterial districts. But because of its nature, it made one vulnerable and ultimately led me to transgress the restrictions. It forced one to be one's own policeman in the underground. Ironically, some people extended the imposition of the restriction, on the grounds that they were afraid of being trapped. The psychological effect of these restrictions forced me to leave the country on 30 September 1974."

He left with a number of other people to arrive in Botswana on that country's independence day. Botswana was a popular base for those aligned to the Black Consciousness Movement and had a close affinity to the PAC. Naturally, the group became exposed to both ideologies.

In the early part of their stay, they had extensive engagements with the leadership of the ANC, such as uThabo Mbeki and uRuth Mumpati. However, because their focus was on academic training and they wanted little or no attachment to any political party, they were sent to Libya in 1975 on a PAC-arranged training programme. They discovered later that what they were handed as an opportunity to further their education was actually a poisoned chalice.

Immediately upon return from Libya, they were faced with a conflict. The PAC claimed them as members, since they had acquired their training on its ticket. USatane and his group did not agree with that thinking and insisted on remaining unattached, maintaining their frail neutrality. Meanwhile, uSatane was in fact silently eyeing the ANC as a likely party to join, should they be forced to make a choice. The basis of this choice was the ideological difference between the PAC and the ANC.

"One of the reasons we were uncomfortable with the PAC was the obvious divisions within that organisation. As a direct consequence, we were abandoned by the PAC and were left to rot at Dar-es-Salaam airport. We were stranded there for about five days. While waiting for help, some familiar faces appeared in the waiting area. These included uJoe Slovo, uJoe Modise and uKeith Mokoape. They overheard our conversation and took an interest. After a while, uKeith approached us."

Their first debate with uKeith revolved around the white element in the ANC and the ANC's policy of accepting people as individuals into its ranks, rather than groups. USatane and his group were a team and could not conceive of being separated. However, this hope of remaining as a tightly knit group was broken, and he finally joined the ANC in 1976.

In 2006, I would meet with uKeith in his capacity as Chief of the SA Army Reserve. He revealed a close relationship he had enjoyed with uThandi in Bulgaria. To me, this further illustrated the extensiveness of the ANC circle.

From 1978 to 1981, uSatane worked at the ANC's London office as Deputy Editor of Sechaba. One of his roles was to set up offices on the continent, addressing meetings and conferences. He worked with people such as Aziz Pahad and Ronnie Kasrils, who were targeting students passing through. He also worked closely with uThabo Mbeki when he was the head of DIP.

In 1981, he was recalled to headquarters in Lusaka, to head a committee with the mandate of building the image of the ANC and developing relations with Africa at different levels. One of the products of the committee was the design of the ANC logo. Another of his early assignments was as member of a team that arranged a youth conference in 1982 in Mazimbu, Tanzania, with the theme 'training diversity'. There was a large MK contingent at the conference.

The youth in him

Until 1987, uSatane was head of the youth league. He was seconded to Swaziland in 1986 with the same responsibility, but dealing directly with the youth in South Africa. He brought his own youthful spirit to this role. I vividly recall his affection for young people and for children. He was like Father Christmas to all my nephews and nieces. He would sing and dance with them as if he were their age. In particular, he liked a hit song of the time by uBrenda Fassie, with the lyrics 'Me do do do do so la do ti'. This would be played repeatedly when he was at Number 43.

USatane is a big man, but his body weight never constrained him in his dance.

I used to sit mesmerised by the contrasts in his character. One moment he would be playing with the children at their level, the next he would be engaged in serious strategic plotting of the liberation of South Africa.

Exposure to Number 43

This is how uSatane relates his first encounter with Number 43: "On my arrival in Swaziland, I was based in Trelawney Park, next to the Uncle Charlie hotel. This was a few blocks from Number 43. The house was secured and handed over to us by uGrace, who in turn introduced us to uMagogo and everyone at Number 43. I had met uGrace in Lusaka and Mozambique. While there, I had heard of Number 43. I had always looked forward to setting foot in this place, which was being talked about across the globe. On arrival in Swaziland, I finally did. It felt as if I had arrived in the Promised Land.

"We spent many hours hanging out at Number 43 with both comrades and friends. For some of us, it was not only a place where we held our strategic meetings and picked up information, it was also home. It was where we had our meals and had access to television. The walk up to Pendray Park, close to Number 43, was always pleasant and remains memorable to this day.

"Not all occasions at Number 43 were uneventful. In fact, life in the house was often punctuated with excitement, tension and sometimes panic. The first alarm I got after arriving in Swaziland was when uGrace burst through my door to report the death of uMaphumulo. We swiftly vacated our safe house and congregated at Number 43. As we were sitting there, analysing the situation and the events that had led to Maphumulo's death, uTodd strode in to report the further killings of uPantsu Smith, uSipho Dlamini and uBusi Majola, in Mbabane. This news left us badly shaken."

My relations

"I came to know most of the people I met and worked with in Swaziland through Number 43. I became one of the regulars who spent their lives kwaMagogo. The only person I never came to know was uSeptember, who happened to be a household name. However, I heard many reports about him through people such as uGebhuza and the Masilela family. I mention uSeptember because I am told he did very good work while in the ranks of the ANC and was one of those closest to Number 43. He was described as extremely courageous and intellectually impressive.

"On the other hand, I started knowing uGebhuza in 1967–68, while staying at Dube and studying at the Morris Isaacson School. There was a library close to where he stayed, to which we had a key, allowing us round-the-clock access. Typically, given the edge we had among the students, we would often visit the library at night together with the rest of our group. Looking back, it is no longer clear to me whether these evenings were used for academic work or for other purposes. But I do remember spending many hours talking politics and doing very little studying.

"Miraculously, we passed high school and proceeded to ONgoye University together with uGebhuza. USteve Biko came to ONgoye during our stay and motivated us to organise ourselves. This we did, and as expected found ourselves in trouble with the security forces. As a result, uGebhuza was expelled in 1971. But despite that, we stayed in contact."

Paul Dikeledi

"Three events that shook me badly were the assassination of uViva on 22 May 1987, and of Paul Dikeledi (whose real name was Sello Motau) and Cassius Make (whose real name was Job Shimankane Tabane), two months later on 9 July 1987. The modes of assassination were very similar and the cars identified in both incidents were the same. We had no reason to suspect that the two were not related."

UViva was killed in a convoy of three cars: a red VW Golf, a Mitsubishi and a white BMW. According to USatane, they had seen one of the cars driving away before they reached Todd's place just after the shooting.

"Around this time, Number 43 was literally under siege, gripped by fear, as uSeptember was said to be prowling Swaziland. We had met uCassius earlier on the day of his assassination, despite the fact that he was no longer supposed to set foot in Swaziland because he was being watched."

UPaul was gunned down along Manzana Road in Lobamba, together with uCassius and a woman who was a Mozambican national, in a drive-by shooting. The taxi they were traveling in was forced off the road by a BMW sedan, with an identical description to one of the cars used two months earlier in the assassination of uViva.

UPaul had been in MK Central Operations, responsible for the Eastern Front from 1976 to 1980, working with uJZ, uJoe Slovo and others. Between 1980 and 1983 he combined this role with that of the Maputo SO Military Command, working closely with people like uManchecker, uGebhuza and uEdwin Dlamini.

On calling Maputo, it was learnt that uPaul, who at that stage was responsible for the Eastern Transvaal machinery, had accompanied uCassius on an investigation of a cache of arms that had gone missing from a DLB. The death of these two senior members of the ANC left a big void in the organisation.

UPaul holds a special place in the heart of the Masilela family. Despite spending relatively less time in Swaziland compared to the others in this book, whenever he was around, his presence was felt by everybody. He had an aura that commanded respect, yet he was one of the most humble people I knew. He was not easily excited, bordering on being introverted, but was very intelligent and highly analytical. He possessed wonderful leadership and negotiation skills. On several occasions, he brokered family disputes in a manner that always impressed me.

USatane concluded: "Among the closest people to me while operating from Swaziland, were uViva, uChris, uGrace, uTodd and uSwazi."

CHAPTER 16

Trail of Terror
by a Trusted Commander

Glory 'September' Sedibe

It was a warm Saturday night on 9 August 1986. I had just started working at the Central Bank of Swaziland, having joined in July. That evening, as was the tradition, we sat in the kitchen at Number 43 with a handful of my former university friends who had an interest in politics, both regional and South African, as well as ANC politics.

We sat up till the early hours of the next morning, philosophising about the progress of the struggle. This included the role of the neighbouring states, in particular of Swaziland, which at that time was perceived by many university students to have sold out, after the secret pact with South Africa signed four years earlier. The impact of Askaris on the liberation struggle was also analysed, uncharacteristically in detail – as if we were having a premonition. There was general consensus about the ultimate success of the struggle and the ineffectiveness of the death squads in halting the momentum towards freedom in South Africa.

Among those who took part in this discussion were uBheki Zwane (a son of Dr Ambrose Zwane) and uBhadala Mamba, a very close friend with whom I had spent my entire school life, shared the same course at the university and later worked for the same employer. Leading the debate was none other than uGlory Lephosa Sedibe, also known as 'September'. To my family and those close to him he was called 'S'bata', a name uMagogo was passionate about. Also in the discussion was uHumphrey Mkhwanazi, now better known as Xolani, who would later be arrested with uSeptember.

For the first time in my brief association with uSeptember, this evening gave me the opportunity to fully appreciate his intellectual capacity and the strength of his convictions about the struggle. Besides him, others whose intellect and leadership I admired were uSatane, uPaul Dikeledi, uPhilipos, uKelly and uGebhuza. By the end of that evening, I was convinced that when South Africa became independent, uSeptember would be one of the high-ranking intellectuals in the new government.

It was not to be.

A few days later, on 12 August, uSeptember and uHumphrey were arrested and held in the Manzini police cells. Two days later, on 14 August, the South African security police, under the command of Eugene de Kock and Paul van Dyk, kidnapped uSeptember from the cells. According to evidence later given by Almond Nofomela, the kidnapping was carried out with the cooperation of the Swazi police. The Commissioner of Police at the time is reported to have ordered that the policemen on duty be unarmed at the station where he was held.

This incident caused many Swazis and others who sympathised with the South African cause to develop reservations about the Swazi government and its police. Evidence heard many years later at the TRC also implicated the Swazi police in the deaths of uZweli Nyanda and uKeith McFadden at Lugaganeni, outside Manzini.

A controversial defection

Around what happened next, debate and controversy continue to swirl. USeptember turned, and the information he gave under interrogation to the enemy inflicted untold emotional, psychological and physical havoc on many people and sent shock waves across not only Swaziland but also the region. He generated great bitterness among people close to him.

Despite all the anger and disappointment that followed the kidnap of uSeptember and his ultimate defection, many people, including the Masilela family, loved him. In many ways, he resembled uTodd, being tall and light in complexion. Many in his machinery had looked up to him as an intelligent and dependable leader with sound political judgement. Respected at the highest levels of the ANC, he had commanded the Eastern Transvaal Rural machinery, together with uJulius Maliba. He was also in the Transvaal Regional PMC with uGebhuza as leader, uPaul, uNtsie Manye and uArchie (Billy Whitehead).

His position in the hierarchy in the ANC and his MK activities made him a valuable target for the enemy, despite some people suspecting that he had always been a plant. Being a direct relative of Ntate Mashego, a close comrade and confidant to Ntate Nkadimeng, this brought immense embarrassment to Ntate Nkadimeng.

Security arrangements in Swaziland and elsewhere had to be redefined, to minimise the risk of this defection. I say 'minimise' because no amount of change to the underlying structure of the organisation in Swaziland would have been enough to eliminate the risk. The risk was just too deep to fathom.

Whilst this may be a source of endless and bitter debate, for me this defection goes down as the biggest in the history of the ANC. The last time the ANC had been confronted with such a significant defection was in the early 1980s, when Bartholomew Hlapane was turned. He gave evidence on behalf of the state in a number of trials, in particular against Bram Fischer. An MK unit would later execute him. In its submission to the TRC, the ANC described Hlapane as "the most senior office-bearer to betray the struggle – he had been a member of the ANC's NEC and of the Central Committee of the SACP."

Trail of terror

September's defection sent fear through the hearts of everybody he had worked with. In the minds of many, he was responsible directly or indirectly for a series of deaths, including those of uPaul Dikeledi, uCassius Make, uViva Dlodlo and uTutu Nkwanyana.

Nevertheless, the question remains about how close he was to all the deaths that were attributed to him. It has been argued by some that his proximity to the events was academic and deductive, since the escalation of the attacks took place after his kidnapping. Given the high positive impact any information he supplied would have had in bringing the enemy closer to the ANC, even if he did not carry out the operations himself, he remained a palpable culprit in the eyes of many. Purists have always argued that "a sell-out is a sell-out".

I have often asked myself the question, "If he were the one pointing out the targets to the South African death squad, and given the amount of time that he spent at Number 43 as well as knowing the concentration of people who were potential targets, why did he not direct the operations to Number 43?"

There were two plausible theories about why Number 43 was left off the list. The first was that the security police saw Number 43 as a central point and a magnet for their targets, whom they would trace from there. An attack on Number 43 would scatter the targets and the house would lose its intelligence value. The second was that uSeptember had grown so fond of the Masilela family and felt so part of it that he found it too difficult to sell them out. Yet both of these theories were obliterated by information unearthed at the tail-end of writing this book.

* * *

In June 2006, I by chance met someone who had worked closely with Eugene de Kock and who is still with the South African police force. He revealed that they always had their own people operating from within Number 43 as plants, and for this reason it could not have been a target. I was shocked by the honesty of the revelation. I could not get over the idea that all along we thought that we were secure and were operating with honest people, yet we had had spies right in our midst, living with us in the house. We had never imagined that this could have been the case.

The discussion, which took about an hour, ended at that point. I did not even want to know who those people were. It was enough to appreciate the extent of the risk that we had lived through. I thanked him for his time and the information he had shared with me. We have never met again.

Surprise Christmas visit to Number 43

I was not to see uSeptember again until an evening in December 1993, when he appeared unexpectedly at Number 43. The family was in the midst of its traditional festivities, with many comrades visiting to spend Christmas. His arrival shocked and angered many who were there. Some reacted violently, even threatening to shoot him.

UTodd and I intervened, pleading for calm. I wanted to ask uSeptember two questions, "What happened?" and "Why did you not point at Number 43?" Unfortunately, the environment was too volatile for any discussion. Amazingly, he was not perturbed by his reception that night. He just carried on as though nothing had happened, displaying his usual friendly and charming character – greeting the old lady and old man, as well as everyone who was then in the kitchen. The only hint of concern was reflected in the amount of time he spent. He was there for a very brief moment, and quickly disappeared into the night, not to be seen again.

He died in April 1994, just before the first democratic elections in South Africa. Rumour has it that his handlers poisoned him. Before his death, however, uPhilipos had the rare opportunity of meeting him, and was able to ask him some of the questions we all wanted to ask. To him, uSeptember confessed that he had indeed talked.

Confessions

The TRC hearings supplied some answers, occasionally unexpected, to some of our questions. It emerged that a woman identified as Nompumelelo Zakade (not a name we knew her by) had been responsible for assassination. She worked deep within the ranks of the ANC. Using her charm, she extracted information from those high in the ANC command.

Nompumelelo would lure comrades to her place, from where they would be tailed by the death squad. In her confession she revealed that in the period culminating in the assassination of uViva, she pointed the squad to Todd's place, where they hid in ambush in the three cars. This was after having traced uViva to a house in Thembelihle, where there was to be a party the same evening.

Three people survived the ordeal. When the assassins returned to inspect the car, they noticed that three were missing. Zakade then pointed to Todd's place as the most likely place the survivors could have gone. The convoy drove back up the hill towards the house, with the aim of finishing them off. The assassins parked outside while she went to knock on the door, but uTodd refused her entry. I shudder when I imagine what a bloodbath would have resulted, had they gained entry into the house. By then it was teeming with operatives, both those who had been there from the afternoon and those who had been summoned. More were filing in.

Zakade later abetted in the assassination of uPaul Dikeledi, apparently using information obtained from uPaul himself, confirming her connections. In June 1986, she was also involved in the death of 'uPantsu' Smith and two other people in Mbabane.

She confessed to having been paid R800 for Viva's death, and R500 for Paul Dikeledi's and Cassius Make's killings. These sums represented the upper end of the range of payments. She typically received amounts ranging between R50 and R200. This clearly shows how cheap life was.

Among all her other confessions, she revealed that she had assisted the security police in the abduction of uSeptember. Nevertheless, doubts about his defection and its motives continue to haunt us. At least the beginning and the ending of the ordeal, as told by the last person he was with before his kidnap, uHumphrey, and the last person he confided in before his death, uPhilipos, have helped in partly bridging the gap. Personally, I remain bitter that we were robbed of an intellectual. If uSeptember had not been a plant and had not been kidnapped he would have been a valuable asset to the new South Africa, as would have been all the other comrades who perished in the hands of the enemy.

CHAPTER 17

Confidant and Friend

Xolani Humphrey Mkhwanazi

Xolani Humphrey Mkhwanazi's political career began early in his school life. His relationship with Number 43 also dates back to the late 1960s. He would later be linked to one of the most infamous kidnappings and would assist in decoding one of the key puzzles in the history of the ANC in Swaziland. He was close to uSeptember and worked with him, up till the point when he disappeared.

Coming from a non-political family, he was born in 1955 in Kwa-Hlabisa in KwaZulu Natal. His father was a worker in a sugar mill at Mtubatuba, while his mother, originally from Swaziland, was a nurse.

He was educated first at kwaKhandisa, and then at Matshali School, staying in Ngwelezane, an area where his mother worked. After his parents separated, he followed his mother back to Swaziland. There, he attended Salesian High School, where he met uTodd in 1969.

Salesian was fertile breeding ground for political activists under the tutorship of people like uStan Mabizela and uRosette Nziba. While uStan was ANC, uRosette was PAC. Despite being in different camps, they were a perfect partnership. These are people who influenced him greatly, both academically and politically. Also contributing to his political development was his uncle, uJoe Mkhwanazi, who was PAC. Like all other youngsters at that time, he was torn between joining the ANC or the PAC. It was ultimately Stan's intellectual flair that appealed to him, swaying him to the ANC.

In 1973, when he completed his Form V, he signed up with the ANC through uStan. However, he decided not to take up formal membership, in order to avoid being exposed, arguing also that his actions would matter more than holding a membership card.

The following year, he enrolled at the Luyengo campus of the University of Botswana, Lesotho and Swaziland (UBLS). In his group were people such as uSolly Makwakwa and uKhanya Dlamini. A significant addition to their number came when they were joined by uTokyo Sexwale in 1975. That year saw a major strike at the university, in which students campaigned against Websters bookstore. What began as a simple protest rapidly escalated, leading the police to barricade the university. Several students were arrested, including the President of the SRC of the time, uStan Kubheka.

While at the university, uHumphrey was invited by uBra Stokes to join what was ostensibly an education committee. Its role was to assist those who wanted to pursue an academic path. It was policy that when people joined the ranks of the ANC, they were allowed to make a choice of path, between academics and military training.

In 1976, as part of the joint university student exchange programme, Humphrey's group was sent to Botswana, a stronghold of the Black Consciousness Movement (BCM). By this point, Lesotho had withdrawn from the university network, which was now called the University of Botswana and Swaziland (UBS). In Botswana they met people like uMandla Langa and uWally Serote. For a variety of reasons, most of the BCM members eventually joined the ANC.

In Botswana, he encountered a certain Vusi, who reminded him of how easy it was to get into trouble in exile. One's dress code, the people one associated with and one's tastes could easily arouse suspicion of collaboration with the enemy. UVusi was mistakenly labelled an 'impimpi' or 'sellout' because of his immaculate dressing. In the late 1970s, he was one of the accused in the Bethal trial. This was the same trial in which the trialists benefited from resources generated from the Las Vegas disco in Manzini, before it was shut down by the Swazi authorities.

UHumphrey returned as an assistant lecturer at the Kwaluseni campus of UBS, where he was introduced to Pat McFadden. He resumed his role in the education committee. However, a friend of Pat's, known as 'Oupa' or 'Spider', invited him to join his unit, as he considered him underutilised by the education committee. Hoping for more interesting and challenging assignments, he accepted.

★ ★ ★

He worked as a courier between Swaziland and South Africa, masquerading as a successful salesman dealing in expensive merchandise. Contrary to the earlier observation regarding people's lifestyles, he could legitimately afford this image, given that it was funded by the ANC. It enabled him to move in and out of South Africa without arousing suspicion, although the risk of exposure was always there. In the early stages of this activity he had no links with Number 43, except indirectly through other people.

Soon after joining Oupa's unit he was introduced to someone who would later become important to his underground activities in Swaziland. This was uVusi 'Sadat' Mashinini. Because of his passion for jazz, uSadat was friends with uBra Stokes, a fervent jazz enthusiast. USadat suspected uOupa of being a sell-out, and as a result he transferred to September's unit in 1981. It was during this period that uHumphrey became directly exposed to Number 43, since both uSeptember and uSadat operated from there. This contact, however, was short-lived, since he left the same year for London to study for his PhD.

On completion of his degree in 1984, he was instructed to return to Swaziland. His arrival coincided with a major military restructuring in the ANC to deal with growing infiltration by enemy spies. In the same year, the Nkomati Accord was signed. As a result, the ANC office in Mozambique was reduced to a skeleton staff. As a member of the underground network in Swaziland, he was active in the sheltering of some of those who were shipped out of Mozambique. He provided safe housing at his UBS residence for a number of comrades, including people like uShezi, uGebhuza, and uPaul Dikeledi. Of these, uShezi would later survive an assassination attempt, while uPaul perished under a hail of bullets.

UHumphrey had a relatively easy time harbouring operatives, as he put it: "I was quite safe from the security forces. Since I had just returned, no one knew me. No one suspected me of being even remotely related to the ANC. This allowed me free movement in and out of Number 43, which turned out to be the ideal meeting point. It became home for me, cemented by the fact that I had studied with uTodd. That academic relationship further reinforced my neutrality. At this time, uGrace finally joined our unit from Mozambique.

"However, my cover was blown in 1986 when a certain Bongani, a former bodyguard of uOR, was kidnapped at the Pick 'n Pay in Mbabane. This was my first scare of that year, and was a prelude to still greater danger. It became clear to us that the net was closing in on us."

Around the same time, uSeptember did something that aroused the suspicions of the ANC military intelligence. He introduced a certain Malaza, who was said to be a policeman in Mpumalanga, into the work of the unit, a piece of information he picked up from uLindi Sisulu. She told him uMalaza had been seen around Manzini with a man named De Boss, whom she was scheduled to meet that evening in Coates Valley. She asked for protection, as she was nervous of meeting them on her own. Two people were called in, uSadat and uTom 'Grenade', to accompany her.

The meeting revealed that uMalaza could have provided sensitive and confidential information to the South African security police relating to operations in Swaziland, although not willingly. The following day he was taken to a safe house in Luyengo for further questioning. He admitted to having been drugged by the South African police, and under a brutal interrogation revealed much information about operations in Swaziland. In particular, he had been questioned about uSeptember.

As a precaution, the ANC sent him to Mozambique. It is not clear whether the events that followed, leading to the kidnap of uSeptember, were in any way aided by his revelations.

Clean out exercise

An instruction was issued from Headquarters in Lusaka to get rid of 'zonke izimpimpi' (all sellouts) in Swaziland. The Military Intelligence (MI) unit was given the task of carrying out this operation. A big budget was allocated for it, and a new car bought from a certain Babane Lukhele. The car was delivered, and the project set in motion.

It was planned that uSeptember would pick up uHumphrey from

the university and uSadat from kwaMagogo. UHumphrey was picked up shortly before 4pm, as uSeptember had a 4pm debriefing appointment with students from Turfloop (now the University of Limpopo) in the vicinity of the Salesian School. Before leaving for this meeting, he suggested they go to the Spar supermarket in Manzini, to meet a friend. In the meantime, uSadat was waiting at Number 43 to be picked up for the mission. Just as they were about to leave the Spar, a force of fully armed police in armoured vehicles landed on them and they were instantly arrested. This arrest caused a major scene in the city, as they were frog-marched to the Manzini Police Station, just around the corner from the Spar.

On arrival at the police station they were immediately separated. Hardly had they spent time in the cell, or had a chance to contemplate what had just happened, when uHumphrey was bundled into a van and driven to his residence, leaving uSeptember behind. His house was turned inside out, but nothing incriminating was found. After the search, instead of being driven back to the Manzini Police Station, he was taken to the Malkerns Police Station. Two days later, he was returned to Manzini. On arrival, the cops disdainfully asked him, "Ye Mkhwanazi, Ulibonile yini liphepha? Nita kufa nine Mkhwanazi! Niwa funani lama ANC?" which means "Hey Mr Mkhwanazi, have you seen the newspaper? You will die! What are you doing with the ANC?"

He was shown the front page of the *Times of Swaziland*, which had a caption 'Jail Bust. . . Hooded Gunmen Lock Up Cops. . . Gang frees ANC man in Raid' (*TOS*, 15 August 1986). He was then whisked to the office of the Station Commander, Eric Dlamini, for an interrogation. The cover story in the newspaper was the focus of the questioning. At the end of the grilling, he was thrown into a holding cell, where the first thing he did was to enquire about September's whereabouts. The inmates told him he had been removed. He immediately sensed trouble.

Indeed, uSeptember had been transferred to Mankayane police station, in a remote part of Swaziland, as part of the orchestration of his kidnapping by the South African security. It was at this police station that his captors broke in before spiriting him out of the country, with the facilitation of the Swazi police.

In the meantime, Sadat had launched a hunt for uBabane Lukhele, the man who had supplied them with the car in which they were arrested. He was suspected of tipping the police off about the car. Months later, though, it was discovered that a certain Andrew Camp could have also been responsible. He is said to have tipped off the police, after spotting uSeptember along Malagwane, as he was driving down to Manzini ahead of collecting uHumphrey and uSadat.

Many years later, in a TRC submission, it was revealed that a woman was involved in furnishing this information to the Swazi police, working with an unknown man. It has not been verified whether this was Andrew Camp, as implied by uHumphrey. It was also learnt later that when uSeptember was sprung from the police cells in Mankayane, someone else was picked up, suspected of being uHumphrey. When the captors discovered that he was not the man they were looking for, he was killed and dumped in the veld.

UHumphrey neither heard from nor saw uSeptember until they met again in 1993, on his return to South Africa. At that stage uSeptember was staying at The Reeds, a suburb in Centurion. Unfortunately, they were unable to engage in any meaningful discussion about the fateful arrest and kidnapping. Even after so many years, uHumphrey remains the closest link to the circumstances that led to the arrest of uSeptember and his thinking up to that fateful point in his life.

CHAPTER 18

Naked Assassination

Theophilus Sidima 'Viva' Dlodlo

The death of uViva was one of three assassinations that followed the kidnapping of uSeptember. UViva died together with uMusa and uTutu Nkwanyana, a close friend of mine, with whom I attended Salesian High School and later the University of Swaziland. They were killed in Mbabane, virtually on Todd's doorstep.

The effect of Viva's loss was both personal and political. He was a warm, sociable and cultivated personality. According to his wife, Felicia Azande Ntshangase, he adored choral music, the Manzini Choir being his favourite. This is a side of him I did not know. More than being surprised about the information I was fascinated, given that I loved the same choir, and uSwazi was one of its leading choristers.

Many people have fond memories of uViva, not to mention uSis' Busi whom I found to have the fondest memories: "To know uViva was indeed a privilege. He had such a smooth character, one that caused most people to be drawn towards him. He was soft-spoken, articulate, tactful and very intelligent.

"He fitted into the family as if he were one of us. The children enjoyed him too. I remember how uZinhle would refuse to be taken to preschool if it were not going to be by 'uMalume Viva'. The neighbour's children, who found him very friendly and inviting, always surrounded him. Whenever he had to leave the house he had to find a way to sneak out, hiding himself from the children.

"This was a man who was very committed to the course of justice, so much so that he ended up losing his life in one of the most brutal deaths that can be imagined at the hands of the enemy. His death left everyone bereaved up to this day."

When the news broke

In this period, a death did not come to us as a major surprise. We lived from day to day, expecting the worst at any moment. The kidnapping and defection of uSeptember had left us helplessly vulnerable. We have always believed that the deaths that followed his defection were related, directly or indirectly, to the information he gave the South African security forces.

★ ★ ★

It was a cold winter evening on Friday, 22 May 1987, when the telephone at Number 43 rang. Someone, I can no longer remember whom, ran from the kitchen, where we were sitting, to the passage to pick it up. On the other end of the line was uTodd who was uncharacteristically emotional. He reported that uViva had been assassinated; his comrades shot and wounded. The calmness that usually defined uTodd was replaced by panic and anger. Coupled with his description of the event, this led everyone to jump to the same conclusion – it was the work of uSeptember. Our intelligence had indicated that uSeptember had earlier been spotted somewhere along the Ezulwini Valley.

He reported that two people had survived and were at his place. A decision was immediately taken to move some of those responsible for security at Number 43 to Mbabane for that night, as we suspected the attackers would strike again. We drove out to Mbabane as quickly as we could. When we arrived, we found the survivors still in the house, being attended to by a doctor I did not know.

I do not have first-hand knowledge of the events culminating in the ambush and assassination of uViva, but uSis' Busi, who was among the last to see him alive, has her own version. Others have slightly different accounts, but these broadly converge. According to uSis' Busi, the following is what happened.

"On the Friday afternoon uViva came around to the house to report that he was going somewhere and would be coming back later. A number of cadres were sitting around and relaxing, helping themselves to what they enjoyed best – Scotch whisky. An atmosphere of celebration developed, as more and more people joined in. By early evening the house was full and buzzing.

"When uViva finally left, the others asked why he was in such a hurry. They tried to delay him so that they could spend a little more time in his company. UZinhle, who adored him, begged him to take her along. For whatever reason, uViva refused. I remember her crying, vowing that she would "never again talk to uMalume uViva". This was unknowingly prophetic, as he never returned.

"He bade us goodbye, then ran away, slamming the door behind so that uZinhle could not catch up with him. A few minutes later, before we had even switched our focus away from uViva's dash out of the house, there was a bang on the door and the sound of someone screaming for help. This was uFelix, better known to us as uShezi, who had been in the company of uViva. As soon as he stepped through the door, he turned his back, revealing that he had been shot several times. He was badly wounded and bleeding profusely. Panic and pandemonium ensued, as people tried to help in any way they could.

"Some went to the scene of the ambush only to find that uViva, together with uMsomi and uTutu, had been shot and lay dead. One of the comrades got hold of Dr Mkhize, who rushed to the house to remove the bullets from Felix's body. He worked throughout the night under very difficult conditions, with the assistance of uZanele, a sister to uSis' Busi, who was a nurse. We could not take uFelix to hospital, as he could have been kidnapped, wounded as he was, and taken back to South Africa. He was a key figure on the wanted list.

"Clearly, on that particular day uViva had been followed by the enemy. The collaboration between the Swaziland police and the South African police was so close that one could not tell who the real enemy was. They set out to eliminate uViva, and did so with such precision, together with his colleagues, on that fateful night. More than fifteen years later the events of that night linger on, reviving all my anger and despair.

"One of the most difficult assignments given to me and uS'busi was to break the news to his wife, Felicia. She had married uViva a mere five months earlier, and was now left with young children to take care of on her own. We had come full circle from celebrating his wedding to the brutal snuffing out of his life, all happening in Todd's house. USis' Busi and I had to find the strength and courage to tell her: "uViva usi shiyile" (uViva is dead). We struggled to come to terms with this task, but we were paralysed, in the grip of emotional turmoil."

* * *

On that fateful Friday, uFelicia had been scheduled to go out with uViva. She sat up waiting for him on the sofa until she fell asleep. When by the following morning he had not returned or called, she became worried. She felt unusually low and depressed, and decided to take a walk with their youngest son, uMaqhawe, around the university. Soon after she returned the phone rang and her father picked it up. It was uJabu on the other end. All he could say was, "Nizwile ukuthi uViva ufile?" which means, "Did you hear that uViva is dead?" That was the last she remembers before she fainted.

They did not know where the shooting had taken place or where uJabu was calling from, but later established that he was at Todd's place. Arriving there, they found uFelix, who told them what had happened. They went to the Mbabane government hospital where the bodies lay. On seeing Viva's body, uFelicia fainted again.

A struggle marriage

Born a South African, uFelicia was taken to Swaziland as an infant and grew up there. She was recruited to the ANC by uZweli and worked with the Natal machinery, alongside people like uFear, uBrazo and uRay. After Zweli's death, she was introduced to uThami Zulu. The closest relationship she had with Number 43 was indirectly through uGrace, with whom she studied at St Michaels. She came to know uTodd through uViva. Later, she studied law at UNISWA and worked as a prosecutor in Swaziland.

She met uViva in December 1983, while he was incarcerated at Mawelawela after being arrested at a Peter Tosh Festival. Theirs was a romantic and serendipitous meeting. She had accompanied a friend who had gone to visit her husband at Mawelawela. Aside from introducing themselves, she and uViva had no chance to talk, but eyed one another throughout the conversation of her friend and husband. Unexpectedly, as they were walking out, uViva asked that she return to pay him a visit. That was to be the beginning of a robust relationship. As uFelicia says, "It was love at first sight."

Their relationship had always been a choppy one, owing to the underground work that they did, in particular uViva, who was constantly in and out of Swaziland. They would go for long periods without seeing each other. After uMaqhawe was born in 1985 they did not meet until late in 1986, as uViva was deported and could not return to Swaziland. She was forced to go to Mozambique to meet with him and it was during that visit that they planned their wedding, which took place in Todd's house on 22 December 1986. Less than six months later, uViva was dead.

Using her position as a prosecutor to investigate matters, uFelicia later established that uNaniki was behind her husband's murder. Through uBrazo she made her report to Lusaka and the two were brought together at the Green House for the hearing. After initially denying any knowledge, uNaniki finally confessed. This would later be confirmed to the TRC.

UNaniki revealed that Eugene de Kock had told her that uViva had been killed by two former policemen based in Middelburg, a certain Frans 'Lappies' Labuschagne and Johan Botha, the latter being the one who actually fired the shots. She learnt that Henry van der Westhuizen fed both men intelligence information. Van der Westhuizen specialised in gathering military intelligence on ANC operatives based in Swaziland. The three former policemen appeared before the TRC *in camera* in a Section 29 hearing where they confessed.

A farewell to uViva

Usis' Busi remembers the tension before Viva's funeral: "The preparations leading to his funeral were made difficult because on the day following the shooting, a contingent of police descended on the house, wanting to know the details of what had happened. Characteristically, they raided the house, unperturbed by the distress of its occupants.

"The day of the funeral was marked by a solemn atmosphere. Some of the cadres who wanted to attend could not, as they would be giving themselves away to the enemy. Those who managed to attend did so at great risk. A few relatives came to bid uViva farewell, including his mother and sister. From the hall in Zakhele, where the funeral service was held, the procession left for the Manzini cemetery where he was laid to rest. Before and after the funeral, both the Swazi and the South African police kept a close watch on the proceedings. Further raids, detentions and torture marked the weeks that followed.

"Paying tribute to uViva, uTodd quoted an anonymous author: 'In a hundred years from now it will not matter what my bank account was, the sort of house I lived in, or the kind of car I drove. But the world may be different because I was important in the life of a child.' Both uViva and uTodd believed in making a difference in the world through children. They held that children should be given values that stretched beyond one's lifetime. I hope uMandisi, uMduduzi, uMaqhawe and uThulasizwe forget the bitterness and instead triumph over adversity."

UViva would have been very proud of uThulasizwe, who completed his PhD studies on South African liberation history at Oxford University, and has paid tribute to his father in his thesis.

* * *

UViva was reburied on 8 August 1998. He now lies in Fourways Memorial Park cemetery. Much as uFelicia has tried to move on with her life, she has found this difficult. She remains deeply attached to his memory. She was especially disappointed about the cleansing ceremony that took place in Swaziland in 2004 (see Chapter 31), only stumbling on the plans two days before the event. She had wanted to be there, but nobody had contacted her.

UViva left a void, not only for his wife and children but for the entire fraternity of friends and comrades.

CHAPTER 19

An Amazing Escape from Death

Candy Sue Mhlahlo

Few people go through the experience of looking death in the eye, and then walking away from it almost unscathed. This is the story of Candy Sue Mhlahlo, one of the three survivors in the assassination of uViva.

Personally, uCandy had nothing to do with the movement unfolding in Swaziland. She was an innocent victim of a hostile onslaught on the ANC, caught in the crossfire. My interview with her was quite revealing, providing for the first time details of how the ambush actually took place, as well as the last words of those who perished.

She was born on 5 March 1966, in Soweto, to Daniel Chocho and Nomasoli. She is the third in a family of four. In 1987, she went to Swaziland, intending to study for her 'O' Level examinations at St Marks High School in Mbabane. On arrival, she was welcomed by a friend, uNaniki, and shared a flat with her during the first month. Later she met uMusa Msomi, who offered her the chance to share a flat at Kuyehlela Flats in Mobeni. The convenience of the offer appealed to uCandy, as they were studying together, so she moved in with uMusa.

UMusa was in Gebhuza's machinery. Because of her responsibilities, she had access to a shared car. This enabled her to get around easily, and was also useful for taking uCandy to school and back, especially since classes were in the evenings. As a result, they were always together during the short period uCandy was in Swaziland.

On the fateful Friday of 22 May 1987, uViva, together with uShezi, came to Mobeni to pick up the car to carry out certain errands. They arranged to pick up the girls later from class. On arrival after the class, they were told there was a party at Thembelihle, to which they were invited. However, uViva and uShezi could not attend, as they had other work to deal with. They agreed to drop off the girls at the party and pick them up later.

Before getting to the party, uViva had to go via Todd's to attend to some business. By now, uTutu, and a third girl, uLungile, had joined them. On the way, they stopped off kwaQobonga, a small shopping centre at Sidwashini, to buy drinks and cigarettes.

The house in which uTodd stayed belonged to the Swaziland College of Technology (SCOT). It was almost at the top of a steep hill, dividing Dalriach to the east and Sidwashini to the west. On the east side, which was the steeper side of the hill, it overlooked the plush high-income suburbs of Mbabane.

Their stay at uTodd's was brief. When they left, they took the easterly direction, down the steep gradient. UViva was driving, with uMusa beside him in the front, while in the back seat were uTutu, uLungile, uCandy and uShezi. They had hardly reached the bottom of the hill when they noticed a car approaching from behind at high speed, with its lights blazing. Someone screamed, "Check, nayi imoto" (Check, here is a car). As if he had a premonition, uShezi replied, "Eish . . . yila bantu" (It is these people).

Both uViva and uShezi reached for their weapons, with uViva simultaneously trying to stop the car, in readiness for the inevitable confrontation. He was too late. By the time he stopped, the car pursuing them was parallel to theirs.

All uCandy could see was a dark kombi, with the side door wide open. This is how she describes the next terrifying moments: "Before I could blink, I heard a queer sound as the kombi swiftly zoomed passed, which went Ggrrrrrrrrr . . . Then there was silence. We were hit.

"Those of us who could still walk jumped out of the car, while uViva made an attempt to turn it around. UTutu kept reaching out to me, clutching me by the arm and saying that I should not go out on my own because I did not know the place. UViva instructed us not to run in the direction of the attackers. He immediately changed his order and insisted we come back into the car. I could tell from his voice and the way he was slouched over the steering wheel that he was in terrible pain.

"He was unable to steer the car properly and drove it into a ditch. Just before it hit the ditch, I tried to jump to the driver's seat to apply the brakes. I did not make it in time. I turned to uMusa and said, 'Msomi, asambe motswala' (Msomi, let us go, cousin). She did not respond but collapsed in front of me. I knew she was dead. Meanwhile, uTutu was still reaching out to me, clutching me by the arm and saying I should not go. He kept repeating, 'Ey sonny, kub'hlung' isisu' (Hey, my tummy is sore). He was hit in the stomach. When I finally left the car, he was still crouching."

Realising she could not help the people in the car, uCandy ran to get help. She went first into a white neighbour's house to raise an alarm. When the occupants emerged she told them what had happened and asked them to call the police. Without waiting for a response or saying who she was, she ran out through the gate and up the hill. On arrival at Todd's, she found uShezi already there. As soon as she entered the protection of the house, she blacked out. She does not remember what happened thereafter, apart from hazily seeing a doctor attending to her.

The next thing she remembers is uTodd and uMatewu coming to Mhlambanyatsi for a debriefing. Then on the Monday following the ambush, she was taken to the police station by Musa's mother, uMa-Msomi, to make a formal report. All the police were interested in, however, was establishing whether she could identify the attackers. When she said she could not describe them, the interrogation took a more aggressive turn. She was suddenly accused of being a sell-out simply because she had survived the attack. It was during this interrogation that she learned the full details and who had died on the scene.

After the ordeal of the interrogation, she was released and heard no more from the Swazi police. She stayed in Swaziland only a week, to attend Musa's funeral. Immediately after the funeral she was smuggled back into South Africa. Later newspaper reports maintained that she had disappeared into the night and was feared kidnapped.

She had, of course, missed taking her 'O' Level examination, the original object of going to Swaziland. Back in South Africa, she took a Secretarial Diploma, followed by Matric in Bophuthatswana in 1988.

Burying deep emotional scars

Candy's survival was close to miraculous, given the seating arrange-ment in the car. On the back seat, uCandy, uLungile, and uShezi were closest to the assassins but were the only ones to survive.

Thinking back to her experience, she says: "I was completely obliv-ious of the people I was dealing with. I was literally caught in the crossfire. The only person I knew before going to Swaziland was uNa-niki. The following morning, when I gained consciousness, I imme-diately called home and related my experience to my mother, though I do not remember what I said."

The experience left deep, long-lasting scars. As one would expect, adjusting to it has been difficult: "Since that event, I cannot be alone in the dark, nor can I drive at night. I get frightfully nervous when a car follows me at night." I would discover that she had never dis-cussed these details with anyone prior to this interview, fearing that it would bring back the nightmares of that fateful night. For the same reason, she deliberately stayed away from the TRC process and avoid-ed following the accounts during the hearings.

Perhaps this explains the difficulty I had persuading her to give the interview. She cancelled twice, after travelling all the way from Bloem-fontein to Pretoria to give the interview. On the third occasion, she refused to drive out to our rendezvous, saying it was too late, though it was only 7pm.

When asked how she felt about the tragedy, she simply said that her future had been shattered and changed forever by the experience. She remains puzzled to this day why the South African police never con-fronted her, even though she noticed that she was being watched and followed wherever she went.

CHAPTER 20

Last Encounter with September

Mamabolo 'Philipos' Nwedamutswu

When I came to interview uPhilipos, I had to drive to Tohoyandou in Limpopo. Despite the tiring journey in the middle of summer, I especially enjoyed seeing his parental home, meeting his mother and siblings, as well as relaxing in a scenic rural setting, with the backdrop of a towering mountain, as if embracing the Nwedamutswu homestead.

This visit fulfilled one of my many wishes, that of knowing more about the people I had lived and worked with in exile, as well as their families. In this case, there was an added bonus. Not only did I meet the family but I met their in-laws. My visit coincided with the Nwedamutswu family receiving their in-laws from Nigeria, in traditional Venda style.

At the time of the interview uPhilipos was the Vhembe Regional Chairperson of the ANC, one of six regions in Limpopo. This responsibility comes naturally to him and is consistent with the political intelligence role he played while operating from Swaziland. It is a pity that we did not really have time to engage on intellectual matters relating to his current responsibilities in the region and the province at large.

UPhilipos, as he was known to those of us who worked with him in Swaziland, was born Mamabolo John Nwedamutswu, to Richard and Florence. The name Mamabolo comes from the place where he was born, near Turfloop. His birth date, 17 April 1952, coincided with the crowning of the Chief of the area. He has always been sceptical about the accuracy of this date, but has learnt to accept it. Incidentally, all his siblings are said to have been born on the same day, 17 April, though of course in different years. He grew up in Vhembe, where his father ran a shop named after the village, 'Matangari'. The shop still stands today, though now operated by someone else on a lease basis.

The name Philipos is a 'tsotsi-taal' version of Philip, which was also an alias. When he arrived in Swaziland, uSeptember decided to call him Philipos. It caught on with everybody. However, it would later haunt him when a manhunt for uNkosinathi was launched in Swaziland. At that time, uPhilipos was in Maputo, but because they shared the name Philip, everybody speculated that the Philip for whom the Swazi police had launched a nationwide manhunt was uPhilipos, assumed to have retreated into Mozambique to escape arrest. The death of uNkosinathi and the subsequent arrest and sentencing of the rest of those involved in the bank robbery that led to the nationwide search finally cleared him.

In order to preserve the name, he has bestowed it on his grandson. He jokes about it and says, "I gave him this name hoping that he will become a priest one day so that it can be associated with good. This would serve as a counterbalance to my choice of becoming a terrorist!" He bursts out heartily, in his deep, rich laugh – his trademark in Swaziland, which earned him the title of 'Spencer' from my siblings.

At first, uPhilipos was concerned about the value of the interview and whether it was worth doing at all. This was because his memory was failing him as a result of events during his life in exile. He revealed that in 1987, while on a mobilisation campaign in Dar-es-Salaam, he was involved in an almost fatal accident, in which he lost a good part of his memory. He never realised the extent of the accident until he saw pictures of the car they were driving in. This condition visibly depresses him and distresses his wife, uThembi.

At the time of the accident uThembi was studying at IFM (Tanzania), supported by funding from Australia. The Tanzanian economy was fragile, lacking basic services, in particular health facilities, with massive shortages of medication. This meant she had to rent a chalet to take care of uPhilipos from home. She did this through the assistance of umaMaseko, then head of the hospital in SOMAFCO. UPhilipos was later sent to the Soviet Union for further treatment. Six months later, he was awarded a scholarship to study in the United Kingdom where he qualified with an Honours Degree in Political Science.

He would later be involved in another accident, while in East Germany for training. UThembi recalls with sadness how frustrated she was after the accident. When it occurred, she was in Swaziland, far from him. She had no direct communication with him, but was forced to rely on reports from third parties. All the reports appeared to claim that he died on the scene, from a back injury. Refusing to accept that he had died, she kept nagging everyone for information. This was not furnished until uMagogo intervened, helping her to trace him to Mozambique where they were reunited. Of course, uMagogo did not do the magic on her own; she drafted Ntate Mashego to facilitate their search.

Beginnings of the life and career of a political commissar

UPhilipos first got involved in politics as far back as 1966, while he was doing his Standard 6 at Pax Training Institute in Pietersburg. Several factors drew him into politics. Firstly, he stayed with a teacher who had strong political leanings, and who influenced him a great deal. Secondly, his sister married a policeman, which drew him into intense debates on the interpretation of South Africa's history. When he went to boarding school, he was taught by teachers from Zaire (now the DRC), as well as African priests who taught the history of the church from an African perspective. For the first time, he began to understand injustice.

In 1969 he was recruited to the ANC and soon after was called upon to organise a strike that led to his expulsion from the school. The strike resulted from what the students saw as an injustice: the missionaries refused residents access to their livestock, once it had crossed the boundaries into the school. Understanding how important the livestock was to the people's livelihoods, the students interpreted this as a contradiction to the very teachings of the missionaries. For the first time uPhilipos came into contact with the security branch of the South African police. So harsh was the response of the police that he attempted to leave the country, but was arrested in 1976 trying to skip into Botswana. Fortunately, no case could be made against him, but he remained under the watchful eye of the police.

In 1979, the security branch discovered a book banned in South

Africa in his desk at school. By now the activities he was involved in included propaganda, leaflet distribution, graffiti, recruitment and building up of cells as well as political education. This was the beginning of the role he would later play in Swaziland as a political commissar. He continued to be responsible for the far northern area of the Northern Transvaal until he was exposed towards the end of 1979, at the time when Venda was granted self-government. He managed to escape to Soweto where he stayed with an aunt, against his father's wish that he should leave the country once and for all.

It was not long before the ANC HQ in Lusaka heard about the danger under which he was living in Johannesburg. A kombi was immediately dispatched from Swaziland to pick him up. When it arrived, he did not suspect anything, even though he did not know who was behind the operation nor the people who had come to collect him. Since then he has come to believe that uBab' Mthenjana or uAmanda Kwadi was responsible. However, he has been unable to verify this.

The day he arrived in Swaziland, he was dropped off at Two Sticks, a small location near Trelawney Park. On the same evening, he was taken to Reggie Mhlongo's place in Zakhele, next to a house that would later be bombed. He was under the guardianship of uMampuru and Ntate Mashego, both of whom were not known to him at that stage. He only grew close to them when uJoe Gqabi indicated he would like to have uPhilipos join him in Zimbabwe, as he was his direct report while operating from South Africa. (UJoe was the ANC Representative to Zimbabwe before his assassination in 1981.)

However, both uMampuru and Ntate Mashego refused, on the grounds that when he was in danger uJoe failed to intervene accordingly. This exchange led to uJoe taking a trip to Swaziland to follow up his demand, with uMoses Mabhida as the mediator. When the negotiations failed, he gave up and went back to Zimbabwe, leaving uPhilipos stuck in Swaziland.

For his first few weeks in Swaziland uPhilipos was holed up in the house for most of the time. He had to stay underground and keep out of sight in order to minimise his exposure. This was a stark change from the active and risky life he had been used to in South Africa. He quickly got sick of his circumstances and started making demands to be transferred to Angola. When his demands became sufficiently strident, Ronnie Kasrils was sent out to convince him to stay in Swaziland and do political work from that base, which at the time was held to be much more important than military training.

His task was ultimately to prepare the conditions in Swaziland for people to transit safely into South Africa. In order to execute this task effectively, he had to take up refugee status, which would allow him to move freely in Swaziland. He was allocated a car, marking the beginning of a long and successful intelligence career in Swaziland, working closely with Ntate Nkadimeng, uArchie, uMampuru, uSeptember, uGeneral, uKelly, uFannie and others.

He was allocated to the political wing, concentrating on rural Transvaal work, which involved monitoring the pulse of political activity in South Africa, servicing units inside the country, receiving new recruits, setting up safe houses, liasing with and infiltrating the South African military, and providing training to operatives based in Swaziland. He would frequently cross the border into South Africa, mainly for reconnaissance purposes.

He does not remember the date when he came into contact with Number 43 for the first time, but estimates that it was early in 1980, soon after he acquired legal status and could drive around. He recalls, however, that he had known about Number 43 long before he got there. He had always equated it with the White House, and considered it as a place for the ANC leadership. As such, he deliberately avoided it, until the senior members of the party such as Ntate Nkadimeng and Ntate Mashego had left Swaziland. Through uCassius, who operated from Number 43, he started frequenting the place.

He recalls that the first time he came to Number 43, it was to drop off Ntate Nkadimeng and Ntate Mashego.

Eighteen men in arms
Despite the fact that uPhilipos had begun frequenting Number 43, there lingered a nagging security worry in his mind, warning him to

stay away. He did not want to be too exposed in case someone was monitoring his movements. He notes that the level of safety at Number 43 varied depending on what period one was looking at. He recalls instances where an entire machinery ready for combat stayed at Number 43 without detection.

He reminded me of an event that had long been erased from my mind. This was an operation that involved eighteen operatives, armed to the teeth, under the command of uSeptember, who found themselves holed up at Number 43 for over a week. Clearly this went totally against our own precautions. The machinery was to be dispatched for an operation involving a research station, but uSeptember was arrested the day before the mission was to be launched. It would later be said that during his arrest he was relieved of money, which was earmarked for the operation. This had an extremely dangerous immobilising effect on the machinery. It could neither proceed nor could it retreat to Maputo.

Apart from this, the arrest led to an extremely unpleasant leadership conflict between uKelly and uPeter Dambuza, resulting in the whole operation being aborted, albeit temporarily. Ironically, these two were very close to each other; they originated from the same area in Venda. Yet this operation almost drove a wedge between them.

Unfortunately, this crisis coincided with Mancheker's wedding, which led to further speculations to the effect that part of the money earmarked for the operation could have been used to finance the wedding. However, nobody could verify this assertion. This notwithstanding, the cadres were prepared to follow through with the operation, despite all the odds.

It was clear to everybody that keeping these men at Number 43 for such an extended period of time was too risky and untenable, both from logistical and security viewpoints. The whole unit was therefore shifted to Todd's place in Hlatikulu. It was at this point that uPhilipos came to their rescue, by providing them with the requisite supplies for the operation to go ahead, in spite of the fact that he did not head that machinery himself.

This operation had massive emotional and psychological impacts.

A few of the comrades were negatively affected by it. It is said that, given the stressful nature of the events that unfolded, one or two of them became mentally disturbed. UKelly was one of those affected. He was extremely angry and bitter, which soured relations between him and his comrades, as well as with the commanders. This led to him making a few rash decisions, including undertaking the operation that would end his life. As did other people, uPhilipos made a determined effort to dissuade him from going, but uKelly was adamant. In June, 1984, he was killed by a bomb that he had gone to plant at a courthouse in the Eastern Transvaal. The details of this event are discussed in Chapter 25.

At the time of his death, uKelly and uPhilipos were very close. However, despite both coming from Venda, they had not known each other until they arrived in Swaziland. In fact, they met at Number 43.

Memories of Number 43

When asked for his view on the theme of the book, uPhilipos responded, "I have no doubt that Number 43 could qualify to be a national monument. However, I am not sure how you could do it, given that it is situated outside of South Africa's borders. I am trying to compare it with many other houses I know, but none immediately comes close to Number 43. It actually has no comparison! Monare's house was short-lived; Msezana's, Stokes's, Rwai Rwai's and the Twala residences do not bear the same characteristics. In my judgement, Twala's residence was more exclusive and not as accessible. Clearly Number 43, in its own right, also produced revolutionaries and participated in developing capacity.

"However, my unit deliberately avoided using Number 43 purely to preserve one of the golden rules of a guerrilla movement, namely that of 'preventing the mixing of different underground units'. But I personally used Number 43 extensively. When I got hungry in the course of doing my work, I always knew that uMagogo would be there to give me food. If I was lucky, which was very often, a beer would also be available!

"It was a critical source of information and networking with other operatives. It was also good for healing. Underground work is very lonely and depressing sometimes. But one never felt alone kwaMagogo."

A personal relationship

The relationship I had with uPhilipos was a very special one. Apart from being intellectually comfortable with each other, our friendship was punctuated by risk-taking and adventure.

I remember a day I had to brave picking up his car, which he had left parked overnight at SEB Mobeni flats in Mbabane, under awkward circumstances. Nervous of being identified, he asked that I go and pick it up. Given the circumstances under which it was left, this meant I had to check for any possibility of booby traps. Unfortunately, I was not trained to sniff for bombs. I had only been exposed to discussions on how to look out for them, but had learned nothing beyond that. Suddenly, there I was, having to practise something I was not trained to do. I was not convinced that I was capable of undertaking such a task but I proceeded with it nonetheless. To avoid being dropped off by someone, I opted to board a bus from Manzini. Throughout the 45-minute journey, I did nothing but brood over the mission I had embarked on. I posed difficult yet pertinent questions to myself, to none of which could I find answers.

I arrived in Mbabane on a cold highveld morning. I walked from the city centre to Mobeni, which took 15 fifteen minutes. It was a lonely and torturous walk, during which the thoughts of the earlier 45 minutes continued to ring in my head.

Then came the moment when I had to do the actual inspection. I discovered the car was parked right in the open, in full view of everyone. This offered comfort in one respect but a huge complication in another. Since it was in the open, the chances of it being wired were slimmer than originally anticipated. The discomfort was that while I was busy inspecting it, people could be watching, which meant I would attract just the sort of attention I did not want. If someone were watching the car, I would be a clear target. I went through the process anyway, inspecting the underside, door handles and bonnet. I did not pick up anything obvious, which was partly comforting.

However, starting the engine and rolling the car for the first 100 metres gave me the coldest sweat of my life. I knew that this stage was the most crucial. If the car were wired, this was the critical distance. Nothing happened. I arrived safely in Manzini, to the relief of everyone, especially myself.

Shock visit

Among all those I interviewed, uPhilipos was the only one who had had an in-depth discussion with uSeptember before he died. This gave him an important insight into his psyche. However, it did not answer many of the Masilela family questions about him.

It would seem as if uSeptember had been determined to make contact with everybody he had worked with in Swaziland. This explained the surprise visit he made to Number 43. In each instance, he would initiate the contact, rather than the other way round. Whilst that would seem to be the right way to go about making contact, it was treated with suspicion by most people. Either he was determined to clear his name or was just lonely, but the end result was the same. According to uPhilipos, he actually drove to Tohoyandou to make contact. Unfortunately, he was not home when uSeptember arrived. On his return, he found a note left with his mother, signed 'Dois' meaning 'two' in Portuguese. This is a name he was given by uFear, while in Swaziland. UPhilipos was shocked; he could not believe he was reading a note from him.

At the time, uPhilipos was no longer staying with his parents. When he returned in 1991, comrades wanting to re-establish contact swarmed around him, while at the same time the security police made endless visits at odd hours. It was difficult for the family and he realised that the state of affairs could not be sustained, at which point he moved out. Surprisingly, the visits by the security police were escalated following the visit of uSeptember. He sought protection from the local police. At that stage he was running a restaurant in Tohoyandou.

He recalls with mixed feelings that when uSeptember was kidnapped, parties were thrown all around Lusaka. He learned through his uncle that uSeptember had made attempts to contact the ANC, but to no avail. It seemed all these attempts were rebuffed in one way or another. They finally met sometime in 1992 at a Metro outlet in Louis Trichardt, to which meeting uPhilipos brought two comrades to witness the discussion. This precaution was important, given that such a meeting could have gone in any direction.

The first question he asked uSeptember was why he had not made an attempt to escape and if he had tried but failed, why did he talk? The response from uSeptember was blunt: "I wanted to save my life because these people were going to kill me." While this response was baffling, uSeptember elaborated on it: "I had expected that, as a golden rule, all plans that I was involved in would be stopped or changed significantly. But this was not done. They continued regardless of my circumstances." As a consequence, several comrades were intercepted at the border, others were killed in drive-by shootings, and many houses were raided in Swaziland.

To me personally, this was a disquieting revelation. I had always wondered what explanation he could have presented after the devastation following his kidnapping. According to uPhilipos, the discussion went on for just over an hour. This is how uPhilipos sums up the experience:

"It was a difficult discussion. His name was completely and utterly tarnished, to the extent that he should have been eliminated. Worst of all, he did not show any remorse. He was plainly arrogant.

"I communicated this to uTokyo Sexwale and uChris Hani. In response, they simply said, 'In MK there are no cowards, but sell-outs and traitors. He remains impimpi, klaar!' I could not disagree with this view. The guiding principle in MK had always been to deal with and kill this thing called fear. Because of his failure to deal with his fear many people died at the hands of the enemy.

"UChris indicated that uSeptember was invited on several occasions to come and explain himself. He never took up that opportunity. This flatly contradicted his assertion that he had made attempts to contact the high command of the ANC."

They never met again before uSeptember met his death in December 1993.

UPhilipos had never known uSeptember until he was exiled in Swaziland. However, he knew people who were close to him prior to his joining the ANC, such as Comrade Sic (Kgose). According to Kgose, uSeptember did not like pain and hardship. He naturally sought an easy life. This view seems to coincide with that of other people I interviewed, diametrically opposed to the impressions I had developed about him.

* * *

When asked what his most difficult experience was, uPhilipos cited the period following the signing of the Nkomati Accord, which he said remains deeply imprinted in his mind. He recalls that comrades who were inadequately processed were pushed through Swazi territory. Inadvertently, they met the cold wrath of the Swazi authorities, who had signed a secret pact with the South African government two years earlier. "There was no sleeping any more. Most comrades we knew in Swaziland ended up behind bars following a blitz to clean up the country and rid it of terrorists – as the authorities put it. It was a trying time until I left Swaziland for Tanzania in 1985."

I had not seen uPhilipos since he left Swaziland until the day we had the interview. It was a pleasant experience.

By the time we concluded the interview it was past 1am, and the guests from Nigeria had long retired, as had the family. It was just the two of us and the serene darkness of Vhembe. UPhilipos looked very tired, after almost nine hours of talking and mind-cracking. I thanked him and quietly walked out of the house, taking care not to disturb the peace, hopped into my car and drove out of Tohoyandou.

For the first time in my experience of driving on South African roads I saw wild animals along the stretch between Tohoyandou and Louis Trichardt. I kept my fingers crossed that I would not get into an accident that would unceremoniously end the documenting of such an important story. However, the reflections from the eyes of these animals helped me to stay awake, as the pressure of the drive and the interview quickly took their toll.

CHAPTER 21

Father to a Freedom Fighter

Dokotela Moses Maseko

The liberation struggle has brought the Masilela family not only many friends but also a substantial number of relatives. Among the latter is the Maseko family in Mamelodi, Pretoria, whom we did not know until late in our lives. Indeed, too late: it took the death of my brother-in-law, uNkosinathi, to bring the two families together. It is a relationship that we cherish and one that has a great deal of meaning for both sides.

It took the initiative of Moses Maseko, known to us as uBab' Maseko, to bring our families together. After one of the most painful experiences a parent can go through, he decided to take the long and risky journey from Mamelodi to Swaziland, to introduce himself to the Masilela family. This followed the precarious condition and ultimate death of his son, uNkosinathi, who had left home five years before to become an ANC freedom fighter.

UBab' Maseko, like uButhongo, has a large family of eight children. Amongst these was uNkosinathi, who was born on 14 April 1959, and grew up in Mamelodi. He went to school in Ndima Primary School in Mamelodi West and completed his Form V at Mamelodi High. Temperamentally, he was an introvert, who never openly took part in debates. His involvement in politics took place covertly, and was kept secret even from his own parents. From this grew a plan to leave the country and join the ANC in 1979.

The only person uNkosinathi told about his activities was uAnita, his sister. In the week before he left, she noticed that he seemed very unsettled. During the commemoration of Solomon Mahlangu, he got himself involved in a clash with the police and was wounded in the head. On the day he left, he placed pictures of himself under Anita's pillow, as a sign that he had gone. It was left to uAnita to break the news to his parents.

Taken completely by surprise at his sudden disappearance, they were devastated to learn its reason. They wanted to know what pushed him to the decision, given that he had never been overtly political. As uBab' Maseko recalls: "We were extremely shocked. After much soul-searching, we reported his disappearance to the police. We were surprised by their initial response, which was unexpectedly calm. All they told us was that we should report his whereabouts should we get any information. Of course we ignored this advice. Just when we thought we were off the hook, the police started coming to the house on a weekly basis to check on whether we had any new information. These visits were not very friendly, a contrast to the earlier response when we reported. We remained worried about his departure."

Communication for the first time

Almost a year went by without any news of their son. Suddenly, one day they received a telephone call from an unknown person who also did not introduce himself, telling them that uNkosinathi was fine and that they should not worry. Shortly afterwards, uAnita received a letter from him confirming this message. About year later, they received yet another anonymous call, telling them that uNkosinathi was in Swaziland. Instead of reassuring them, this news made them all the more anxious.

In his frustration, uBab' Maseko contacted a brother, uEzekiel, asking him to help trace uNkosinathi. He followed this up with a visit to Swaziland, taking uMaMaseko with him. The search took them as far afield as Mhlume, on the eastern side of Swaziland, but drew a blank.

Together with a friend, uFreddy Shongwe, uEzekiel led the search through Swaziland. These two would later inform uBab' Maseko about Number 43 and how uNkosinathi related to the place. This piece of information became valuable for uBab'Maseko after the death of uEzekiel on 20 May 1983, following his involvement in the Pretoria Church Street bomb blast. At the time, uNkosinathi was operating from Swaziland and was instrumental in the planning and launching of the attack. However, uBab' Maseko was oblivious of his son's activities, as well as the link between him and uNkosinathi, until after his death. As he put it: "He deliberately kept this vital piece of information away from me because he knew how bitter I was about the ANC and the disappearance of my son."

He and his wife returned to Pretoria, where after a long time they received a call from uNkosinathi himself to confirm that he was fine, and that they need not worry. They later learned that he had called them from Number 43. After several more telephone conversations, they arranged another trip to Swaziland, where they met him at Sicelwini, a township west of Number 43.

This is how uBab' Maseko remembers this meeting: "Our discussion revolved around his unannounced departure and his education. He assured me he was looking after himself and his education. We took several pictures. Telephone communication continued long after this meeting. Interestingly, on several occasions during our discussions he mentioned a Masilela family. In all these instances nothing tangible came out about this family. I also did not pursue the matter."

By now, uNkosinathi was both politically and personally part of the family at Number 43. By 1980, he had begun a relationship with uJoana. The first news of this for his parents came when uBab' Maseko received telephone call: "Suddenly, one day he called to tell us that uJoana, a daughter of Mr Masilela, was going to have his baby. It was not long before we were told that uJoana had given birth to a baby girl, uSibongile."

* * *

Meanwhile, Nkosinathi's undercover activities in Swaziland had taken a new turn. For me, because I did not do a great deal of political work with him, the brother-in-law relationship overshadowed the political one. I would describe our relationship as close but cautious. One of the reasons, I have been told, was that he found me too serious. As a result, he tended to be closer to my friends who frequented Number 43.

Among these friends was uDumisa Dlamini. He and uNkosinathi were involved in a disastrous bank robbery, which earned uNkosinathi the title of 'Mr Big' in the Swazi press. It was after this that he was forced into hiding. Curiously, while he was in hiding, the police on several occasions mistook me for him. A raid would always follow my arrival home from university, and the police would claim that uNkosinathi had been seen walking into Number 43. The description of the clothes he was said to have been wearing always coincided with mine. In each instance, we were able to show that I had been mistaken for him. For some reason, this never sank into the minds of the police. They were probably too desperate to make their arrest.

Towards the end of December 1993, when the Swazi police intensified their pursuit, during the time of the infamous Peter Tosh music festival, uAnita and uMaphupho took a trip to Swaziland. This was the festival used by many South Africans to get emergency passports to flee the country, under the pretext that they were going to attend the festival. Busloads of South Africans, who never returned, descended on Swaziland.

When the two arrived at Number 43, they found only uGranny and uSwazi there. UJoana, uMagogo and I had been arrested. It was arranged that they meet uNkosinathi at the Uncle Charlie's hotel. UMaphupho would later arrange that he be smuggled through South Africa en route to Botswana. UNkosinathi's family knew nothing about this plan.

Last home visit

It was agreed that Botswana would be a safer place, until the situation calmed down. UNkosinathi, however, decided he could not go past South Africa without visiting home. So, on the night of 2 January 1984, he paid his parents in Mamelodi a surprise and final visit. With him was a Matlala friend, known to the Maseko family, who is suspected of having later sold him out to the police.

The visit was very brief. Rather oddly, given that according to what we knew his destination was supposed to be Botswana, uNkosinathi told his parents he was heading for Lesotho. During this short stay, he made a plea to his parents, one that was to have long-term consequences for both families. He requested uBab' Maseko to fetch uSibongile from Swaziland so she could grow up under his guardianship in Mamelodi. Soon after that, he disappeared into the night.

Two days, later, on 4 January, the Masekos were raided. It was an unprecedented raid in the history of Mamelodi. The whole block was sealed off, and the house surrounded. The security police demanded that they produce uNkosinathi, which they clearly could not, since they did not know where he was. The house was searched and ransacked. When no trace of him was found, the family was instructed to go to sleep, while the police kept guard, hoping that he would show up. In the meantime, uMaphupho was taken away for interrogation. Surprisingly, without a word, the police suddenly left. This left the Maseko family quite confused, yet relieved that their freedom had been restored.

Anxious and distressed, when morning broke the family set about its daily chores. UBab' Maseko drove his kombi to the taxi rank, for his usual daily rounds, but for some reason he could not concentrate on his work. With a sense of foreboding, he decided to stop business for the day and went back home. On arrival, he was told that uNkosinathi had been killed in a house in Mamelodi East. That explained the premonition.

He drove there immediately, but did not find the corpse at the scene, as the police had already removed it. The only evidence of his son was his shoe. He went to the mortuary where he found the body thrown on the floor. Unlike other corpses, it had not been placed in the cooler. They were told that his burial could not take place until police from Swaziland had come to identify the body. By the time the corpse was released, it was badly decomposed.

Contrary to their worst fears, however, the Masekos were allowed to bury their son with dignity. They had made a request to the Masilelas that Nkosinathi's baby be brought over to Pretoria for the funeral. This was a major mission, involving risk on both sides of the border. Given the danger, the ANC was deliberately kept out of it. The Masilelas arranged that the baby be smuggled through the border into South Africa and back into Swaziland.

The child in the centre of this whole episode was finally moved to her grandparents in Mamelodi and attended school there. At the time of writing this book, she was a trainee in the South African National Defence Force, instinctively following in her father's footsteps.

Meeting of the families

The tragedy of Nkosinathi's death finally brought the two families together. For the Masekos, trips to Swaziland were not easy, as they were always followed by unpleasant police visits and interrogations. Undaunted, they undertook the journey, establishing bonds of friendship which remain deep to this day.

When they arrived to introduce themselves for the first time, uMagogo, Ntate Manthata and I received them.

It was an emotional moment for all of us, but uBab' Maseko seemed to have come to terms with the loss of his son, and accepted that uNkosinathi had found a new family in Number 43, one which offered him the fulfillment of his destiny and to which he had grown very close. He had resigned himself to his son's fate, recalling the experiences of other families who had children joining the fighting ranks of the ANC.

CHAPTER 22

A Wife's Deep Scars

Annah Maseko

Just like me, many people have questions about events during the days of struggle, why they happened and how they happened. One of these is uAnnah Maseko, the surviving wife of uEzekiel Mloywa Bakayi Maseko, one of those killed at the scene of the Pretoria Church Street bomb blast. UAnnah has always wondered what happened to her husband, when and how he became involved with the struggle and with whom he was involved. When I approached her about this book, she was quite appreciative and ready to give an interview, as she hoped that her unnerving questions would finally be answered. This is what she had been longing for ever since that fateful day, which changed her life and that of her family forever.

She knew she would never be settled in her mind until she found out what had really happened. All she remembered being told about her husband's death was that he died not of the blast but of a bullet wound. She was shown photos of uEzekiel just before he was taken to hospital in an ambulance. She had also been told that he had died calling for his wife and children.

Whilst it was clear to me that I could not provide answers to her questions, I did motivate that at least part of the story should be documented, for her children and her grandchildren to learn and cherish what happened to their father and grandfather. She was comforted by knowing that we were together in the cause of searching for the truth.

Mysterious behaviour

This is how uAnnah recalls the events that she witnessed unfolding in the period leading to Ezekiel's death. A friend of Ezekiel's, uFreddy 'Mageza' Shongwe, arrived on the afternoon of Wednesday, 18 May 1983, looking for him, but he was not at home at the time. In an urgent and worried tone, he said they had to make a trip to Swaziland. UAnnah wondered how her husband could plan to travel to Swaziland when he did not have a passport.

It was not until about 9pm that night that uEzekiel returned home. When quizzed about how he would travel without a passport he just smiled without answering. On Friday, 20 May, uFreddy showed up again, indicating that he had just returned from Swaziland. He asked to park a car, a white Colt sedan, in the yard. UAnnah noticed he was travelling with other people in the car, but did not take much notice of who they were. Later on she inspected the parked car, and noticed that it was unusually dirty. She still did not ask any questions.

Later that day uEzekiel returned home and immediately began washing the parked car. It was unusual for him to be home at that hour, but uAnnah still did not ask any questions. After washing the car, he left in his own, only to return later with uFreddy. They immediately became conspicuously busy, moving in and out of the house without saying a word to uAnnah. They worked on this now seemingly special car with electric grinders and drills. Promptly after the activity stopped at around 3.30pm, they left in both cars still without a word. This was the last time she saw her husband alive.

She remained in the house awaiting his return, as they were scheduled to go to a prayer meeting later that day. He failed to return for the prayer meeting, but uAnnah was not too concerned, and simply put it off. Little did she know that he was gone for good, never to return.

Breaking news

Under normal circumstances uAnnah and uEzekile would have had dinner at about 6pm. On that evening, when she finally went to sleep at about 11pm, he had still not returned. The next day, when news bulletins brought reports of a bombing in Church Street, these did not catch her attention, despite her children following them with keen interest. She was too preoccupied and frustrated by Ezekiel's absence. He had never behaved like this before, which gravely worried her.

The first time she developed an interest in that particular news item was on the Saturday following the blast. At that point she still did not suspect that her husband was a critical part of it.

On the following Tuesday, Freddy's wife came to uAnnah to enquire about Freddy's whereabouts. Throughout that week, uEzekiel's friends also made enquiries. Despite her anxiety, uAnnah remained hopeful that he would be coming home. Towards the end of the second week, however, the family ran out of food, as well as coal to cook and warm the house. It was winter and the situation rapidly became unbearable. One of the children, uSipho, needed school shoes, which uAnnah could not provide. The reality started sinking in: the breadwinner was not coming home.

On the following Friday, 27 May, as she was making up her bed, she accidentally dropped Ezekiel's leather jacket onto the floor. On impulse, she searched through it in the hope of finding money. Indeed, her prayers were answered. In the inner pocket, she found cash amounting to about R3000. Without doubt, the money came in handy, but by then her hopes of her beloved husband coming home were fading.

Search intensifies

The next day, uSipho went to buy the shoes he needed from Marabastad. Curious, he walked past the bombsite to see for himself what had actually happened. Nearby, he spotted his father's kombi, covered with a thick coat of dust after being there for over a week.

He rushed back home to report. As an elder brother of uEzekiel, uBab' Maseko was immediately called and told about the kombi being found. On the Sunday a tow truck was hired to take the kombi to Mamelodi. In the car, a leather jacket, a paper bag with jumper cables inside and a small radio were found.

UAnnah immediately resumed her search for her husband. The first place she went was Kalafong Hospital, followed by HF Verwoerd Hospital. In both places, she drew a blank. Meanwhile, she kept hearing announcements on the radio calling on the public to come and identify relatives who might be involved in the bombing. She did not take these calls seriously. At no point did she think her husband could have been involved in the blast, let alone that he might be dead.

On her return she tried the radio that had been found in the car, but it was difficult to turn on. She put it aside and kept it on top of the wardrobe. Presumably, this was a transmitter to be used to detonate the bomb remotely, but this has not been verified.

By 31 May, she still had no news, at which point she decided to call her parents, notifying them about her husband's disappearance. By now, fear was beginning to overwhelm her. In the meantime, uBab' Maseko took the bold step of making a search in the district mortuaries.

At the same time, a cousin in Daveyton insisted on coming over to Mamelodi to assist with the search. Just as he arrived, uBab' Maseko also arrived to report the death of uEzekiel and the circumstances. He was carrying his clothes as evidence.

First visit by the security police

UAnnah was devastated, but her nightmare was just beginning. The following Wednesday, 8 June, Dirk Coetzee arrived at her home. She did not know who he was, thinking he was just another Afrikaner policeman. She only found out his identity many years later, during the TRC hearings. The irony is that Coetzee was only interested in establishing whether she knew how her husband had died. When she told him she did not know, he immediately left with no further questions.

The following day, Freddy's wife arrived, accompanied by a horde of white men, who harassed her and prevented her from mourning her dead husband. From then on, the interrogation gathered momentum. The questioning was carried out in Afrikaans, which uAnnah did not understand. Two black police officers, known to her only as Mtshali and Jerry, did the translation. She was surprised to find that most of the harassment was directed at Freddy's family, not at her. She learned later that Freddy's wife was suffering more because her husband was closest to the blast. It is said that his body was ripped apart by the impact, and the only thing that was recognisable was his leg.

The questioning never stopped despite the fact that the families were in mourning and had to plan for funerals. UEzekiel was finally buried on 11 June 1983.

Given the unending interrogation and harassment, uAnnah removed the radio from the house and kept it with a neighbour.

The torture begins

Two days after Ezekiel's burial, on Monday, 13 June, Dirk Coetzee and Eugene de Kock burst into Annah's house at about 7am. She was forced to dress in front of them, and was taken to the Silverton Police Station. As she recalls: "I spent the whole day under continuous interrogation as well as abuse. At about 4pm, I was put into a cell, where I spent the rest of that week."

For about three weeks she was starved and ill-treated, which led to her developing severe stomach cramps. She was taken to Louis Pasteur Hospital, in the centre of Pretoria, after which she was taken to the Pretoria Central Police Station. Further interrogations took place in Compol, a building next to the Department of Home Affairs in Pretoria Central. During the interrogation she was insulted and ridiculed. On several occasions, De Kock threatened to take her to "Vlakplaas", hurling abuses such as "Jy sal jou ma sien" (You shall see your mother). According to uAnnah, "In the meantime the black officers were advising me to cooperate. I did not know what that meant or how to cooperate because I did not know anything relating to what they wanted to know."

By the end of her stay in Compol, which was between two and three weeks, she had completely lost her voice. She recalls how terrifying it was. She was kept alone in a cell, but as she was being taken in and out, she could not help noticing that the staircases and doors at Compol had thick chains and big padlocks. Even more frightening to her was that neighbouring cells were marked with the names of people who were facing long-term sentences, some of whom had died. In her distress, she imagined herself ending up in the same position as those people. She would be kept for days on end without being allowed to wash or change her clothes. However, one of the black policeman, uMtshali, offered to assist in bringing her clothes from home from time to time.

The radio

At one stage the interrogators insisted on knowing what uAnnah had found in Ezekiel's car. At first she said she found nothing. But after persistent badgering and torture, she finally succumbed and admitted having found a radio. She was driven home to point it out, and it was retrieved from the neighbour, a certain Nhlapo. Throughout this, she was more concerned about exposing her neighbour than of the pulverisation that would follow.

When the paper bag was opened, the police went into a panic and scattered in all directions. They radioed back to the police station, describing what they had found. There was a long discussion on the phone. When the decision was finally taken to bring the radio to the station, a lengthy debate followed as to who should carry the paper bag. None of them wanted to get close to it, so uAnnah was forced to carry it. To any rational person, if this was a bomb it really did not matter who carried the bag, since they all traveled in the same car. But this logic seemed to have escaped the police.

When they got back to Compol, the interrogation started afresh. This time it was rougher, with more threats and insults. After a long, painful process, the police described to her the bombing and how uEzekiel had been involved.

★ ★ ★

Finally, uAnnah was arraigned in court, with the families of the victims present. She recalls that, "It was dramatic. I was never given an opportunity to speak. Instead, the recordings of the interrogations were played back to the Court. After all these had been heard, I was simply released and dropped off at home, by the same Mtshali. I never heard from the police again. Just like that".

In all, she estimates she spent about three months under interrogation.

Reliving the blast

Following the incident, for several years white people would assemble at the spot on the anniversary of the blast, in a ceremony that was used to hurl insults and denigrate the ANC and black people. UAnnah only started recovering from the ordeal after 1994 when this pilgrimage was halted.

Despite the fact that she was finally acquitted, her suffering did not end with the interrogations and the court hearing. On her release she was told to go and pick up her husband's death certificate from an office along von Wielligh street, which she did. She was made to wait for over an hour before the certificate was handed over to her. When she finally got it and read it, she was astonished by the cause of death, written in Afrikaans: "Ruptuur linker femorale arterie en vena met bloed in wat opgedoen is tydens 'n bomontploffing wat deur homself en Freddie Shongwe bewerkstellig [sic] in nadat hulle deur die . . . Van African National Congress opdra . . . (16 September, 1983)" (Rupture of the left femoral artery and veins with bleeding following on a bomb plot by himself and Freddie Shongwe . . .)

The death certificate became a major source of pain and misery for the family. It made it impossible to secure decent service from any government department. The children could not use the certificate to obtain ID documents. It seemed as if the world was caving in on the family. They were forced to apply for another death certificate with toned-down wording. This took another two years to be cleared. They only received it on 20 November, 1985, with the inscription, "Raptuur linker femorale arterie en vena met bloeding – Bomontploffing [sic]".

Battling to make ends meet, the following year uAnnah found a job as a cleaner at the South African Reserve Bank (SARB). She was desperate to earn a living, as she was now the sole support for her children. She arrived at 8am on her first day. By 10am she had been fired. She was told to collect her money for the two hours' work, and that the Bank did not want anything to do with her ever again. Deeply shocked, hurt, disappointed and scared, she went straight home, ignoring the offer of payment for that day. A certain Mahlangu, who is a family friend, offered to collect the money on her behalf.

Despite her bitterness, uAnnah has some positive observations about her experience: "I may say that there was some humanity in the police. When on several occasions I would request to come and see my children at their respective schools, this would be granted. While I was allowed to visit, I was not permitted to step out of the car. But because my presence attracted a lot of attention from the other students and the rest of the school, one headmaster finally stopped the visits, arguing that they were disruptive to the school. I was deeply hurt by this decision."

While uAnnah was in custody, her aunt and daughter to her brother-in-law had to stay at home with the children as they were still very young. There were five children, uSipho, uJabu, uVusi, uPhumzile and uMandla. The youngest was only nine years of age then. USipho, who was the eldest, was eighteen. Since uSipho's name always came up in her interrogations, the police had on many occasions threatened to lock him up as well. Fortunately, this threat was never put into action.

Before the rebuff at SARB, uAnnah had worked at Woolworths for a year. In between, she got a temporary job with Maizecor, where she earned R15 per week. She struggled to get by on this meagre salary. Her children had no decent shoes, no uniform or other necessities for school. When uPhumzile started high school, she struggled to secure a bursary. Appeals to the ANC for help came to nothing. She only received a bursary in her second year of university, from the South African Council of Churches. Life was tough, to say the least.

Today uAnnah and her children have outlived this ordeal and live a normal life like any average family. They stay in the same house in Mamelodi. They are not bitter about their past, despite the way the ANC treated them at a time of dire need.

CHAPTER 23

An Armed Robbery that
Went Badly Wrong

Dumisa Edgar Dlamini

Dumisa Dlamini is an old friend and schoolmate of mine. His role in this book is a critical one, not only for me but for the entire family. He was one of the last people to spend time with uNkosinathi and the only one in whom he confided. Their association came to an end rather sourly, however, when he was given a death sentence for a double murder and nine years for armed robbery. The sentence was subsequently commuted to twenty years in prison. When it was first passed, however, I did not think I would ever see him again.

UDumisa was born on 10 June 1962, in Jabulani, Soweto, into a family of five. In 1968 his family moved to Swaziland and settled at Elwandle, an outlying area south of Manzini. All his formal education took place in Swaziland. In 1970, he started primary school at the Nazarene, in Manzini, and began his high school education at Salesian in 1977, where we first met and became friends.

Shifting friendship

As a friend, uDumisa frequented Number 43, both during and after our high school days. When I went to university in 1982, he became involved in a variety of activities, among them car theft. By now, I was spending less time at Number 43. It was during this period that he met uNkosinathi, who showed an interest in buying some of the cars for his underground work. From time to time, uDumisa would provide him with this transport.

Their friendship matured in various directions. He recalls that on several occasions uNkosinathi would forget guns in his car, including one that he ended up not collecting. Instead, he asked uDumisa to keep it, arguing that he had no use for it. Later, he asked him to take a sub-machine gun for safekeeping.

A combination of the activities that uDumisa was involved in, as well as this consignment, ignited ideas that might otherwise not have come into being. UDumisa and two of his other friends, a certain Vezi Mabuza and a taxi driver, hatched a scheme to stage an armed robbery. This idea was broached with uNkosinathi, who reluctantly agreed to join. Usually, uNkosinathi worked alone, which minimised the likelihood of being double-crossed. Agreeing to participate in this exercise was out of character.

The planning of the robbery began at Number 43 – without the knowledge of the family – before being shifted to a less risky venue, the Coronation Park, next to the Manzini Post Office. As part of the plan, they considered using a car provided by a certain 'Makhabizitsha' who worked for Mbabane Motors at the time.

Barclays Bank in Matsapha, at Tommy Kirk's shopping complex, was their first target. The attack was staged on 8 December 1983. The plan was for uDumisa and uVezi to storm the bank, while uNkosinathi kept watch in the car. However, the operation was bungled because of a lack of understanding of the bank's security system. Fortunately, they were not identified as they were wearing balaclavas.

Disappointed and with fingers still itching for action, they immediately drove to Bhunya, a small industrial town in the northwest of the country. According to uDumisa, "At that stage we were desperate for action. Unfortunately, Bhunya seemed an impossible target. We decided to go to Mhlambanyatsi instead, which is less populated." There, they attacked Frasers Supermarket. On entering the supermarket, they ordered everyone to lie down. Unfortunately, one woman did not co-operate and in the midst of the panic she was shot. They got away with an insignificant amount of money, taken from the cash register.

They retreated to Manzini. Not satisfied with the results of their operation, they proceeded to rob a pub called Gum Tree, east of Manzini. The proprietor, a certain Mr van Heerden, was held up at gunpoint. An employee who came to his assistance was shot. This operation was also abandoned. Listening to the radio, as they were driving back to Manzini, they heard that both the woman shot at Mhlambanyatsi and the pub employee later died of their wounds. By now they knew they were in big trouble.

At the end of the day, uNkosinathi was dropped off at Number 43. When uDumisa came by the following day, he was told the Swazi security police were there in search of uNkosinathi. Nobody in the family knew why, nor would uNkosinathi link it for us to what had happened the day before. We could only speculate that it was for his underground military work. Of course this was not the case, but uDumisa was not about to reveal anything.

Later that night, uNkosinathi appeared at Dumisa's place to explain what had gone wrong. At the Mhlambanyatsi scene, a Chinese man, travelling with his gardener, had spotted them. The Chinese lived four houses from Number 43. The gardener later described uNkosinathi to the police.

I was not surprised that uNkosinathi knew all this, since he had amazingly effective information networks. He would always be the first to know about planned raids on Number 43, and of course would walk away just before a raid and return soon afterwards. If he knew that the police would camp on the premises, he would simply not return. It baffled us how he could be so well-informed.

Nationwide manhunt

A massive nationwide manhunt was launched for uNkosinathi with a reward of R500 for anyone who could give the police a lead. Two days later, uDumisa returned to Number 43 to find the place had been turned into a police camp. This time he was apprehended, questioned and threatened with bodily harm unless he revealed where uNkosinathi was. He would not say anything, so was taken to the Manzini Police Station for further questioning. On arrival, he found uButhongo and uMagogo already there.

For some reason, uDumisa was left unguarded in an open office. Seeing his chance, he dashed out of the police station and headed for home. He was desperate to know the whereabouts of uNkosinathi, who by then had completely vanished. He went back to Number 43 later that day to check on him again, but to no avail. It was then that he decided to go into hiding at an uncle's place. He recalls that, later that evening, uNkosinathi came to his mother to report that he was leaving Swaziland. UDumisa never saw him again.

Dumisa's cover was blown and he was arrested on 14 December 1983. To his relief, he was only charged with car theft, not armed robbery, and kept at the Lobamba Police Station. A few days later a policeman, Stanley Bhembe, came to tell him that his friend uNkosinathi had been killed. At that point, uVezi was still at large. Driven by greed he continued with more armed robberies, using the same guns they had used earlier. When he was finally caught, he revealed all the details about the earlier robberies. His confession led to a change in Dumisa's charge from that of car theft to double murder and armed robbery.

The trial lasted until August 1984, when they were sentenced. The capital sentence was commuted to life, equivalent to 20 years, when King Mswati III was installed. Dumisa served about 13 years of his sentence and was released on 12 June 1997. I vividly recall the night of his reception in Two Sticks, at his in-laws'. It was a night filled with a lot of emotion.

To this day, uDumisa remains a close friend of the Masilela family. He seems fully reformed and runs a driving school and taxi business of his own.

CHAPTER 24

Survival by Mistaken Identity

Cassius Phahle Motsoaledi

Also known to us as 'MaCash Cash', uCassius Phahle Motsoaledi is one of the few people who worked in Swaziland in the underground but returned later to work legally. He held office as First Secretary, Political, in the South African High Commission to Swaziland from 2002 until July 2004. In both these periods in Swaziland, he was very close to Number 43. He would later preside over the preparations that led to the hosting of the ANC cleansing ceremony in Swaziland. This event is discussed in the last chapter, as the closure of the work of the ANC in exile, as carried out from Swaziland.

Born into an ANC family, he joined the fighting ranks of the ANC at a tender age. He is one of six sons of uElias Motsoaledi, one of the Rivonia trialists, who died in 1994, on the same day uMadiba was inaugurated.

UCassius trained in Angola and Russia. When he returned in 1978, he was based in Maputo. In the same year, he was infiltrated into South Africa, through Swaziland. His first mission into South Africa was to recruit people to the ANC. As he was sePedi-speaking, he was sent to the Northern Transvaal (now Limpopo) to recruit. Two people, known only as uDick and uBernard, later instrumental in several missions launched from Number 43, were among those he recruited while on this operation.

In 1981 he was sent on a reconnaissance mission to Bushbuckridge. During this mission, he suffered a series of misfortunes. One of these resulted in him being part of a mass arrest, where a number of people suspected of witchcraft were rounded up. This was a clear case of mistaken identity, but one to which he did not object, accepting that witchcraft was a much lesser crime than the one for which he could have been arrested, namely sabotage. It would be stretching it to say that he prayed, given his communist inclinations. He was incarcerated for ten days before being released on bail. Interestingly, the Chief of the area paid for the bail, reasoning that his subjects should not be subjected to such an arrest.

While incarcerated, all their fingerprints were sent to Pretoria, as was normal procedure. The report on the fingerprints revealed Cassius' real identity and Pretoria promptly sent a special task force to pick him up. Fortunately, luck was on his side yet again, because the bail was granted on the morning of this discovery. By the time the task force arrived, he was already a free man. With helicopters hovering above, he made a dash for the border. He was pursued into Swaziland, so to avoid capture he trekked further into Mozambique.

This was not the only time he escaped through mistaken identity. On many occasions, the Swazi police mistook him for a schoolboy. He would literally walk through police roadblocks and cordons.

UCassius is a very small man, looking about a third his age. Even today, if he is in short pants he could pass as a lower high school student. It is this feature that helped to make him so elusive, giving him a non-threatening, even innocent appearance. In reality, he was one of the bravest and most cunning freedom fighters, responsible for some of the bigger operations carried out by MK from Swaziland.

Responsibilities in Swaziland

In 1982, uCassius was made Chief Logistics Officer for the Transvaal rural machinery. This involved the infiltration of materials and ANC personnel into South Africa. His commander, uSeptember, introduced him to Number 43 in the early part of that year. Initially, he operated from one of the safe houses managed by uSwazi. It was only at a later stage that he moved to Number 43, a base from which he operated until his departure from Swaziland. Given the role he played as Chief Logistics Officer, all the operations for which he was responsible were managed from there. Number 43 became the central meeting point for the planning, strategic decision-making and the final launching of operations. Among those who worked closely with him were 'uSeptember' as commander, 'uKelly' as commissar, 'uThemba Automatic' as the reconnaissance officer, and 'uBaba Rich' as an operative and mechanic.

Major operations that uCassius directly managed included the Tonga army outpost and police station as well as the Hectorspruit fuel depot missions. The materials used in both operations were kept in the wardrobe in my bedroom. They included full arsenals of AK47s, Makarov pistols, limpet mines and both offensive and defensive hand grenades, as well as thermite (used to improve the effectiveness of the limpet mines). The stuffing of the limpet mines was actually carried out in the bedroom, before the units set out on the operation.

It was common practice to keep these materials at Number 43, but we were careful not to keep them for more than a day in the house. This principle was applied very strictly. On launching an operation, we made sure the room was cleaned of any trace. However, gremlins did creep in from time to time. This led to an unfortunate event in January 1983 when a grenade detonator was forgotten underneath my bed. It was among the materials used for the Tonga operation. Police discovered the detonator during one of their raids. It led to one of the most publicised cases in Swaziland at the time, during which I was arraigned in court. Out of all the arrests I experienced, this was the only one that culminated in a court hearing. Luckily, the state did not have enough evidence to convict.

UCassius left Swaziland in 1985, after he was captured in a raid on one of the safe houses. He was deported to Lusaka. However, before he was deported, he made it onto the infamous list of most wanted ANC operatives. Despite this, he kept close ties with Number 43 until he returned in 2002 with his newly acquired official title.

CHAPTER 25

Lion of the Great North
David Malada (Peter Dambuza)

Known to us as Peter Dambuza, David Malada first came into contact with Number 43 in 1980. He hails from Venda in the northern part of South Africa. Peter was one of those I met, but with whom I never spent sufficient time to know and understand well. I only came to understand him better during the writing of this book, drawing on his vast experience and leadership role in the Transvaal rural machinery. During his stay in Swaziland, he spent more time with uMagogo. Because of his quiet demeanour and towering height she named him 'Thutlwa', which is 'giraffe' in seSotho.

While he did not spend a long time in Swaziland, he nevertheless left an indelible track record. He hit the headlines in the Swazi press on many occasions. On 29 December 1984, the *Weekend Observer* carried a picture of him on the front page, with the caption, 'WANTED'. On the third page of this issue he was paraded with other comrades. Strangely, I could not find this page anywhere in Swaziland during my research. I dug through the UNISWA Swaziana section, the Swaziland National Archives, the *Times of Swaziland*, and the *Swazi Observer* itself, with no success. Ironically, the National Archives has a copy of the issue, but with the third page neatly torn out. The officials were taken aback when I pointed this out to them. They had never noticed that the page was missing, prior to that day. The family possesses an old battered version that we kept in the Masilela specialised archive – Magogo's wardrobe.

Nothing ever leaves this wardrobe. While you may not find something, given the particular 'filing system', it will certainly be hiding somewhere in the many corners, bags and envelopes. There is a great deal of history behind this wardrobe. Aside from its contents, it has a history in its own right. It is as old as the marriage between uButhongo and uMagogo, having been given to uButhongo when he was discharged (honourably) from the army at the end of the Second World War.

At the time of this newspaper report, in the eyes of the Swazi public, uDambuza was the most sought after person, even more so than uGebhuza. It is not clear why this was the case, though it may be partly attributed to his role in the Venda Police Station attack in 1981 and a jailbreak he masterminded in Simunye, a town in eastern Swaziland, forming part of the sugar belt. In the period leading to the infamous jailbreak, he coerced the station commander into knowingly delivering money for an operation to uMagogo. This money was found on them when they were arrested.

★ ★ ★

We reunited with uDambuza in June 2004, during a visit to Swaziland for the ANC cleansing ceremony, as part of the Freedom Park initiative. I had last seen him in 1982. He visited again in December 2004, this time with his family. It was during this visit that I had my first interview with him. Indeed, it was the first interview for this book. Several trips to Limpopo followed the initial interview for further discussions with him and to be introduced to the families of other comrades with whom he had worked.

While driving around Limpopo collecting data, my understanding of uDambuza deepened immensely. I had the opportunity to explore his innermost feelings and preferences. Unlike the days in Swaziland, there were no boundaries, as we covered topics from marriage and children to business and politics. I discovered that he is a man with a large, forgiving heart and has a passion for freedom in all its aspects.

★ ★ ★

When uDambuza first came to kwaMagogo, he was on a mission under the command of uKelly, who was also known as uJonas to the Masilela family. UKelly was a fascinating character, highly intelligent, a calculating strategist, and frighteningly brave. He was the Chief of Staff for the North-Eastern Transvaal, under the command of uSeptember. Owing to an interesting turn of events, he would later be demoted and uDambuza would become his commander. According to uDambuza, this never created any ill feelings in uKelly, and they continued to work closely until the latter's death in June 1984.

The death of uKelly

The death of uKelly is shrouded in deep mystery. Everyone I have talked to about it has a slightly different version of how it happened. Even his family does not really know, apart from the fact that "he was blown up by his own bomb, as explained by the police."

On 5 November, 2005, I had the great pleasure of speaking to his eldest sister, uJoyce Raphotle, after being kindly introduced by uDambuza. She told me that after uKelly left in 1976 they never saw him again. At the time of his departure, the family was living in Dobsonville, Soweto. He simply disappeared without a word. Two days later, his disappearance was reported to the police. A few months later, the family received a letter telling them he was in Botswana waiting for a passport to proceed to Tanzania.

The next correspondence was not until about three years on, when they received a letter from Swaziland, through an unknown person. While she does not remember the entire contents of the letter, uJoyce does recall three words that jumped out at her, 'I am naked'. Moved by these words, the family hastily organised clothes for him and these were ferried across to Swaziland. They would later identify a jacket they had sent him when they came to inspect his corpse in Bethal in 1984. It was one of the ways they confirmed it was him.

Following his departure from home, the family was terrorised by the South African police. These actions were directed more at the elder brother, uJoel, who was tortured on a number of occasions. Each time someone came to deliver a message, the police would know about it and would pay them the dreaded visit.

* * *

Prior to my visit, uKelly's family had never heard of Number 43. The only address they remember was in Kwaluseni, but they had never been there. The whereabouts of uKelly remained a mystery up to his death. My visit filled an important gap in the family's knowledge and quest for information. The mere fact that they had met someone who stayed with uKelly seemed like a big relief.

They learned about uKelly's death through his father, who was an officer in the Venda police force. His superiors simply informed him that they had identified the body of his son in Secunda, and that he had been involved in an attempted bombing of the Magistrate's Court in Delmas, on 16 June, 1984. With no time to digest the news, the family had to rush to Secunda for the funeral which was decided in haste, after they were told that the authorities there were not prepared to release the corpse to them. On arrival, they made a rather depressing discovery. Contrary to earlier information, they were now told that the body had all along been ready to be released to the family but that the Mphephu government would not grant permission for uKelly to enter the borders of Venda, let alone be buried in his village, or indeed anywhere in the vicinity of Venda. So the problem was not with the South African authorities, but with the Venda authorities. This deeply affected the family.

Pauper's burial

UKelly's family were left with no option but to play witness at the burial of their beloved in Bethal, away from his village of birth. It was a pathetic sight, a typical pauper's funeral. UKelly was thrown into an old coffin with no handles or lid. Sacks tied together to make ropes were used to lower the coffin into the grave. There was no priest. His father had to give the benediction. UJoyce, however, consoles herself by noting that, "At least he was not thrown into a mass grave like the other people who were being buried at the same time. Thank God we were there. It earned him a little decency, even though it was far from what he deserved."

She recalls that while all this was taking place a dark kombi was parked at a distance, its occupants watching every stage of the proceedings. Soon after the burial was over, the kombi drove off. To this day, she does not know who those people were.

Asked whether there was any approach from the ANC regarding

the death of uKelly, she says there was none that she could recall. All she remembers were four blankets delivered to her father, but she cannot say where they came from.

* * *

We left Thohoyandou with heavy hearts. We drove out of the vicinity in complete silence. In the car were uDambuza, uNonhlanhla and my niece, uZinhle. It took us a while to start conversing, as we each tried to deal with the information we had received and the emotions. This was one of the few interviews, which were extremely emotional. UKelly was like a brother to me. He was one of the few comrades who lived permanently at Number 43 – and we shared many good moments. Each time uJoyce sobbed during the interview, which happened several times, I fully shared her feelings. A bond was developed.

UKelly was born George Mpho Ou Baas Ramudzuli on 15 March 1955. He was the third of a family of five children. At the time of our first visit to his home, a process was under way to exhume his corpse from Bethal and give it a more fitting burial in Thohoyandou. The reburial was finally performed about a year later, on 23 September 2006, in a royal ceremony at the residence of King Vho-Thobela M.P.K. Tshivase in the presence of Chief Vha-Musanda Vho-Takalani, as well as Minister Sydney Mufamadi and the Premier of Limpopo, Sello Moloto. On the same occasion, a bond between the Ramudzuli and Masilela families was forged, with a public handing over of a picture of Number 43.

Preparing for combat

According to his recollection, uDambuza spent three days at Number 43 during his first visit, which was around June or July 1980. He had joined MK in 1975, and trained in Angola from 1976 to 1980. Some of the comrades working with him, such as uCassius, followed much later. He found people like uJanuary 'Che' Masilela, the Director General of Defence at the time of writing the book, and uGebhuza.

At the time of the interview with uDambuza, I was reading Chris Hani's biography, which inspired a number of interesting questions.

One of the facts I wanted to establish was at which stage he had met uChris. His response was that it was extremely rare to meet with leaders of the ANC during training, which corroborated the frustration of some cadres as reflected in the biography. He met uChris for the first time in 1981, six years after joining the fighting ranks of the ANC. This coincided with the completion of his training programme, after which he travelled through Zambia and Mozambique into Swaziland.

UDambuza's mandate was to enter South Africa, to establish military bases within the country and to develop DLBs in the northeastern part. The bulk of these DLBs were in the mountains of the Soutpansberg range. The difficulties of this operation were compounded by the fact that his only means of travel across South Africa was on public transport or on foot, which made moving around extremely cumbersome.

His first combat operation, in 1981, was a complicated and dangerous one, the planned assassination of Chief Mphephu of Venda. Underlying the operation was a philosophy to destabilise the governments of the Bantustans through fear, with the ultimate aim of eliminating them. A team of three undertook the mission, the other two being uBernard and uSimon. UBernard would later arrive at Number 43 with bullet wounds suffered while retreating from the operation.

One evening, as I was walking past the carport at Number 43, I heard a hushed voice calling to me, "Professor, Professor, zwakala yi". When I checked, I found uBernard with bullet wounds in his side. I quickly alerted uMagogo, who arranged for a doctor and had him attended to and moved.

To the best of my recollection, that was the last time I saw uBernard. For years to come, I would puzzle about how he had reached Number 43 in the state he was. During the writing of this book I literally stumbled on the answer while talking to a Swazi lady who had voluntarily offered to give an interview, but requested to remain anonymous. She revealed her involvement in bringing uBernard to the gate of Number 43 earlier that evening. This was a surprising revelation to me, as she is a person I would least suspect of having had dealings with Number 43, let alone be involved in the activities of the ANC.

Not only was I surprised, I was also relieved that a question I had harboured for so long had at last been answered.

UDambuza recalls that when they left Swaziland for this operation, starting from Mbabane, they were allocated a driver in a light blue Ford Cortina van. He no longer remembers the driver's name, but from the description it sounded like uStan Simelane with whom I worked on several operations. UDambuza was very impressed with his driving skills, since it was quite dangerous driving across South Africa during this period. To make the journey even worse they ran out of petrol in the vicinity of Turfloop University.

They tried to get help with the fuel from a lecturer at the university, known to uDambuza, who refused to assist, fearing victimisation. They were forced to spend the night on the road, only filling up the car the following day, by which time they had been noticed and were being trailed by the police. Thanks to Stan's driving skills, however, they were able to shake off their tail near Louis Trichardt, after which they proceeded to Venda, the point of their operation.

Failed attempt on Chief Mphephu

The team spent about two months on a reconnaissance exercise, before they launched their attack. The plan as finally drawn up was to ambush Chief Mphephu's motorcade as it exited the parliamentary complex. They had carefully mapped his movements and routes, but on the day of the planned attack, for an unexplained reason, the motorcade went out through the rear exit. It remains a mystery to the team how this happened and a mark on the record of uDambuza, who headed the operation.

Despite their disappointment, they were determined not to retreat without sending a message to the governments of South Africa and the Venda homeland. Thus on 26 October 1981, they attacked the Venda Police Station. Four policemen were killed, without returning fire, with one escaping, though according to newspaper reports only two policemen were killed. Before leaving, they bombed the police station using limpet mines, razing it to the ground.

To allow for a cooling off period and to avoid being tracked down, they retreated to the mountains, where they set up camp. They spent three weeks in hiding before making their way through Gaza Province in Mozambique and back into Swaziland. The retreat was not an uneventful one, since the South African security net was still thrown wide. Their move was picked up and they were pursued into Mozambique. During this operation, uDambuza hurt his left hand while launching a bazooka. It was during this retreat too that uBernard was shot.

When asked why they had embarked on an unmandated operation, uDambuza was at first uncomfortable, but eventually explained that it was a reaction to the frustration of their failure to kill the Chief. He argued it was meant to send a stern warning to the government – the same explanation offered to the authorities of MK in their report back.

UDambuza returned to South Africa on 14 August 1991, a date he remembers vividly. He is now settled in one of the elite suburbs of Polokwane.

CHAPTER 26

Rejected by Father, Adopted by Masilela Family

Madoda 'Linda' Motha

ULinda is one of those people who had an exceptionally close relationship with the Masilelas from very early in his life, to the extent that he became part of the family. Until he left Swaziland, he maintained this closeness, albeit with due respect for security precautions.

He was born Madoda Mahlomola Vincent Motha on 5 November, 1962, to Fana Hamilton and Mamoruti Alice, in Soweto, Orlando East. In his infancy, he was moved between his maternal and paternal grandparents, while his father taught in Swaziland.

His parents married in 1968. Soon after the wedding the whole family moved to Swaziland. When he enrolled at Salesian Primary School, his name 'Mahlomola' was changed to 'Sostinus'. He recalls that this was at the insistence of Fr Patrick Ahern, on the grounds that he needed to have a proper Roman Catholic name. It would seem this was a common tendency at this time in Catholic schools in Swaziland.

In 1970 his parents separated, an event that exposed him and the rest of his family to uMagogo. His mother had just given birth, and because of her marital circumstances sought shelter with uDr Margaret. There she met uMagogo, as uDr Margaret was a common friend. Soon after her recovery from the delivery, his mother returned to South Africa, leaving the rest of her children in the custody of their father.

It was not long before his father married a second wife. The life of the children deteriorated as a result of these changes. In February 1974, uLinda was sent back to South Africa to join his mother. He was smuggled across the border by an uncle, without his father's knowledge or approval. This precipitated the crisis between the parents; as a result uLinda finished the rest of his education in South Africa.

In 1976 when the student uprising engulfed Soweto, he found himself in the midst of the upheaval. He was elected one of the student representatives, and as was to be expected, found himself from time to time in trouble with the law. He was soon introduced to a friend of his uncle, who was a leading activist in the township. This spelt the beginning of a long road in the struggle. In June 1982 he fled South Africa, headed for Maputo through Swaziland. He did not stay long in either country. Within five months, he had proceeded via Lusaka to Angola.

He ended up in the Soviet Union in January 1983, where he was given anti-tank guided missile training, a course that lasted three months. He returned to Angola, to find himself side by side with the MPLA on the eastern front, fighting to push back UNITA. His involvement in this war continued until early 1984. The ANC's participation in these activities attracted a lot of criticism from within and without its ranks. It led to a mutiny, which was harshly dealt with by the ANC.

Working with deviousness

ULinda later joined a crack squad of twelve combatants, to be trained in a special sharpshooters programme. They also received specialised training as an assassination squad to be launched into South Africa from Mozambique. Their mission was first delayed, then made redundant by the signing of the Nkomati Accord. They were forced to retreat to Zambia and ultimately to Botswana. Those involved included uSwazi, uSibusiso Radebe, uMiracle 2000 'Ngemtho', uElliot and uBrian.

While in Botswana they stayed in a safe house in Maru-a-pula, a suburb of Gaborone. Unfortunately, they were soon discovered and hurriedly vacated the house. On the same night, the house was bombed. It is believed that one of them, who had always been suspected of dubious activities, had a hand in the bombing. After two weeks of hiding in another house, in Mogoditsane, the Botswana police raided them. After a fierce exchange of gunfire, they gave themselves up, mainly because they realised the raid was conducted by the Botswana

Defence Force (BDF) and not the South African security forces. The whole group was promptly deported to Lusaka.

On 25 December, 1985, part of the team was deployed in South Africa. They were based in Krugersdorp under the guardianship of a certain Sister Ncube, a Roman Catholic nun. Unfortunately, their operation was never to materialise, as they were arrested in a raid the following morning. On this occasion yet again one of them was the main suspect. He had gone out the previous night, never to return.

In February 1986, uLinda fell under the command of uPaul Dikeledi and uGebhuza and headed for a mission in Swaziland. On arrival he was posted kwaGrace at Woodmasters, where he spent two nights. On the third day he was moved to Number 43, to meet with uJabu Omude for a debriefing exercise and to choose a safe place. Owing to his familiarity with the area, he chose to stay with his father in Zakhele.

Rejection by father

This plan, however, was quickly changed. ULinda's father refused to accept him in the house, saying he was uncomfortable with the work he was doing and that his presence would attract the security police. As a result of this rejection, he was forced to go back to Number 43. On the same night, his father's house was raided. When uSwazi brought the news, uLinda was instructed not to move from Number 43. It was feared that if he went anywhere else he would be tracked down and killed. He strongly suspects his own father of alerting the police.

After a while at Number 43, he was moved to Sindi Mthembu's, in Fairview, where he stayed for about a month, while his identity documentation was being processed. He finally settled down at the George Hotel flats, after a short stint in Moneni. By now he was in possession of appropriate documentation and could write contracts that allowed him to rent the flat. During this period he frequented Number 43 for various forms of business, with no problems at all.

* * *

He recalls that during one of the visits, uMagogo reminded him of the difficult times his family had been through, which had led them to seek shelter at Dr Margaret's place with their mother. He was surprised and deeply touched, never expecting that uMagogo would remember that episode as well as display so much concern.

He has fond memories of Number 43: "I spent many long days at Number 43, for all manner of reasons. Most importantly, I enjoyed the company of my comrades and the Masilela family. It also allowed me to spend what I considered to be family time away from home, in particular listening to a wide variety of good music with uElias.

"As I frequented Number 43, I would think of all sorts of scary possibilities, such as the cross-border raids in Matola and Maseru. I would shudder to imagine the extent of damage that would be caused by a similar raid on Number 43. Surprisingly, because I always felt at home there, I never carried a firearm whenever I visited. One way of avoiding attention, though, was to masquerade as one of the men who worked with uButhongo. This allowed me to naturally merge into the family.

"When I re-entered Swaziland in 1986, I assumed the name of 'Linda', which I inherited from a comrade who perished in an ambush in Piet Retief. Towards the end of 1986 I met uKhosi kwaGrace, in Woodmasters, who later became my wife. This added a great deal to the value of my relationship with the Masilelas. Given that my own family rejected me, I adopted this family as my own. I treated uElias as if he were my own brother."

* * *

In the latter part of his stay in Swaziland, uLinda was made responsible for the safekeeping and distribution of guns and ammunition in the country, a role earlier played by uCassius. He would also be responsible for setting up DLBs in South Africa. However, he carried out these responsibilities from a different location, not from Number 43.

He returned to South Africa in January 1989 to set up a base. In February of the same year, the ANC was unbanned. In July 1996 he was absorbed into the South African National Defence Force (SANDF), after an experience in the TEC during the period 1993–1994. This was followed by a job in a security firm with other comrades. In the intervening period he attended a course to secure national key points. At the time of his interview he held the position of captain in the army. We remain close to this day.

CHAPTER 27

Loneliness in the ANC . . . and in Death

Kopi Ben Baartman

The life stories of those who operated in Swaziland are widely varied. Quite a few of them are not so pleasant. They include the story of Ntate Baartman, told through his daughter and son-in-law, uMary and uHarry Nxumalo. These are close family friends. My relationship with uHarry began as a professional one. I first met him in the early 1990s when we established the Swaziland Staff Association for Financial Institutions (SSAFI), a union for senior managers in the financial sector. I had no clue then as to who he was, and it was only later in our relationship that I discovered his background.

Ntate Baartman passed on in July 2002, before he could tell his own story. What follows is an infusion of memories and recollections from uMary and uHarry. In particular, I was fascinated by Harry's depth of knowledge about his father-in-law.

The story of the Baartman family is one of those that uncover a concealed unhappiness and bitterness towards the ANC. The family feels that the ANC deserted them at a time when they needed it most – when Ntate Baartman passed on. According to uMary, not one of those they had always considered close friends and confidants of Ntate Baartman offered their condolences, let alone came to the funeral. Instead it was the PAC leadership, in particular uJoe Mkhwanazi, who worried about him. "He was lonely in his death," was how uMary described it. It was a repeat of his life of isolation, before he went into exile.

This contrasts with Mary's experience when she married uHarry on 30 August, 1975. On that occasion, the entire high command of the ANC in Swaziland was present. She fondly recalls that uGebhuza and uThabo Mbeki were part of the bridal party. In particular, uThabo drove the bride and groom in his green and white Peugeot 404.

When he remembers the events of that day, Harry marvels about Thabo's driving skills. He recalls that he had to negotiate rough and dangerous terrain to get the bride and groom to Harry's homestead in Elundiyaneni, in Shiselweni in the southern part of Swaziland. While many cars, including pick-up vehicles, could not negotiate the road, uThabo manoeuvred the sedan up to the homestead.

Once the festivities had started, uThabo commented on the slaughtering of the beast for the ceremony, "I am an African, but I did not think I would ever witness this procedure." He himself had married just the year before. That is how close the ties were between the ANC and Ntate Baartman while he was still alive.

Harry would later bump into uThabo in London in 1978, and was pleasantly surprised that uThabo immediately recognised him.

From solitary confinement to a lonely death

Ntate Baartman arrived in Swaziland in 1960, from Worcester. He was among the first refugees to enter the country. Before this, he had been slapped with a banning order by the South African authorities and in 1959 had been confined to Ngwavuma. There he lived in the open veld, in a tent with no access to food or water. He only survived through the generosity of people in the neighbourhood. Given the conditions under which he lived, it became a matter of urgency that he left South Africa.

According to uHarry, "He woke up one morning and just decided he would leave his confinement and cross over into Swaziland, and that is precisely what he did." It is not clear whether he was under any surveillance while under banishment but clearly on that particular day there was none. He simply walked across the border into Swaziland. There Dr Ambrose Zwane, who in turn introduced him to Fr Hooper at St Michael's Girls' High School, received him. Fr Hooper provided him with temporary accommodation on mission property.

While all this was unfolding, Ntate Baartman had left three very young children behind in Worcester, his wife having died in 1959. The children stayed under the guardianship of their uncle, who would later facilitate their passage to join their father in Swaziland. Ntate Baartman arranged passports, train and bus fares to Manzini, which was not an easy exploit given the economic conditions at the time.

To support himself, Ntate Baartman took a driving job at Dr Margaret's surgery in Manzini. UDr Margaret was one of the many prominent black South African professionals in Swaziland at that time. While working there, Ntate Baartman met his second wife, uJustina Thabede, a teacher at Little Flower, now St Theresa's Girls' School. They married in 1964, and in the same year Ntate arranged for his three children to join him in Swaziland.

When the children arrived, he could no longer stay at the mission. A certain John 'Sgegede' Nhlapo, who lived in Trelawney Park, just behind the White House, accommodated them. Later they moved to a place called Sithwethweni.

Ntate Baartman's residence became an important meeting point for the ANC high command and naturally attracted several raids from the Swazi police. His role was to house and find passage for operatives, either going for training or returning. He was also responsible for the distribution of rations. The life of the Baartman family was little different from that of the Masilela family at Number 43.

Soon after the signing of the Nkomati Accord, Ntate Baartman was arrested together with many others who were rounded up. They were held in Manzini, before being moved to Sidvokodvo. In both places they were kept in packed prison cells. They ended up at Mawelawela, a refugee camp just outside Manzini, before being deported to Lusaka. He left the responsibility of looking after his family to uHarry as the eldest son-in-law in the family. When Mary's sisters got married, uHarry played the role of father, by handing them over.

Ntate Baartman only returned in December 1991. One reason for his return was to prepare for a trip to Bulawayo to attend the wedding of his son, Seedwell. Joshua Nkomo was a guest at the wedding. On returning to South Africa, he went back to Worcester, where he found his house in the hands of other people.

The consolation that the family hangs onto is that Ntate Baartman died and was laid to rest where he belongs.

CHAPTER 28

Six Days

Elias Masilela

The year 1981 was a major turning point in my life. My academic future hung in the balance. This was because of an arrest that coincided with my Form V 'O' Level examinations. I faced an abyss, only to be saved by Fr Larry McDonnell, who went out of his way to ensure that I wrote the exams despite being virtually behind bars.

Fr McDonnell was headmaster of Salesian Boys' High School, one of the finest schools in Swaziland. The pupils and students affectionately called him 'iNyoni', which means 'bird' in isiZulu and siSwati. The name derived from the position of his office, which was on the upper floor of the building. From there, he would conduct assembly, looking down over the students and the rest of staff on the ground floor. A multi-storey building was still a fascinating novelty in those days in Swaziland. Salesian and the Swaziland Warehouse, which is now Builders Warehouse, were among the first such buildings in Manzini.

The year in question was a trying time for me, not only because of the arrest but also because of its further implications for my life. I had been arrested several times before, and was to be again, but this instance was uniquely challenging.

* * *

Several members of the family had been arrested, all for similar reasons. For instance, in the mid-1980s uButhongo was detained at Maphiveni, close to the border with Mozambique, for transporting operatives, and was held for two weeks before being released. This event and further developments following his release created acute tensions between Number 43 and the ANC command in Swaziland.

It was to be expected that those arrested in the course of doing business for the ANC would be assisted. In this case, when uButhongo was faced with the legal challenges of the arrest, the ANC leadership disappeared into the woodwork. However, when he was finally released, along with the car, they immediately reemerged. They promptly visited Number 43, not to deal with problems uButhongo faced but with the sole objective of recovering the car. To their surprise, uButhongo refused to hand it over until his legal bills had been settled. It took the intervention of uStan Mabizela and uMabhida to resolve the matter.

UMagogo was among the most frequent guests in the Swazi police cells. It was not clear why she was picked on. But at no point was she arraigned in court. She would be detained for a few days and then released. While this was not the same as having to spend weeks behind bars, followed by more days in court, it was extremely inconveniencing and humiliating if not dehumanising both to her and the rest of the family.

On one of the occasions when she was arrested, she was beaten up by the police and badly tortured. Hospitalised as a result, she remained under the treatment of a certain Dr Douglas in Matsapha for several months. She was advised both by the doctor and the ANC leadership in Swaziland that she should sue the Swazi government. This came as an attractive proposition, but on countervailing advice from attorney Peter Dunseith in Mbabane, she decided against it. Dunseith argued that while uMagogo had a solid case legally, the political odds were stacked against her. Indeed, at that time, there was a high probability that she and the family could be deported from Swaziland. Worse still, she could simply disappear like so many other people. Given the odds, more weight was placed on Dunseith's advice.

* * *

I had been in and out of detention several times. However, three instances stand out in my mind. The first was in 1980, the second, which is the subject of this chapter, in 1981, and the third in January 1983. On the third occasion, the Swazi police raided Number 43 as part of their routine. The raid followed closely on the Tonga operation, resulting in a grenade detonator being found under my bed, mistakenly not removed with the rest of the material for the mission.

The dreaded Sunday

The second arrest took place one warm Sunday afternoon. I was standing at the side of a dusty road in Kwaluseni, Matsapha, waiting for a bus to take me to Manzini after visiting my uncle Aphane and cousins. A car, unfamiliar to me, screeched to a halt and reversed to give me a lift. It was uGeneral, a comrade who was responsible for transport logistics, both in Swaziland and Mozambique, who also helped Ntate Nkadimeng set up the White House.

On the way to Manzini, he proposed that I help him with what he termed 'a small operation', ferrying cars to the Lomahasha border. It was urgent, he said, as the cars were needed in Maputo the following day. As always, I was willing to assist, but forgot to enquire about the 'cleanliness' of the operation. I assumed it had been appropriately planned with the requisite safeguards. Nor did I bother to call home to say where I was going, as I thought it would be a quick exercise. The trip to Lomahasha is only 104km, so I reckoned to be back in about three hours. Little did I guess that this would turn into six of the most horrific days of my life.

We proceeded past Trelawney Park, headed to the east side of Manzini, next to Manzini Café, now a Kentucky Fried Chicken outlet. This has always been a very busy part of town. There we met with a group of people, in a convoy of about five cars. I did not know any of these people. After a few minutes' discussion, we continued with the journey. On arrival at Lomahasha, I was advised to remain in the car to be used for our return journey, while the others drove across the border.

They were all prepared for the operation. They had their passports and were to drive across legitimately. UGeneral himself crossed over to the Mozambican side on foot using the Luthuli highway, one of the often-used illegal routes. He was to meet with the convoy on the Mozambican side. That would be the last time I ever saw him. My attempts to meet with him for the book never materialised.

* * *

193

I had been waiting for about 45 minutes, when a plainclothes policeman knocked on my window. He asked if I was Elias Masilela, and
I told him I was. He wanted to know about the owner of the car, and
I knew immediately I was in trouble, since I had no idea who the
owner was. I asked the man why he was questioning me the way he
did. His response was to order me to drive the car to the police station, where I would get my answer. Clearly, I had not bargained for
this turn of events.

On entering the police station, no questions were asked. Instead I
was instructed to remove my belt and watch, and was thrown into
the holding cells. Already there were the others with whom I had been
driving in the convoy, all except uGeneral. For the first time we introduced ourselves to each other. Unfortunately, owing to my state of
mind at the time, I cannot remember a single name.

My biggest worry was that my arrest coincided with my exams. I
had written only one paper, the previous week. The following day,
which was a Monday, I was meant to write a compulsory English paper, the rest of the papers following during that week. When I explained this to the police and requested that they release me to go
and write or arrange for the exam papers to be brought to the cell, I
was told, "You have chosen terrorism. This cannot be combined with
academics. Besides, you have no right to enjoy Swazi education, if you
are a terrorist." Repeated requests to communicate my whereabouts
to my family or the school were met with deafness.

I spent the first night on my feet, unable to sleep. The second day
came and went, as did the third and fourth. By then, I had lost hope
of ever making contact with anyone who could help from outside.
UGeneral was also nowhere to be seen. It turned out he never communicated to my parents what had happened.

On the Thursday, early in the morning and with no explanation, I
was called out of the cell, handed back my belongings and bundled
into a police van – all alone. I asked where I was being taken, but was
answered only with cold silence. All I could tell was that the van was
headed in the direction of Manzini. Many thoughts went through my
mind. The predominant one was that I was going to be handed over

to the South African security police, a growing trend at that time in Swaziland.

A moment of hope and excitement when the van entered Manzini was quickly dashed as it drove right past Manzini in the direction of Mbabane. I was taken to the Mbabane Police Station, where I was shaken by the amount of security that was immediately thrown around me. I was treated like a top-rated criminal. I concluded that I was in much deeper trouble than I had anticipated. Flustered and in deep distress, I gave up all hope of being released any time soon.

By now, I had accepted that my exams and what I saw as a potentially bright future would elude me.

No one spoke to me and the communication among the policemen was by way of deliberate whispers and sign language, so that I could not follow what they were saying.

Yet again I was thrown into the holding cells without a word. Another night went by without my knowing what was going to happen next. Interestingly, though, at no point was I tortured or even manhandled.

Early the next morning, the Friday following my arrest, I was taken out of the cells. Yet again, no explanation was given. I was bundled into another van, which drove off in the direction of Hospital Hill. This is the geographical centre of power of the Swazi Executive, with the Cabinet offices, government offices, one of the larger public hospitals in Swaziland, the current High Court and, more relevant to my trip, the country's police headquarters. That was where I was being taken.

My respect for the Swazi police begins

When we entered the cold grey concrete building my handcuffs were removed and the ring of security police around me dispersed. As if I were an important guest, I was ushered into the elevator and taken to what I thought must be the top floor of the building. I could not help noticing the difference in treatment since the Sunday of my arrest. I found this change of mood rather queer.

On exiting the lift, I was shown into a massive boardroom. My ushers just dissolved behind me. I stepped timidly into the room, to be confronted by one of the longest boardroom tables I had ever seen. On the other side were at least a dozen stern looking men, all dressed in black suits, black neckties and white shirts, and perfectly coordinated. I could have sworn that everything else they were wearing was matching!

This was the top brass of the Swaziland police force, with the then Commissioner of Police in the chair, right in the middle, splitting the gathering in two perfect halves. On my side of the table was one forlorn chair, deliberately positioned to intimidate, to which I was beckoned. As I sat down, I felt as if I were sinking into an electric chair, ready for execution.

Indeed, I was entirely at their mercy. I felt very afraid, but at the same time found myself amused and respectful of the intelligence of the Swazi security police. They had effectively intimidated me, and I thought, "They have succeeded in their psychological game".

I knew I had been brought in for interrogation. I had expected there would be people from the South African security police, but that was not the case. Not a single Afrikaner was in the room. All the people there were black and Swazi. That really astounded me.

Among them I recognised a certain Dlamini, a policeman whose sister, uMakhosazana, was a tenant at Number 43. He was one of the very few friendly cops in our life. From time to time, he would alert us to any planned raids on Number 43 and other safe houses in the country. On several occasions during the interrogation he came to my rescue by either posing mitigating questions or merely diverting the heat, which I really appreciated. To return the favour, I tried to avoid eye contact to prevent any suspicion that he was known to me. He would later die in a car accident.

The interrogation started promptly at 9am and was extremely rough. Several times I was threatened with deportation because I was found to be uncooperative. This went on until around 3pm without a break. When they realised they were not getting the information they wanted from me, I was simply told that the interrogation was over, and that I should go home and wait to be contacted in due course. I was released onto the street, but was never called again.

The fear of being released to my own custody

Throughout my six days in custody, I had not washed. I was still wearing the same clothes I wore when I went to church the previous Sunday, a white shirt and a pair of powder blue pants. I was filthy and smelly, and both scared and embarrassed at being on the street at that point. I was scared because I did not know who was watching and waiting to pounce as soon as I stepped out of the safety of the police headquarters. I did not know which was safer, the streets, the holding cells, or the interrogation room I had just been in. I just wanted to get back home.

My biggest predicament was that I had no money for a bus to Manzini. At that time, uSwazi was working at Business Machines in Mbabane, but when I went to check on her for money, she was not in her office. I resorted to hitchhiking at the Mbabane Hospital bus stop. Luckily, it was not long before someone stopped and gave me a lift directly to Number 43. To this day, I do not remember who that person was. I was simply too bewildered to remember.

The big search

I did not know until I arrived home that while I had been in custody, uMagogo and Fr McDonnell had been on a crusade to find me. UMagogo became worried on the Sunday night when I did not return home. She called my uncle's place in Kwaluseni, to be told I had left much earlier in the day. That was when the warning light came on.

Meanwhile, Fr McDonnell guessed I was in trouble when I did not show up for the English exam paper. Because English was a compulsory subject, every student was expected to sit for it. In that year, one seat was empty in the exam hall and that seat was mine. In my entire history at Salesian I had never missed classes, which made him conclude that something was wrong and triggered him into action.

According to uMagogo, he came to Number 43 to enquire about my whereabouts early on Monday morning. On being told the family had no clue where I was, he insisted they check the Nazarene Hospital and then the police. At both places they drew a blank. When he further suggested they check the mortuaries, uMagogo flatly refused, saying she was not ready to make such a discovery. If anything of that sort had happened, she would rather have the news come to her than go herself to find it. So that option was not pursued.

It was not until Tuesday that the school got a call from the Manzini Police Station, telling them I was incarcerated at Lomahasha. UMagogo and uButhongo, accompanied by uSis' Tsali Malaza, directly drove to Lomahasha. When they arrived at the police station, the police refused them access, saying I had moved to Mbabane. This was of course not true. They hurried to Mbabane, where they were told I was still in Lomahasha. Given the complete lack of cooperation from the police, the attempt to find me had to be abandoned. At least there was a hope that I was still alive, somewhere.

On the Wednesday morning, a friendly police officer named Sifundza came to the house, to inform my parents of the state of affairs, and how seriously the case was being taken. It was not merely the fact that cars were being driven across the border that made it serious in the minds of the Swazi police, it was the link they had finally made between uGeneral and Number 43. UGeneral had been on the priority list of so-called notorious ANC operatives in Swaziland for a while.

The ultimate risk

In the meantime, Fr McDonnell was pulling out all stops and engaging in hurried negotiations with the police to allow me to write my exams in the cells. He had also taken one of the biggest risks any headmaster could take. He had given instructions to his colleagues that the envelopes carrying the scripts should not be sealed until that weekend. He did this in the hope that I would show up, in which case I would be given the opportunity to write, after which the envelopes could be sealed and forwarded to Cambridge. He advised uMagogo to bring me to the school as soon as I arrived, making sure that I did not have any contact with other students.

I am certain no other headmaster, anywhere in Swaziland, would have taken such a risk. For this, I remain deeply indebted to Fr McDonnell and the entire Salesian community.

As soon as I arrived at Number 43, uMagogo swung into action in her usual resourceful manner. Because uButhongo was not home to drive us to the school, a taxi was called. I was bundled into it and quickly driven to Salesian. When we arrived, we found an entourage of priests standing in front of the Rector's office, waiting to welcome me. They were visibly elated, even more indeed than my own mother. I was instructed to return to the school at 8am the following morning, which was a Saturday, to sit the exam.

Indeed, the next day, I wrote all the remaining six or so papers in one marathon sitting, under the invigilation of Fr Patrick Ahern, popularly known as 'Gwinya' (large stomach, as if he had swallowed something) among the students. Contrary to the concerns of those around me, writing an entire exam without any preparation did not worry me. I was just very grateful that I had been given a golden opportunity, much against the wishes of my captors of earlier that week.

I started at 8am and was done by around 5pm on that day, ending in a state of total exhaustion.

I was one of those who passed with a First Class for the year 1981. That thrilled Fr McDonnell. His efforts and risk-taking, and that of the entire school, had paid off. And of course uMagogo was over the moon!

CHAPTER 29

Golden Age of Salesian

Frs Larry McDonnell and Patrick Ahern

The perspective of the South African liberation struggle as seen through the eyes of the Salesian priests, in a school where many South Africans either worked as teachers or attended as pupils, is a humbling one. During one of my visits to Swaziland to interview people, I took time to have a discussion with Fr Larry McDonnell. I was very pleased when, with very little persuasion, Fr Patrick Ahern joined us. They displayed the same abundance of care and sensitivity as they had during our days as students.

When asked about his view of the events in the school during his days as headmaster, Fr McDonnell responded in a startling manner: "My reaction was that of deep ignorance about the things that happened, not only around me but right under my nose. Where these things really came to challenge me was at the funeral of an old colleague and friend, Stan Mabizela. When his obituary was read, I could not resist the temptation of asking myself questions about this person with whom I had worked so closely, yet knew very little about. It amazed me how he was never late for class, yet he would have been out all night, for nights on end, carrying out all sorts of clandestine activities. I feel I was stupidly innocent. History just passed us by."

He recalled many events of historical importance for the school, including the fact that Robert Sobukwe's son was a student at Salesian. Speaking about the assistance that he extended to this particular student, he said: "I never realised I was dealing with great people and important documents. We were unknowing and extremely naive." On many occasions, he acted as intermediary between people in Lusaka and Swaziland, since some of the correspondence came through the telex, postal and fax facilities at the school. He simply did not pay much attention to the private business of students and teachers.

Fr Ahern remembers two prominent calls during his tenure at the school. One was from uRobert Sobukwe himself, when a teacher, uRosette B Nziba (simply known as RB), died. The other was from uOR to check whether uStan had left Swaziland. Fr Ahern too did not give much attention to these calls.

Fr McDonnell acted as intermediary for messages from all sorts of places, sometimes including odd lines such as "Great-grandfather died" or "Your mother has been involved in an accident". At first, these appeared innocent enough. In time, though, he worked out that they were far from innocent, but were in reality coded messages. What convinced him was that he often received the same messages to the same person at different times. As he reflected: "One can only lose two grandmothers. If you lose three to four grandmothers in one life-time, there must be something wrong."

He summarised his situation: "As I saw it, all we did was from the goodness of our hearts. One could not deny people all these things."

The beginning of a golden era

Fr McDonnell arrived in Swaziland as a young missionary in 1970, at the age of 35. Among the first South African teachers he worked with was RB. He did not know how famous RB was until after his death. He recalls a bold headline in one of the local daily newspapers, 'The Great RB is Dead'. This headline was reflective of the legacy RB had left in Swaziland, both as an educator and political activist.

Unknowingly, RB touched a chord in Fr McDonnell, who had to give mass at the funeral, an experience that continues to linger with him to this day, as he remarks: "Here was this little white male from Ireland dealing with veterans. Here is an exile dying in exile. . ." was the thought that ran through his mind. To a large extent, it defined the paradox of his relationship with RB, even in his death.

He continues: "It is very hard to be factual about that period because it was all done in both innocence and ignorance. There was an intricate relationship between the school and the South African exiles who sought refuge not only in Swaziland but in the school as well.

Our success was a direct result of the quality of people we had at that time, both students and teachers. Needless to say, these were all South Africans. They created and preserved the social and scholastic calibre of the school."

In his view, it was not only the academic results that mattered. There was a host of other factors that set the school apart. He recalls meeting a certain Mandla Hlatshwayo, a former student at the school and an outstanding activist in his university days at UNISWA, who asked why Salesian was able to produce so many outstanding people and leaders across all sectors. Fr McDonnell could not explain this phenomenon, apart from saying, "The school was blessed with bright, wise and highly dedicated individuals. Indeed, the bulk of these were South Africans."

No immunity

The story would not be complete, though, without including the sad side of those days. Fr McDonnell remembers the bombs going off in Zakhele, and having to go and give absolution, which left a vivid imprint in his mind. Among his many activities was running a home for street children in Manzini, predominantly boys. At one point, these boys uncovered a large arms cache in a ravine in Ngwane Park. On inspection, the police found an assortment of arms, from rocket launchers to grenades and AK 47s. Later they discovered that one of the boys had taken an AK47 to sell to soldiers in Masundvwini for pocket money.

Despite this dark side, Fr McDonnell has good memories of receiving letters from students who had left Swaziland, either to study further or undergo military training. His work on academic boards allowed him to keep in touch with some of these students. Among these bodies were the World University Service (WUS) and Ephesus House in Swaziland, financed by the International University Exchange Fund (IUEF) in Geneva. This responsibility exposed him to all sorts of atrocities. In particular, he recalls with a mixture of sadness and disgust how Craig Williamson closed down Ephesus House in Manzini. It is reported that prior to its brutal closure, Williamson broke into the offices at least three times.

Jacques Pauw describes Williamson as South Africa's super-spy and later member of the President's Council and a National Party politician. While studying at Wits University he was a fervent police informer, but achieved notoriety when he infiltrated the IUEF as an Assistant Director. He made extensive contacts with MK in Europe and fed information to the South African security services. When his cover was blown in 1979, he simply walked out of the IUEF with a sum alleged to be about R50, 000. This money he later used to purchase a secret police farm similar to Vlakplaas. In 1985, he testified against Dirk Coetzee.

Williamson came to Salesian on many occasions for meetings with the teachers and headmaster, under the guise of discussing students sponsored by IUEF. At that stage he was the Deputy Director responsible for the funding office. On several of these visits, he suggested the meetings be held at the George Hotel where they could also have drinks. UStan Mabizela, however, firmly refused, noting that the place was infested with spies. Ironically, this was the same hotel uThabo Mbeki and uJZ had frequented in the mid-1970's before they left Swaziland – an interesting role-change for the George.

At the time, Fr McDonnell did not understand what uStan was talking about. It was only much later, when Craig Williamson was finally exposed, that he came to appreciate his concerns. Marissa Rollnick, a teacher at St Michael's Girls' School, had always shared Stan's suspicions and openly argued that Williamson was a spy.

Challenges of being headmaster and team leader

Fr McDonnell has had very good relationships with his teachers, but on occasion has had to deal with deep misunderstandings. One of these involved uGerald Mohlathi, who at one point labelled the headmaster a racist. It took Stan's wise intervention to diffuse what was potentially a disastrous ending to a good professional relationship.

Another not so pleasant experience was with a certain Jackie Moreke who was widely suspected of having been behind the Zakhele bomb blast in 1984. He was later arrested and deported from Swaziland, Fr O'Dea being given the job of driving him back to South Africa.

Fr McDonnell remembers that uMoreke bought a car, one of the more conspicuous luxury vehicles of the time. Fr McDonnell made a comment about how expensive the car must have been, a remark that attracted a very interesting response: "There was dead silence. You could hear a pin drop," was the way he recalled the reaction. UMoreke later gave evidence *in camera* against another South African teacher who had served briefly at the school.

Fr McDonnell took over the headmastership of the Salesian High School in 1971. Over and above this responsibility, he had many others, including dealing with church and development work, as well as managing Manzini Youth Care. He also worked at the Bishop's office as an administrator, and has been involved in social outreach and Aids projects. In January 2005, he took over the Rectorship from Fr Ahern, who had been Rector for three successive terms.

There is no doubt that the Salesians played a vital role, not only in educating both Swazis and South Africans but also in the liberation of South Africa, albeit unknowingly. It may not have been a contribution of a military nature. Indeed, it was much more substantive, being concerned with the spiritual and the academic, as well as in the development of leadership among the students and teachers who passed through the school.

CHAPTER 30

Apex of Sacrifice for the Movement

Victor 'Mtolo' Fakudze

It was certainly not South Africans alone who waged the struggle for the liberation of South Africa. In contrast to the political stance of the Swazi authorities across three decades, many Swazis participated. Not only did they provide moral support as sympathisers but some went as far as laying down their lives for the cause.

The cross-border raids launched by the South African security forces into Swaziland resulted in many Swazis being maimed physically and psychologically, abducted and killed. One abduction that caused a major diplomatic scare was that of four people on 12 December 1986. These were two Swazi nationals, Grace Cele and Danger Nyoni, as well as two Swiss nationals, Dr Daniel Schneider and Corinne Boschoff. Two people were killed during this raid.

In collecting information for this book, I spoke to a number of Swazi nationals, most of whom were unwilling to have their identities re-vealed. These ranged from close friends to people I knew only vaguely, as well as complete strangers. Many interesting stories were shared with me, about relationships these people had with Number 43. In doing so, they helped solve some of the many puzzles that have always troubled me. These recollections ranged from bringing arms and am-munition to Number 43 for safe custody, while their own houses were being raided, to directing people who had escaped persecution in South Africa to seek assistance from Number 43, to delivering, under cover of darkness, operatives who had suffered wounds in combat. The conclusion to be drawn from the sum total of these names and events is that many Swazis suffered deeply as a result of the struggle as it took place in Swaziland.

★ ★ ★

Among this sea of brave people who overtly shared a vision of a bigger future for the continent, one Swazi national stands out in the context of Number 43. This is uVictor Fakudze, popularly known as 'Mtolo', a name taken from his praise name. Those he trained with in Tanzania also knew him as 'Shaka' or 'Commissar'.

UMtolo was born and raised in Swaziland. He attended both primary and high school at Luyengo. He became involved in active politics in 1977, pretty much by default, while working for Barclays Bank in Mbabane. He was never directly recruited, but was drawn in by osmosis or association. He was a keen collector of music, and this attracted people of various walks of life to his house. One of the first activists he became acquainted with was uBricks, who had earlier visited Swaziland as the drummer of a band called the All Rounders. According to uMtolo, "When he returned to Swaziland in 1977, however, he was a changed person."

He befriended many other activists, including uTokyo Sexwale, uSelaelo, uBuddy and uSipho Twala. The latter would in turn introduce him to uGebhuza. At that point, he was staying at a place called Corporation in Mbabane, popularly known as 'Kopis'. He comments that, "As part of the social engagements we had, I was gradually initiated into the struggle. My place became a mini Number 43, because it became an alternative to Number 43 where people could meet, be delivered and collected. This involved mainly the Transvaal and Natal Machineries."

UGebhuza and uJabu eventually became his handlers. He also worked closely with uViva. His responsibilities included transport between Mozambique and Swaziland, which meant he would frequently spend weekends in Mozambique.

Sacrificing the job

UMtolo's employment with Barclays lasted exactly ten years. His political activities put him in direct conflict with his employer. The South African security police had been making persistent enquiries with the bank about his extramural activities. Meanwhile, the Swazi police began a campaign of direct harassment. He would be picked up at random for questioning. This did not go down well with the bank. Though his work had never suffered, under pressure from the South African police, his employer confronted him. Rather than pick a legal fight, he decided to bow out. In June 1984 he chose the struggle and walked away from his job.

This decision coincided with the period in which Swaziland experienced a major influx of operatives, following the Nkomati Accord. Many went underground, while many others left Swaziland. Unemployed, he felt quite alone and with no support from the movement. Because he could no longer sustain payments on his bond, he lost his house, the only asset he had. Despite this, he went on to share his clothes and other valuables with those operatives who remained in Swaziland. Describing this period, he simply says, "This was the apex of my sacrifice to the movement!"

For a long time, he heard nothing from any of the people in command. It was a trying time and each day felt like a long, torturous year. Then, in 1985, uBricks returned. Shortly afterwards uGebhuza also emerged. With no questions asked, he resumed work with uGebhuza, spending most of his time in Mozambique. They stayed underground in both countries. By now, he was receiving a monthly allowance for his upkeep.

During Operation Vula, uGebhuza had to go deeper underground. When this happened, uMtolo started working more closely with people like uTodd, uSkorokoro, uShezi and uViva. Towards the end of 1987, uSipho Twala introduced him to uBullet, who became his new handler.

In October 1988, he was taken to Tanzania for a year's military training at the Cassius Make training camp. On his return, he spent a few months re-socialising in Tshaneni. He was eager for combat and excited about the prospect. This excitement was dampened by the announcement that a settlement had been negotiated in South Africa and that people would be repatriated to South Africa. He was not alone in being disappointed by this turn of events. Many were itching for action, but the times had suddenly changed, no longer allowing for combat.

UMtolo had been introduced to Number 43 by uCassius and uKelly.

He estimates that this was probably in December 1979 or early in 1980. As he recalls: "The Masilelas were the only family I could run to when in real trouble. They were more than what I would define as my family – they were like a shield. That was the second best place for me after my own house. The first time I went to Number 43, we had just bought a new Ford F250 registered under the name of my late brother, uBuddy. That was the car used to attack Secunda in Sasolburg." He remembers being arrested at Number 43, together with uTZ (uMabhontjies), during one of the raids launched in search of uNkosinathi. They walked into one of the many ambushes laid by the Swazi police.

UMtolo concluded the interview with a nostalgic comment: "I am proud to have had the chance of participating in such a noble cause. More so, since as a Swazi my contribution will add to the annals of both South Africa and Swaziland. My activities did not stop in Swaziland. They extended to Shell House, which makes me even more proud."

He does, however, have reservations. He would be happier if the ANC government looked after the welfare of veterans such as himself. They made enormous sacrifices, yet today they are left to die as mere paupers, not as heroes. However, he is quick to qualify: "It is not money that I am talking about".

PART IV
Closure

SD TO HOST CEREMONY FOR
South African freedom fighters

BY LINDOKUHLE SITHOLE

MBABANE – A cleansing and healing ceremony for South African freedom fighters who died in Swaziland during the apartheid era will be hosted by the kingdom in a two day spiritual ceremony proposed to be held at the end of this month.

The ceremony comes at an opportune time, when the Kingdom of Swaziland and the Republic of South Africa are in the process of signing the Bilateral Joint Commission.

According to the Deputy High Commissioner of the Republic of South Africa to Swaziland, Lucas Mokoena, the ceremony, which is still in its early planning stages, is meant to, amongst other things, take the spirits of freedom fighters who died in the country back to where they belong—back home in South Africa.

"This entails a number of

South Africans who ran away from South Africa and were killed by former apartheid regimes while in Swaziland," he said.

The ceremony, which has been hosted before by neighbouring countries such as Mozambique and Botswana and is yet to proceed to other countries, comes after a decision taken by the South African Government in the 1990s that there was a need to put a symbol in place through a Memorial Park.

The memorial park will show the property lost, the land as well as the people who sacrificed their lives during the apartheid era.

A South African committee responsible for the significant event, the Freedom Park Committee, was in the country in the middle of last month to hold meetings with the Ministry of Foreign Affairs and Trade where representatives from the country and South African delegates shared ideas and information about the ceremony.

"The significance of the healing and

cleansing ceremony is to maintain the African culture so that when a person dies in a foreign country, African rituals are performed to take that person's spirit back home," explained Mokoena in an interview with this newspaper.

In this instance, traditional healers keep bowls called *Isivivane* in a building at the Freedom Park in the Republic to keep the spirits of those who passed away during the struggle.

Event

Although the planning of the ceremony is still in its early stages, there are high chances that the Deputy President, His Excellency Dr. Jacob Zuma, will grace the occasion since he is the one who played a major role during the struggle; representing the Swazi government will be His Excellency the Prime Minister, A. T. Dlamini.

According to Mokoena, the programme for the ceremony will be done in two days. Information gathered by this newspaper

MBABANE - Lucas Mokoena (deputy commissioner of SA High Commissioner) during an interview. On the left is Casheous Moatsaledi (first secretary at the South African High Commission) (Pics: Walter Dlamini)

discloses that traditional healers from both countries will, on the first day take the spirits from the various

graveyards and identified places.

The second day will involve the Council of Churches and this is when

government will take the lead.

Emphasis was placed on the significance of the role of traditional healers from the country because they will be tasked with handing over the spirits to their South African counterparts who will then receive and accept them.

Traditional healers are also to make sure that the spirits are redressed so that ancestors may be satisfied and if there is a need to combine the spirits they do so in a respectable manner.

The First Secretary and Deputy to the Republic of South African High Commission to Swaziland, Casheous Moatsaledi and Lucas Mokoena respectively, emphasised the importance of African people to talk to their ancestors, saying that the ceremony is a typical way of paying their respects to the people who died for the new South Africa.

"It is our culture and we cannot run away from it," said Mokoena.

Another South African who was buried amid the apartheid struggle at the Manzini cemetery.

... AND SA ON A MISSION TO GATHER NAMES OF ITS FREEDOM FIGHTERS

BY LINDOKUHLE SITHOLE

MBABANE – After 10 years of democracy, the Republic of South Africa is on a mission to gather the names of its freedom fighters that died in Swaziland and some other countries that harboured these freedom fighters on their lands during the apartheid era.

Although it has been quite difficult for the South African Committee tasked with investigating the names of South African freedom fighters that were killed by former apartheid regimes in the country, the Republic of South African High Commission in Swaziland is in possession of about 20 names of these people and some of their families.

"It has been quite a task as some of the freedom fighters used code

names as disguise during the apartheid era. This has meant that some of the names in our possession are not their real names with the original names still not known to us," said the Deputy High Commissioner, Lucas Mokoena, when relating how far they have gone with finding the names and families of freedom fighters who died in the country.

Reverend Alpheous Nxumalo, a man who was actively involved and was in the know during the times of the South African struggle for freedom, has revealed that in his well kept files is information of some instances where Swaziland saw some South African freedom fighters being murdered by soldiers of the former South African apartheid regime. Some sources assert that even Swazi police were involved at some point

in the murder of these freedom fighters.

INSTANCES IN REVEREND NXUMALO'S FILES INCLUDE:

■ The death of Gebhuza Nyanda, brother to Siphiwe Nyanda who is current Army Commander in the Republic of South Africa - killed in Lugaganeni.
■ The murder of Casius Maake and two others.
■ 3-5 other South African freedom fighters who died in the famous Ngwane Park shooting.
■ Those that were kidnapped from Manikayane Police Station and murdered.
■ A large number of South African Freedom fighters that died at Mobeni Flats.

OTHER SOURCES DISCLOSED THESE FURTHER DETAILS:

■ Theophilus Dlodlo who was shot and laid to rest at Manzini cemetery.
■ Tutu Nkwanyana, then a student at the University of Swaziland, who was shot at Thembelihle in Mbabane.
■ Paul Dikeledi and others murdered at Elangeni.

CHAPTER 31

Cleansing Ceremony in Swaziland

The events of many years at Number 43, dating back to the 1960s, ended in a gratifying manner in June 2004, in the Swaziland ANC cleansing ceremony hosted by the Freedom Park Trust. This was a cleansing and healing ritual for those South African freedom fighters who perished in Swaziland during the liberation struggle. The two-day event, hosted jointly with the Swaziland government, was meant to take the spirits of the fallen South African heroes back to their motherland, symbolised in the Freedom Park in Pretoria, Tshwane.

While to some of the organisers this event might have been simply an official procedure, for those of us who had lived through the struggle as waged from Swaziland it was a major milestone. It allowed us to take stock of the events and the risks that had led to the liberation of South Africa. We could evaluate what freedom actually meant and how we could maximise the potential benefits it afforded, not only for South Africa but for the entire continent. More importantly, it provided a real closure to our past.

To the Masilela family, it also gave us an opportunity to formalise and normalise the relationship between Number 43 and the Swazi authorities. Even though attitudes had already started changing and the authorities had begun to consider residents of Number 43 in a different light, we had never before heard the kind of conciliatory and congratulatory statements uttered repeatedly throughout the proceedings.

Finally and most importantly it provided, for the first and perhaps the last time since 1994, an opportunity for many of the operatives who have had a relationship with Number 43 to reassemble at the house and reminisce about the 'good old' torturous days of the struggle. It was a truly historic moment, and one I will never forget.

It marked the end of a long struggle, filled with fear but also driven by a determination to fight the ugly scourge of the apartheid regime in South Africa. To many comrades, the visit to Swaziland for the cleansing ceremony, and to Number 43 in particular, was an immensely important pilgrimage. It defined a final chapter in a long, painful journey to which, while it was being travelled, there appeared to be no obvious end.

Other popular interests

While the official objective of the cleansing ceremony was as stated above, many people had their own peripheral objectives which I found equally relevant.

The press was out to unearth facts and experiences that could not have been revealed or spoken about, even in hushed voices, during the struggle. Various cases were investigated and analysed in Swaziland's leading newspaper, the *Times of Swaziland*, in its Sunday edition, over several weeks before and after the ceremony.

Number 43 and the activities that took place there were central to these investigations. Among the reports was an article entitled 'I am scared of Swazis!' taken from an interview with uMagogo whose name could not be revealed at the time of going to press; instead an alias, Molefe, was used (*TOS*, 20 June 2004). Another report attempted to solve an old puzzle concerning the whereabouts of Thabo Mbeki's son, said to have died in Swaziland. Part of this investigation was covered in an article entitled 'Mbeki's son dies in SD' (*TOS*, 20 June 2004).

To those who were close to the struggle, this whole process of trying to unearth the unknowns brought back deep distress and longing.

Proceedings

Notwithstanding these darker memories of the past, the cleansing ceremony was a graceful occasion. It began on Friday, 25 June 2004, at the Swaziland National Trade Fair grounds. A number of cows and goats were slaughtered for the people who had braved the bitter winter temperatures of uMzimnene River. In true African tradition, the Swazi government and the Manzini City Council donated the beasts.

The ceremony drew in people from all walks of life, including those we knew as the staunchest critics and persecutors of the ANC in Swaziland. Despite their differences, all felt a sense of oneness between the two societies, Swazi and South African. The programme included visiting places where people had died and those gravesites that could be identified. From each of these sites, soil and stones were gathered as a symbol of collecting the spirits of those who fell. These were placed in a basket woven of natural reeds, which was later handed over to the South African delegation headed by the Minister of Foreign Affairs, Nkosazana Dlamini-Zuma, to carry back to the symbolic Memorial Park in Tshwane.

The festivities continued till the early hours of the following morning. They were concluded the next day with an official ritual carried out in the Manzini Cathedral. I was impressed by the convergence of religions, cultures and beliefs, a phenomenon I would never have dreamed of before that day. In all my years at the Salesian School, the Cathedral was treated with deep reverence, such that non-religious music was banned inside it and even confetti was not allowed in the grounds.

On this day, however, we witnessed mass celebrated in a unique cleansing fashion. It was a multi-denominational service, which included traditional healers and leaders. The Bishop of the Roman Catholic Church in Swaziland, Ncamiso Ndlovu, shared the pulpit with priests from three other denominations as well as Swaziland's leading traditional healer, Nhlavana Maseko, who is the President of the Swaziland Traditional Healers Association. Filling the whole Cathedral was a rich incense which was burned side by side with 'isichelo', traditional African herbs sprinkled from the altar using a branch of a sacred tree. At the same time, the Cathedral was turned into a political platform, with placards emblazoned with the words 'Freedom wasn't free'. Bearing witness to these words was a long list of names read during the proceedings, of people who died in Swaziland, together with their families who represented them on the day. In all, about 62 names were read out to the gathering. This was done while the families were assembled at the altar.

To many, this ceremony was seen both as an historic closure and as the start of the next stage of our liberation as a country and as a continent. For the Masilela family, it was an important opportunity to pay our respects to those who fell, siblings, comrades and friends.

May their souls rest in peace!

Important Dates

5 **August 1925** – UButhongo is born in Middelburg (although he strongly believes he was born the previous year)

12 **December 1928** – Birth of uMagogo in Hammanskraal

7 **September 1939** – Death of uMoraka, father to uButhongo

1943 – UButhongo is forced to join the army to earn an income for the upkeep of his mother and siblings

1945 – UButhongo and uMakgomo meet in Hammanskraal

20 **May 1945** – Death of uBatseba, mother of uMakgomo

1 **August 1951** – UButhongo and uMakgomo get married

1958 – UButhongo first visits, and then considers relocation, to Swaziland

1960 – Ntate Baartman enters Swaziland as one of the first ANC refugees

11 **July 1963** – Liliesleaf farm raided; high command of the ANC arrested

6 **June 1964** – Death of uAbraham Jambo Kekana, father to uMakgomo, an event that delays the migration to Swaziland

January 1965 – UButhongo and uMakgomo settle at Number 43 Trelawney Park, on a temporary basis

28 **May 1966** – UMagogo develops complications while giving birth to uAngel, which causes uButhongo to relocate to Swaziland permanently, leaving his job in Johannesburg

1971 – Main house at Number 43 in commission, after about five years of construction

1974 – UThandi starts working at George Hotel, where she is exposed to uThabo Mbeki and uJacob Zuma

1976 – UThandi leaves for Bulgaria

1976 – Ntate Nkadimeng arrives in Swaziland; sets up the White House in Trelawney Park

25 **June 1978** – UJabu Masina assassinates Det.-Sgt. Chapi Hlubi in Soweto

1978 – USwazi deals with her first batch of activists arriving from South Africa

1979 – ULucky leaves for Mozambique

4 **June 1980** – Zakhele bomb blast

9 **August 1980** – Bishop Mandlenkosi Zwane dies in a mysterious car accident, along the Mbabane–Manzini road

30 **January 1981** – South African security forces attack homes used by the ANC at Matola, murdering 16 South Africans and one Portuguese national. UGrace survives the attack.

1981 UElias is arrested at Lomahasha, resulting in him virtually writing his 'O' Level exams behind bars

February 1982 – Swaziland and South Africa sign a secret non-aggression pact

28 May 1982 – Limpet mines used in attack on Hectorspruit depot and power transformer

June 1982 – Liqoqo (supreme body) established by King Sobhuza II

21 August 1982 – King Sobhuza II dies; laid to rest in Shiselweni

1982 – White House is closed down; Ntate Nkadimeng forced to leave Swaziland

January 1983 – UElias arrested and charged for the possession of an arm of war (grenade detonator) and subversive materials

20 May 1983 – Pretoria Church Street bomb blast, outside the South Africa Air Force HQ; 19 people killed, 217 injured

20 May 1983 – UEzekiel dies of a bullet wound during the Church Street bombing

26 May 1983 – South Africa Air Force jets and helicopters raid Maputo, killing at least 5 people and injuring about 30, in retaliation for the Pretoria Church Street bombing.

11 June 1983 – UEzekiel is buried

13 August 1983 – USibongile is born to uJoana and uNkosinathi

22 November 1983 – UZwelakhe Nyanda and uKeith McFadden killed in a grenade and rifle attack in Manzini – two others survive.

08 December 1983 – UNkosinathi and uDumisa stage bank robbery

14 December 1983 – UDumisa is arrested

23 December 1983 – UJoana is arrested and is put into solitary confinement, in Malkerns, following the disappearance of uNkosinathi

December 1983 – Peter Tosh concert in Swaziland, used by many South Africans as a legitimate excuse to leave the country

4 January 1984 – UNkosinathi killed in a police raid in Mamelodi East

16 March 1984 – Signing of Nkomati Accord between the South African and Mozambican governments

16 June 1984 – UKelly dies in Bethal

21 December 1984 – Certain comrades are declared wanted and their names posted on all print media in Swaziland: Sidima Theophilus Dlodlo (alias Sipho Victor Simelane); Sphiwe Nyanda (alias Gebhuza, alias Tebogo Kgope); Thami Zulu (alias Mandla John Kunene); Lefoshi Glory Sedibe (alias September); D.P. Motsoaledi (alias Cassius); Zondi Rollar Molape (alias Selby); M.D. Malada (alias Peter Dambuza); Mduduzi Cecil Sithole (alias Trevor Vilakazi, alias Belgium); Edward Gabriel Lawrence (alias Cyril Raymonds); Collingwood August (alias Maphumulo); Vishnathan Pillay (alias Ivan); Rakgakgane Daniel Seopela (alias Kwaitos); Terrence Russel Tyron (alias Leonard);

N.N. Hlongwane (alias Nsizwa); S.P. Ntuli (alias Nsimbi); B.A. Mlambo (alias Solly); Selby Simelane (alias David Zulu); Moses Molotwana (alias Ace); Sello Peter Motsa (alias Paul Dikeledi); Keith Mokoape; Michael Moche (alias Fanie); Cliff Mashinini (*TOS* 21 December 1984)

1985 – In a sanctioned arrangement, uSwazi meets with South African security police at Ezulwini valley

25-27 April 1986 – King Mswati is crowned in a three-day ceremony

April 1986 – Liqoqo is dissolved

12 August 1986 – uSeptember and uHumphrey arrested in the Manzini city centre

14 August 1986 – uSeptember kidnapped from Mankayane police station

16 August 1986 – Ephesus House, in the Central Chambers building in Manzini, is broken into – a file containing names of students funded by Ephesus House is taken away from the premises

22 December 1986 – UViva marries uFelicia at Todd's place

1986 – Operation Vula launched, mainly as a response to the Nkomati Accord

22 May 1987 – UTheophilus 'Viva' Dlodlo, uTutu Nkwanyana, uMildred Msomi killed in a drive-by shooting in Mbabane – three others survive

09 July 1987 – UCassius Make, uPaul Dikeledi and uEliza Tsinini

ambushed and killed along Manzana road in Lobamba

14 August 1988 – UJabu Shoke is attacked at his flat in Thokoza, Mbabane, escaping with serious bullet wounds

24 April 1990 – UGrace dies

19 November 1990 – UMadiba visits Swaziland for the first time as guest of the King (the five-day visit coincided with the PTA heads of state conference, hosted by Swaziland in that year)

1992 – UPhilipos meets with uSeptember, in Louis Trichardt

December 1993 – USeptember makes a surprise visit to Number 43, to the irritation of many

April 1994 – USeptember dies

21 July 1994 – UGol' Annah dies

1996 – UBhomo sells the house at Number 466, Mofolo North, to the Manyapye family

06 May 1999 – UAngel dies in Manzini after a motor vehicle accident

21 June 1999 – UGranny dies in Manzini, of illness

July 2002 – Ntate Baartman dies

24 March 2003 – UTodd dies in Pretoria after a long illness

20 May 2003 – Unveiling of Ezekiel Maseko's tombstone, where for the first time I make a link between uPhumzile Maseko and uNkosinathi Maseko

25-26 June 2004 – ANC Cleansing Ceremony performed in Swaziland

11 February, 2005 – Ntate Nkadimeng is recognised by the President, Thabo Mbeki, in the State of the Nation Address

05 November 2005 – I meet Kelly's family in Venda for the first time, and I talk to his elder sister, uJoyce Raphutle

23 September 2006 – UKelly is re-buried in his village, at the royal residence of King Vho-Thobela MPK Tshivase, in Tohoyandou

Essential Historical Facts

466   House number of the property that uBthongo owned in Mofolo North, in Soweto, before the family relocated to Swaziland, in search of an alternative to Bantu Education. He sold the house to his brother, uBhomo, who in turn sold it to a Manyapye family in 1996.

1964   This was the year in which the first attempt was made to start the long journey to Swaziland. It would have been the year in which the planned relocation was implemented, had it not been for two factors that prevented uButhongo from effecting his plan. Firstly, was the birth of his eighth child, uElias, on the 27th of April of the same year. This date, the 27th of April, would later be declared South Africa's Freedom Day. Two months later, in June, Abraham Jambo Kekana, the father to uMakgomo, died. Together, these events stopped the migration.

466/64   If you combine the numbers above, you end up with Madiba's prisoner number. The first part of the number is Madiba's individual prisoner number. The second part of the number is the year Madiba was arrested and sent to prison on Robben Island.

Index